Shark of the Confederacy

The Story of the
CSS *Alabama*

CHARLES M. ROBINSON III

NAVAL INSTITUTE PRESS
ANNAPOLIS, MARYLAND

© 1995 by the United States Naval Institute
Annapolis, Maryland

LIBRARY OF CONGRESS CATALOGING-IN-PUBLICATION DATA

Robinson, Charles, M., 1949–
    Shark of the Confederacy : the story of the CSS Alabama / Charles M.
Robinson III.
        p.   cm.
    Includes bibliographical references and index.
    ISBN 1-55750-728-7
    1. Alabama (Steamer)   2. United States—History—Civil War,
1861–1865 — Naval operations.   3. Privateering—United States—
History—19th century.   I. Title.
E599.A3R58   1994
973.7′57—dc20   94-13816
                                                              CIP

Printed in the United States of America on acid-free paper ∞

3   5   7   9   8   6   4   2

Frontispiece: CSS *Alabama* (U.S. Naval Institute Collection)

FOR MY FATHER,
Charles M. Robinson, Jr.
1909–1980

Contents

CONTENTS

List of Illustrations

Author's Note

*M*ANY PEOPLE AND ORGANIZATIONS WERE INVOLVED IN THE development of this book. I especially wish to thank Dr. Norman C. Delaney of Corpus Christi, Texas, for reviewing the initial draft of the manuscript, and for his comments and suggestions. More than that, he gave me his friendship, expressed in a constant stream of letters of advice and encouragement on the *Alabama* and many other subjects.

My interest in the American Civil War was first encouraged by my father, who grew up in Wilmington and Fayetteville, North Carolina, at a time when many of the old vets were still alive. He listened to their stories and passed them on to us.

I also wish to acknowledge Jeff Burke and the late Chuck Rose, for sharing with me their experiences in the discovery of the *Hatteras* and encouraging my writing on that ship and the *Alabama;* Malcolm MacDonald of the University of Alabama Press, for his advice and encouragement; the W. Stanley Hoole Special Collections Library, University of Alabama, for furnishing the contemporary descriptions of the *Alabama* found in Appendix 1; the University of Georgia Press, for permission to reproduce the English translation of the song "Here Comes the Alabama" from W. Stanley Hoole's *Four Years in the Confederate Navy;* and Bernie Klay of the South Street Seaport, New York, for tracking down Civil War material.

Finally, I thank the United States Department of the Interior, National Park Service, Adams National Historic Site, Quincy, Massachusetts; Yolanda Gonzalez of the Hunter Research Room, Arnulfo Oliveira Library, Fort Brown, Brownsville, Texas; the San Benito, Texas, Public Library; and my wife, Perla.

SHARK OF THE CONFEDERACY

Prologue

*T*HE AMERICAN CIVIL WAR EXCITED CONTROVERSY FAR BEYOND the borders of North America. In Great Britain, the ruling class was fascinated with the idea of the Southern states rising up and—they hoped—defeating the pushy and sanctimonious Yankees. France, preoccupied with settling long-standing disputes in Mexico, welcomed the war as a means of rendering the United States powerless to intervene below the Rio Grande.

But the verdict was not unanimous. The Russians supported the American Union because it served as a counterweight to their hated enemies, the French and British. Throughout Europe, intellectuals marveled that the American government would drench itself in blood to preserve an ideal and to liberate an oppressed people. Among Europe's ordinary citizens, a Union victory meant the end to the odious institution of black slavery on the North American continent, while a victorious South meant it would continue.

Against this background of international passions, a lone ship cruised the oceans of the world, waging a single-handed war against Northern commerce. To her enemies, she was a pirate who attacked helpless merchantmen. To her admirers, she represented the South in the one place it had any chance of success—the high seas. She was conceived in chaos by a struggling government that had no clear aim or direction. She was built amid spies and Byzantine intrigue.

She sank in foreign waters, far from a home that she never saw. But while she sailed, she carried the flag of a new republic to the far corners of the earth, and she captured the imagination of the world.

Her name was *Alabama.*

This is her story.

1

The South Goes to Sea

*A*LABAMA. THE NAME STRUCK TERROR INTO NORTHERN SHIP-owners and captains. She was the bane of U.S. Secretary of the Navy Gideon Welles, who had to maintain ships in every ocean to look for her. To the North, the *Alabama* was a pirate ship, and her captain, Raphael Semmes, no better than Blackbeard or Sir Henry Morgan.[1] To the beleaguered South, and to the world at large, the ship was near legendary, and Semmes, the embodiment of a classic swashbuckler.

Pirate or dashing hero? Actually, the proud, aloof Semmes was neither. He saw himself as a naval officer doing his duty. He believed in his ship and in the young republic he served. Like many naval officers of his day, he was touchy on points of honor, and this attitude would ultimately have some bearing on the *Alabama*'s fate.[2]

The ship herself? Contemporary accounts describe her as a beauty. She was long and sleek and rode well in the water. Semmes likened her to a swan.[3] In appearance she may have been, but looks were deceiving. She was a shark, swimming among the minnows.

The *Alabama* was as much the product of serious miscalculation as anything else. When the Confederate government was formed in the provisional capital of Montgomery, Alabama, President Jefferson Davis appointed Stephen R. Mallory as his secretary of the navy. The choice hardly could have been better. Mallory was probably the most competent man in the Davis cabinet and the only one to serve in the same position for the government's entire existence. He had been a U.S. senator from Florida for ten years—from 1851 until that state seceded—and had spent much of the time as chairman of the Senate Committee on Naval Affairs. He viewed secession with distaste and for that reason was distrusted by many members of Congress and the government. Davis practically had to coerce him into accepting the navy portfolio.[4]

Yet Mallory's years on the Naval Affairs Committee had given him an understanding of the value of sea power.[5] His counterpart in the North, Welles, is generally regarded as the greatest secretary of the navy in history, but Mallory was nearly his equal. According to Commander James Bulloch, Confederate naval agent in Europe, Mallory "had a thorough knowledge of the organization, equipment, and general disciplinary rules of the United States Navy. If he had been placed at the head of that service, he would have been a popular and efficient administrator, but at Montgomery he was like a chieftain without a clan, or an artizan without the tools of his art."[6]

The singular difference between the two secretaries was in the support they received from their respective presidents. Abraham Lincoln realized the role naval power would have in winning the war, and he backed Welles in every possible way. Both knew that the U.S. Navy lacked ships and manpower to enforce the blockade. Welles's job was to get the ships, and Lincoln made sure he had the means to do it.[7]

Davis, on the other hand, could not grasp the need for a navy. Unlike the North, with its vast New England merchant fleet, the South had no maritime tradition. In 1861 the United States had the second largest merchant marine in the world, but only one-tenth of the total tonnage belonged to the Southern states. Although ten Confederate states were coastal, their leaders had a land-bound mentality. A soldier's education—at West Point, Virginia Military Institute, or The Citadel—was considered essential to well-rounded Southern youths, even if they did not enter active service upon graduation. Little thought was given to the sea or naval affairs. Davis, a West Pointer and former U.S. secretary of war, was a product of this background, and Mallory was left to fend for himself.[8]

CSS *Alabama*
(from Ellicott, *John Ancrum Winslow*)

Captain Raphael Semmes, CSN
(from *The Photographic History of the Civil War*)

Secretary of the Navy Stephen R. Mallory,
Confederate States of America

The secretary's troubles began almost as soon as the government
was formed. The new nation's cotton merchants, hoping to starve
the European mills into recognizing the Confederacy and paying
Southern prices, announced an embargo. Mallory contended that
Southern cotton should be shipped to Europe immediately, before
the blockade could become effective. The South should use the money
gained to build a navy capable of keeping its ports open. Yet the
government refused to intervene. Meanwhile, the British mills, well
supplied from 1860's bumper crop, continued production despite
the embargo.[9]

Mallory's chance to get his navy came in the winter of 1861. After
the disastrous Indian Mutiny, the British East India Company had
surrendered its sovereignty to the crown and was now liquidating
its assets. For two centuries, the company's giant ships had linked
Great Britain to the East, but when the Royal Navy and British
merchant fleet assumed that role, these ships were no longer necessary.

In Britain, Charles K. Prioleau, president of Fraser, Trenholm and Co., the Liverpool branch of a Charleston shipping firm, had located a fleet of ten first-class East Indiamen for sale at less than half their original cost. Like all ships of their type, they had been built not only for cargo but to carry armament and move troops as the need arose. All were steam-driven and could be easily converted to warships. Total cost of buying, arming, and delivering them to the Confederacy was estimated at $10 million, or about forty thousand bales of cotton. Port Royal, South Carolina, which had been used as a U.S. Navy coaling station before the war, was ideal as a base for this fleet. Brunswick, Georgia, was also suitable. Prioleau submitted the proposal to Charleston, where his senior partner, George A. Trenholm, forwarded it on to the government in Montgomery.

Incredibly, the offer was turned down. Rather than accept a ready-made fleet, which could have blown a hole in Welles's blockade before it could organize, the government expressed more interest in commerce raiders that could harass and destroy the U.S. merchant fleet. A decision of such far-reaching consequences could only have come from one of two men—and because Mallory understood the importance of a navy, that leaves Davis. It was a once-in-a-lifetime opportunity, and it had been lost forever. The Indiamen were acquired by the British government.[10]

While Mallory worried about a fleet, Gideon Welles was obtaining ships as fast as they could be found. Virtually anything that could float and carry a gun—passenger liners, river steamers, tugboats, ferryboats, yachts—was pressed into service, armed, and sent South.[11] Slowly the noose was tightening, as Mallory knew it would. His chance to break the blockade by naval force lost, he concentrated on weakening it. If enough Confederate cruisers could reach the high seas as commerce raiders and wreak havoc among U.S. merchant ships, he reasoned, the result would be twofold: it would hurt the United States economically, hampering the American government's ability to sustain the war, and U.S. warships would have to be diverted from the blockade in ever-increasing numbers to hunt the cruisers down.[12] There was wisdom in this decision, particularly because the South had no merchant marine of its own. As naval historian James Soley noted: "In a warfare against commerce, the Confederates could

Secretary of the Navy Gideon Welles,
United States of America

strike heavy blows, without fear of being struck back. Accordingly, it was against commerce that they immediately took the offensive; and they maintained that position until the end of the war. . . . The Federal Government, on the other hand, could not make use of commerce-destroyers because there was no enemy's commerce to destroy."[13] Thus the *Alabama* and her sisters were born.

A naval board met in New Orleans in the spring of 1861 to inspect light, fast steamers that could be converted to warships and sent to sea. The results were disappointing. Nevertheless, reports were prepared and sent to Mallory. On April 17, Commander Raphael Semmes of the Light-House Bureau called on Mallory to discuss commerce raiding. The secretary went over the problem and handed him a report on one such ship, the *Habana,* of 520 tons, built for trade between New Orleans and Cuba. She was propeller-driven, with a low-pressure steam engine capable of driving her nine or ten knots, and the deck could be strengthened to carry four or five guns. But she could carry fuel for only five days and had no accommodations for the large crew needed to man a warship. Accordingly, the board had condemned her as unfit.

"Give me that ship," Semmes said. "I think I can make her answer the purpose."[14]

Mallory agreed and telegraphed the board to accept the *Habana,* which became the first Confederate warship. The following day, Semmes received orders detaching him from the Light-House Bureau and appointing him to assume command of the ship, now named *Sumter* "in honor of our recent victory over Fort Sumter." His officers were listed as Lieutenants John McIntosh Kell, R. T. Chapman, John M. Stribling, and William E. Evans; Paymaster Henry Myers; Surgeon Francis L. Galt; and Midshipmen William A. Hicks, Richard F. Armstrong, Albert G. Hudgins, John F. Holden, and Joseph D. Wilson. Holden drowned in an accident in the Mississippi before the *Sumter* sailed. Several of the others would later serve on the *Alabama.*[15]

Both Mallory and Semmes were Roman Catholics, the former born on Trinidad to a Connecticut father and an Irish mother, the latter descended from Catholic refugees from Normandy, who had settled in Maryland in 1640. He was born in Charles County, Maryland, on September 27, 1809. Orphaned as a boy, he was reared by his uncle, also named Raphael. In 1826, another uncle, U.S. Representative Benedict J. Semmes, secured him an appointment as a midshipman from President John Quincy Adams. Ironically, this appointment would cause many sleepless nights for the president's son, Charles Francis Adams, who became Lincoln's minister to Great Britain.[16]

Naval service was leisurely during the first forty years of the nineteenth century. After long periods at sea, officers were entitled to extended leaves and often used the time to develop other interests. In Semmes's case it was literature and the law, the latter of which he read with his brother Samuel, an attorney in Cumberland, Maryland. Upon returning from his first cruise in 1832, he was admitted to the bar but opted to remain in the navy. Promotions were slow at the time, and it was not until 1837 that he was appointed lieutenant. Five years later, he moved to Alabama. During the Mexican War he commanded the brig *Somers* on blockade duty. He was chasing a suspicious sail when the *Somers* was hit by a storm. She sank, and

Semmes was one of the few survivors. He commanded a shore battery during the siege of Veracruz, then accompanied General Winfield Scott's march to Mexico City, serving as a volunteer aide to General William Worth.[17]

In 1849 he moved to Mobile, which would be his home for the rest of his life. He left active service, established a law practice, and entered local politics. He also wrote his memoirs, *Service Afloat and Ashore during the Mexican War,* which one contemporary called "a spirited and valuable contribution to the history of that conflict." Settled for the first time, Semmes became more Southern than the archtypal plantation owner. He was, in fact, a "period piece," representing everything that was both good and bad about the Deep South of his age. Yet he was also a highly capable officer, and the Navy Department could not let him go for very long. In 1855 he was promoted to commander and subsequently recalled to active duty. He was sent to Pensacola, where he served as inspector for the Eighth Light-House District with responsibility for lighthouses on the Gulf Coast. He also served as secretary to the Light-House Board in Washington. During his tenure in Pensacola, he was defense counsel in the court-martial of four midshipmen, one of whom was Francis Clarke, who had saved his life when the *Somers* went down. Another was John Kell, who would serve Semmes faithfully as executive officer in the coming war. The charges were trivial—the men had failed to obey an order to light candles for relief lieutenants coming on watch. Even so, Semmes lost the case, and all four were dismissed from the service, although they were later reinstated through political influence.[18]

In the 1860 presidential election, Semmes supported Stephen Douglas's candidacy against the more popular Southern choice, John C. Breckinridge. His views were similar to those of Georgia politician Alexander H. Stephens, who would remember Semmes after he became vice-president of the Confederacy. A month after Alabama seceded, Semmes resigned from the U.S. Navy and, through Stephens's influence, received a commission as commander in the Confederate navy. President Davis sent him north on a procuring mission, and he obtained large quantities of powder for the Confederacy before hostilities broke out. On his return, he was appointed chief of the Light-House Bureau, and it was in that capacity that he had called on Mallory the day he was given the *Sumter*.[19]

Although the war was scarcely two weeks old when Semmes arrived in New Orleans, he found that the city was already feeling its impact. The lucrative trade with Cincinnati, Pittsburgh, and other Northern river ports had been severed. "The levée in front of the city was no longer a great mart of commerce, piled with cotton bales, and supplies going back to the planter; densely packed with steamers, and thronged with a busy multitude," he wrote. "The long lines of shipping above the city had been greatly thinned, and a general air of desolation hung over the river front. It seemed as though a pestilence brooded over the doomed city, and that its inhabitants had fled before the fell destroyer." The *Sumter* lay across the Mississippi at Algiers, and as he crossed every morning to supervise her refit, he noticed that on some days there was no activity at all on the river.[20]

Workers were set to removing the ship's deck cabins and top-hamper and making other alterations. It was a frustrating job. In the past, Semmes had refitted ships in navy yards that had skilled laborers and well-equipped shops. Here everything had to be improvised from water tanks to gun carriages and primers. He not only had to determine the alterations but make drawings and plans which the local yard crews could understand. Meanwhile, the confused Southern transportation system was creating other problems. When Virginia seceded, the Confederacy acquired Gosport Navy Yard at Norfolk. Mallory had dispatched orders giving the *Sumter* top priority for guns, shot, shells, and cordage. The guns had been shipped immediately but failed to arrive. After several weeks, Semmes sent a lieutenant, who found them one by one at various points along the railroad lines, where they had been offloaded to make room for other freight.

Once the guns were in his possession, Semmes did not bother with Gosport again. A former customs employee set up a shop in the old customs house and built carriages for the pivot gun out of railroad iron. When they were finished, Semmes said they were the best he had ever seen. A local foundry produced satisfactory shells and solid shot.[21]

The ship was taking shape. The main deck was strengthened to support the battery, and a berth deck was installed for the crew. The engine, part of which was above the waterline, was protected with extra woodwork and iron bars. Officers' quarters were rearranged, and the ship was rerigged as a barkentine. Finally, she was armed with an eight-inch shell gun to be pivoted amidships and four light thirty-two-pounders in broadside.[22]

Meanwhile, events elsewhere were shaping the future of the Confederate navy. On April 19, 1861, Lincoln issued a proclamation declaring that any Confederate ship that molested a U.S. ship on the high seas would be regarded as a pirate. He also made the blockade a legal reality. On May 14, Great Britain responded with a proclamation of neutrality, recognizing the Confederate States of America as a belligerent power. The example was followed within the next three months by France, the Netherlands, Spain, and Brazil.[23]

As May drew to a close and Semmes fretted over delays, the blockade became effective. The USS *Brooklyn* appeared off the mouth of the Mississippi on May 26 and was joined shortly thereafter by the *Niagara* and *Minnesota*. The river was now closed.[24]

Finally, on June 3, the *Sumter* was commissioned and the Confederate ensign was hoisted for the first time. The next two weeks were spent in final preparations and trials along the river. Semmes was disappointed in her speed, which never exceeded nine knots. Although he had expanded her coal bunkers, she could carry fuel for only eight days. And when she was under sail, the propeller created a drag. "It was with such drawbacks, that I was to take to the sea, alone, against a vindictive and relentless enemy, whose Navy already swarmed on our coasts, and whose means of increasing it were inexhaustible." Still, Semmes was undeterred. "The sailor has a saying, that 'Luck is a Lord,' and we trusted to luck."[25]

On June 18 the *Sumter* eased downriver and took on powder. Then, at 10:30 P.M., she got up steam and headed for the sea, anchoring under the protection of Forts Jackson and St. Philip at 4:00 the next morning. Three days later, Semmes received his sailing orders from Mallory in Richmond, the newly designated permanent capital. More Union ships were now on station so it was not until June 30 that he was able to run the blockade and put to sea. After a quick run to Cuba, the *Sumter* overhauled the seven-hundred-ton U.S. bark *Golden Rocket*. The ship was condemned, and after the crew had been removed, she was burned. The Confederate navy had captured its first prize. For the next six months, Semmes took the *Sumter* through the Caribbean and Atlantic, capturing various prizes.[26]

The new year found the *Sumter* in need of repairs and short on fuel. She had been battered by a storm, was leaking, and her machinery needed work. Semmes had hoped to cruise a few days off Cadiz before putting in for repairs, but on January 2 the chief engineer reported that the leak was too bad to continue. The following day, the ship put into Cadiz, where Semmes notified the U.S. consul that he had forty-three prisoners of war on board who wished to be repatriated on parole. The consul refused to acknowledge Semmes's official right to parole such prisoners.[27]

In Spain Semmes first encountered the bureaucracy and diplomatic tangles that were to hound him throughout his career as a Confederate officer. First, he was ordered to sail within twenty-four hours. Upon replying that his ship was in too bad condition, he was allowed to take her into the government dry docks, where Spanish naval authorities examined her to establish that her condition was as bad as he had represented. The hull was found to be basically sound; the leak was in the propeller sleeve. Repairs were allowed, but the Spaniards refused to authorize an engine overhaul on the grounds that low steam pressure could still be maintained. Furthermore, Spanish authorities refused to return nine deserters, whom Semmes maintained had been enticed away by the U.S. consul and were being sheltered in the consulate.[28]

Semmes contended that U.S. representatives were creating all the obstructions. In fact, Spanish authorities had no idea what to do. His arrival had created an unusual situation. Although the Confederacy was a recognized belligerent, the war had not progressed far enough for any Continental power to develop a policy toward Southern naval vessels. The United States, by contrast, was an established power with protocol abroad, and its representatives were protesting vehemently. Finally, the Spaniards resolved their predicament by ordering the *Sumter* to leave the country.[29]

The ship was now reasonably seaworthy, and Semmes got up steam and headed for Gibraltar, arriving there on January 19. Shortly before entering British waters, however, she captured two final prizes. The

Neapolitan, loaded with fifty tons of sulfur and bound for Boston, was burned. The *Investigator,* also of U.S. registry, carried cargo under British consignment for Wales and was therefore bonded.[30]

In contrast to the Spaniards, British authorities at Gibraltar received Semmes with all the courtesies due to a foreign naval officer. Permission was given to land the prisoners, who were paroled and sent ashore. But U.S. consul Horatio Sprague persuaded local merchants to withhold coal from the Confederate ship. Semmes then sought to buy coal from the government. The request was telegraphed to London and a week later was denied.[31]

Semmes decided to send Paymaster Myers and T. T. Tunstall, former U.S. consul, who had opted for the South, to Cadiz to buy coal there. En route, their packet stopped at Tangier, and they went ashore for some sightseeing. They were arrested by Moroccan authorities at the request of the U.S. consul in Tangier, who claimed that they were U.S. citizens wanted for piracy. After being held in irons in the local prison, they were transferred to the U.S. merchant ship *Harvest Home,* whose captain ordered their heads shaved and had them confined in irons for the duration of the trip to the United States. Semmes never forgot the incident, and several Yankee crews would pay for it later.[32]

Meanwhile, the U.S. warships *Tuscarora, Ino,* and *Kearsarge* had arrived and were cruising off the coast, waiting for the *Sumter* to come out. Semmes knew he was trapped. He telegraphed Confederate commissioner James Mason in London for permission to discharge all but a caretaker crew, then took most of his officers to Great Britain. The *Sumter* was put up for auction and sold to Fraser, Trenholm and Company for use as a blockade runner.[33]

Although he had lost his ship, Semmes was pleased with the results of the cruise. In all, the *Sumter* had captured seventeen ships. The U.S. Navy had been forced to divert new steamers from blockade duty to look for him. "The enemy kept five or six of his best ships of war constantly in pursuit of her, which necessarily weakened his blockade, for which, at this time, he was much pressed for ships," he reflected.[34] It seemed as though Mallory's plan for weakening the blockade might work after all.

The *Sumter*'s success was largely owing to Semmes and his officers, particularly Kell. During the cruise they had established a working relationship whereby Semmes handled the administration of the ship and made all major decisions while Kell oversaw day-to-day operations and dealt with the crew. This quiet understanding—Semmes confided in no one, including Kell—was invaluable because the majority of the officers on both the *Sumter* and *Alabama* were young and relatively inexperienced.[35]

The cruise of the *Sumter* showed that converted coastal steamers were poorly suited to the task that lay ahead. Yet she was typical of what the South could provide at home. Except for a few odd merchant steamers already on hand, the Confederacy had no means of producing a navy. Therefore, it was understood that future commerce raiders would have to come from abroad, where they could be built to exact specifications. The job of procuring them went to James Bulloch, Mallory's naval agent in Europe.

2

The Secret War of No. 290

JAMES BULLOCH'S JOB WOULD HAVE KEPT A DOZEN MEN fully occupied. He organized the supply and shipment of war matériel to the Confederacy. He acquired specially designed blockade runners for the Confederate government. He arranged accommodations and transportation for Confederate officers and crews and kept them under wraps until time came for them to depart for their various assignments. He arranged the construction or purchase and outfitting of Confederate warships. He walked a tightrope with the British to avoid violation of their neutrality laws and Foreign Enlistment Act. And he had to circumvent the highly organized spy system set up by U.S. minister Charles Francis Adams.

Bulloch was exceptionally well qualified for his job. He had served fourteen years in the U.S. Navy and eight years in merchant shipping. He was discreet, and he was honest. In the course of his dealings, Bulloch handled large amounts of hard currency, and it amazed Semmes that he was able to maintain his integrity. Bulloch lived simply on his government salary and such personal funds as he had available. Like many people caught up in the war, he came from a family of divided loyalties. His half-sister Martha was married to New York merchant Theodore Roosevelt and had a small son, also named Theodore, who would one day become president of the United States.[1]

After Bulloch's arrival in Liverpool on June 4, 1861, one of his first acts was to commission construction of a warship with the firm of William Miller and Sons. The design had to be unique. The ship would need to carry all necessities, especially for ordnance. She had to function equally well under sail or steam so that frequent coaling would not be necessary. Miller's drawings of a Royal Navy gunboat were modified for greater length to allow sharper lines on the hull, which would increase her speed. The rigging was greatly increased to carry more sail and make her more maneuverable. The engines were discussed in detail to be certain they would meet all the requirements. She would be called *Oreto* and was officially destined for the Italian government, although Bulloch contracted for her in his own name.[2]

While he was negotiating for the *Oreto,* Bulloch visited another shipyard, the Birkenhead Iron Works, owned by the firm of John Laird and Sons. There he discussed the possibility of a dispatch ship with specifications similar to those of the *Oreto.* An agreement was reached, and Bulloch began preparing the model and plans. Most British ships were then built of iron, and Bulloch wanted wood. The Lairds told him it would take more time and be more expensive than the usual ship. The financial arrangements were made, and the contract was signed on August 1, 1861, again in Bulloch's name. This ship was designated simply as Hull No. 290.[3]

While his warships were under construction, Bulloch purchased a light, fast ship, the *Fingal,* loaded her with rifles, artillery, munitions, medical supplies, and uniforms, and personally ran her through the blockade to Savannah. Then he returned to Liverpool, where his polish and sense of style appealed to his British hosts.

Bulloch's absence while delivering the *Fingal* created delays with 290. Laird's intended to build a first-class ship, and because Bulloch was unable to look after his interests personally, the company was all the more concerned with doing the job right. Bulloch himself noted, "They were especially critical and hard to please in the selection of the timber for the most important parts." Several times a sternpost had already been fitted and bored for the propeller shaft when someone at Laird's noticed a defect and ordered it scrapped.[4]

Semmes arrived while construction was under way. After the *Sumter* was laid up, he and Lieutenant Kell went to London and rented a

Commander James D. Bulloch, CSN
(from *The Secret Service of the Confederate States in Europe*)

set of rooms together on Euston Square. Even though it was still early in the year, the lawns were green, the trees had leaves, and flowers were in bloom, which they appreciated after so many months at sea. They enjoyed Virginia-style hospitality from Commissioner James Mason and were entertained by Southern sympathizers among the local population.[5] Mason informed Semmes that the *Oreto* had recently sailed for Nassau, where she would be commissioned as the *Florida*. Adams was in a fury because Thomas Dudley, U.S. consul in Liverpool, had established beyond any reasonable doubt that she was bound for the Confederacy.[6]

While the *Oreto* was at sea, Bulloch was pushing for completion of No. 290, which was behind schedule. Already she was attracting attention. Passengers on the ferries steaming up the Mersey past Birkenhead could not help noticing her, especially when they were accustomed to seeing cumbersome iron ships on the ways. This worried Bulloch. "No doubt," he wrote, "remarks were often made in respect to her fitness for a cruiser, and it is not therefore surprising that she should have aroused the suspicions of those whose business it was to keep watch over the interests of the United States."[7]

Indeed, there was no question in Adams's mind that No. 290 was destined for the Confederate navy. There was even a rumor that she was designated 290 because she had been funded by 290 Southern sympathizers, although, in fact, she was the 290th hull built by the company. In March, Dudley hired Matthew Maguire, a private detective, to hang around the yards, watch the ship, and question the workmen. From various sources Maguire managed to piece together enough rumor and fact to confirm American suspicions.

The ship was similar to the *Oreto* but of superior construction. She was built of "the best English oak that could be obtained. . . . Every plank and timber of which she is built was strictly examined after being worked up," Maguire reported. "A large quantity of this oak was condemned, for what, the carpenter says, was no detriment whatever. . . . The stern gear is all copper and brass, in fact the gentleman who superintended her construction says, 'they could not turn out anything better from Her Majesty[']s Dock Yards.' "[8] Affidavits were made that Bulloch had been enlisting men to serve on her for the Confederate navy, a charge he denied.[9]

Bulloch was fully aware of Maguire's activities. He consulted his attorney, who advised him that he was doing nothing illegal and should maintain a low profile and complete the ship as soon as possible. No effort was made to conceal the ship, but absolute secrecy was maintained about her purpose. Neither the Lairds nor their employees were given any more information than was absolutely necessary. According to Bulloch, "they did not know for what purpose the ship was intended when they agreed to build her."[10]

Bulloch's denial notwithstanding, it is hard to imagine that the builders did not suspect that No. 290 was a warship. Maguire was convinced that the "Lairds themselves [and] the foreman carpenter" knew her purpose. Her specifications called for features that would be useful only on a naval vessel such as carlings "requisite for Gun Pivots &c," shot racks, a magazine and light room, and a shell room.[11] Iron water tanks were placed forward and aft of the magazine and shell room for protection. After the war, Bulloch speculated that this arrangement of tanks may have doomed the *Alabama*.[12]

The ship was launched on May 15, 1862. She was called *Enrica,* the Latinized form of the name of the woman who sponsored her. Bulloch and his wife attended, along with "several American gentlemen," and these events were duly reported by Maguire. Two tugs took her under tow immediately and moved her over to the graving dock. Before she was secured, the cranes began loading her machinery. Laird's was embarrassed over construction delays and hoped to make up the time by fitting her out as rapidly as possible.[13]

Mallory had ordered Bulloch to command the new ship, but he offered to relinquish that honor to Semmes. But there were no orders to that effect, and because Semmes found nothing else available for himself or his officers, he felt it better to return to the South and wait for further instructions. This was good news for Kell, a strong family man, who wanted very much to go home. Together with Surgeon Galt, they obtained passage to Nassau on the *Melita*. This ship was owned by a firm of blockade runners, and they were allowed to sail free of charge. Semmes ascertained that the *Melita* was making a legitimate voyage to Nassau and would not try to run the blockade, which meant that he and his officers would be safe if she was overhauled by a U.S. warship. The voyage was made without incident, and they arrived in Nassau about 2:00 P.M. June 13, 1862. From there, they planned to catch a blockade runner into Norfolk.[14]

If the war had wrecked the New Orleans economy, it had been a windfall for Nassau. Not long before, it had been a fishing village, dependent on a trade in sponges, sea turtles, and conch shells. Now it was a center for blockade runners. "All was life, bustle, and activity," Semmes wrote. "Ships were constantly arriving and depositing their cargoes, and light-draught steamers, Confederate and English, were as constantly reloading these cargoes, and running them into the ports of the Confederate States." Docks were piled high with cotton shipped out of the South, and warehouses were full of supplies waiting to be shipped in. The streets were jammed with commerce by day and drunken revelry by night. Both Semmes and Kell noticed that many of the businessmen were U.S. citizens hoping to make quick fortunes by selling arms and equipment to the Confederacy.[15]

The *Oreto* was already in Nassau, and Semmes met with Commander John Maffitt, who had come to commission her as the *Florida* and assume command. Another recent arrival was Commander Terry Sinclair, who brought a letter from Mallory ordering Semmes back to Europe to assume command of No. 290. She would be called the *Alabama*.[16]

Semmes immediately wrote to Mallory and accepted the command. He said he planned to return with Kell and Galt, along with Lieutenant B. K. Howell of the marines, who had arrived in Nassau a few days earlier, as had Lieutenant Stribling. Semmes wanted Stribling to go back as well, but Maffitt asked that he be transferred to the *Florida*. Consequently, Semmes proposed to promote Midshipman Armstrong, still with the *Sumter* in Gibraltar, to fill Stribling's spot as lieutenant.[17] Then he wrote Commander J. H. North, another Confederate agent in Great Britain, saying he would return as soon as possible. In the meantime, he asked North to "do me the favor to inform Bulloch immediately of this change, and to request him to proceed with the preparations of the ship precisely as if he were to command her himself. Detain also any of the *Sumter*'s officers who may be still in London or Liverpool, without informing them, however, of the object of their detention, lest through indiscretion they may speak of it." He also asked North to contact Armstrong in Gibraltar and call him to Britain to join the command.[18]

Aware of the difficulties involved, Semmes wrote Mallory:

> It will, doubtless, be a matter of some delicacy, and tact, to get the *Alabama* safely out of British waters, without suspicion, as Mr. Adams, the Northern Envoy, and his numerous satellites in the shape of consuls and paid agents, are exceedingly vigilant in their espionage.
>
> We cannot, of course, think of arming her in a British port; this must be done at some concerted rendezvous, to which her battery and a large portion of her crew must be sent, in a neutral merchant-vessel. The *Alabama* will be a fine ship, quite equal to encounter any of the enemy's steam-sloops, of the class of the *Iroquois, Tuscarora,* and *Dacotah,* and I shall feel much more independent in her, upon the high seas, than I did in the little *Sumter*.[19]

While Semmes worried about the ship, Kell faced yet another separation from his family. "God grant it may be for the best!" he wrote to his wife. "At least the sacrifice is made for our beloved country, and it must be done with a good will and a cheerful spirit.

Charles Francis Adams, U.S. minister to Great Britain
(Adams National Historic Site)

The fortitude with which you and my dear mother bear this separation sustains me through it all, and for every duty."[20]

Semmes was correct in assuming that Adams would make trouble. The American minister's primary weapon was the Foreign Enlistment Act. This law, passed in 1819, prohibited any British subject from equipping, furnishing, fitting out, or arming any vessel that was intended for service by a belligerent power. On June 23, Adams notified the Foreign Office that he suspected the ship was being outfitted in violation of the act. The note was referred to legal officials who said that if this was the case, "the building and equipment of the vessel were a 'manifest violation of the Foreign Enlistment Act, and steps ought to be taken to put that act in force and to prevent the vessel from going to sea.'" The British, however, insisted that evidence be submitted before any action could be taken against offenders. With that proviso in mind, Adams instructed Dudley to gather all available evidence of the *Enrica*'s true nature and present it to Samuel Price Edwards, collector of customs in Liverpool. Dudley got a sworn statement from an apprentice shipwright that Bulloch had asked him to sign on 290 as carpenter's mate and that the ship was to be a Confederate man-of-war. This and other statements concerning the ship's magazines and reinforced deck were presented to Edwards, who took them as hearsay and insufficient to warrant detention of the ship. Exasperated, Dudley finally demanded that Edwards seize the ship. Dudley's firmness together with Adams's constant badgering in London prompted the foreign secretary, John, Earl Russell, to order an admiralty inspection of the *Enrica*. This was at least the second such inspection, and once again the ship was found to be unarmed and with no war matériel on board.[21]

There were several reasons for British inaction. First, Confederate legal advisers had thoroughly researched the Foreign Enlistment Act and found it riddled with holes. It would have been a violation to build, arm, and equip a warship in a single operation, but as Adams's son later noted, "there was nothing in the act which made illegal the building of a warship as one operation; and nothing which prevented the purchase of the arms and munitions to equip such vessel, when built, as another operation. But the two must be kept distinctly separate." Then, in July 1862, the North suffered a series of military disasters that made the likelihood of a Southern victory very real. Government ministers in both London and Paris were considering the possibility of mediating between the United States and the Confederacy as separate powers. Failing that, Lord Palmerston, the prime minister, and Lord Russell agreed that it might be necessary to recognize the Confederacy as an independent nation. Against that possibility, the British government was careful to avoid offending the South.[22]

Adams was equally indifferent to British legalities and Southern military success. He had only one interest, and that was to stop the *Enrica,* which, he learned, had gone out for her first trial on June 15, with representatives of Fraser, Trenholm and Company on board. The *Tuscarora* arrived in British waters, and he sent word to her commanding officer, Captain T. A. Craven, to position himself to intercept the *Enrica* if she tried to put to sea. Bulloch, however, was one jump ahead. He made arrangements with a friend in Southampton to keep an eye on the Union ship's movements while he personally watched out for Adams.

"We knew that the American Minister was pressing the Government to seize the ship," Bulloch said, "and the frequent inquiries addressed to the builders by the Customs authorities at London, and the active watchfulness of the local officers of that department at Liverpool, warned me that the situation was critical." The *Enrica* was coaled and all stores were put on board. A British master was necessary so the ship could receive her certificate from the Board of Trade, and for that purpose Bulloch retained Captain Mathew J. Butcher, a Royal Navy reservist and former Cunard man. He detailed Lieutenant John Low, CSN, to help complete arrangements and accompany the ship. An outstanding seaman, Low was a Liverpool native who had become a de facto Confederate because he was living in Savannah when Georgia seceded. Everything was ready for a fast departure.[23]

Adams presented his case to Robert Porrett Collier, judge advocate of the British fleet and the country's leading authority on maritime law. Collier was convinced that the ship was in clear violation of the Foreign Enlistment Act and that if she were allowed to sail, the U.S. government would have "serious grounds of complaint." Armed with this opinion, Adams went to Russell, who agreed to take the case to Sir John Harding, queen's advocate.[24]

On Saturday, July 26, Bulloch received reliable information that it would not be safe for the *Enrica* to remain in port for another forty-eight hours. He moved fast. He already had a verbal agreement with Laird's that the ship could have a second trial with a full load. Now he told the company that he wanted her to have a day-long trial in the Irish Sea. Butcher was ordered to ship more hands and have everything ready to come out on Monday's tide. Privately, Bulloch told him to load more coal and complete his stores because the ship would not return. Low and other trusted Confederate officers were also sent aboard.[25]

Luck was on Bulloch's side. The queen's advocate had suffered a crippling stroke, and his wife "allowed the package to lie undisturbed on his desk for three days."[26] On his own initiative, Russell sent an order to detain the *Enrica*. He was too late. At 9:00 A.M., July 28, she came out of the dock and anchored. The following morning, she was dressed out in flags, with a party of invited guests for the trial cruise. Low had contracted the tug *Hercules* to accompany the ship as a tender. Hidden in the tug's hold was spare equipment that had been left off the *Enrica* in the rush to get her ready for sea. At 4:00 P.M., the *Hercules* took Bulloch and his guests off, and the *Enrica* headed toward Moelfre Bay, on the Welsh coast, where she anchored.[27]

The next morning, Bulloch was at the landing stage ready to return to the *Enrica* when he was handed a telegram from his contact in Southampton. It said that the *Tuscarora* had sailed and was believed to be heading toward Queenstown on the southern coast of Ireland. This meant that Craven planned to intercept the ship if she followed the usual route down the Irish Sea and through St. George's Channel. She would have to sail north, past the Giant's Causeway and around Ireland.[28]

It was stormy by the time the *Hercules* delivered Bulloch and the spare equipment aboard the *Enrica*. Butcher feared for the ship's safety, and Bulloch himself confessed that under ordinary circumstances he would have sought shelter. But these were not ordinary circumstances, and at 2:30 A.M., July 31, she steamed out into the Irish Sea. That evening, as she passed the Giant's Causeway, she hailed a passing fishing boat, which took Bulloch and pilot George Bond ashore. Captain Butcher pointed the ship around Ireland on a course that would take her down the Atlantic to Praya Bay on the island of Terceira in the Azores. Bulloch had learned of the bay when he had stopped the *Fingal* at Terceira for water. It was an ideal rendezvous point. Upon arrival, Butcher was to meet the supply ship *Agrippina* and take on guns and stores. "Fill the bunkers from the coals on board the *Agrippina* and keep both vessels ready for a start on short notice," Bulloch wrote. "Captain R. Semmes, of the C.S. Navy, is the officer who will I hope very soon relieve you." Obviously, Butcher knew the true nature of the voyage and had known for some time. Among his instructions, Bulloch told him: "You are to consider yourself as my confidential agent, and I shall rely upon you as one gentleman may upon another. If you have an opportunity at any time, send me a line, and get out of the reach of the telegraphic stations as soon as possible. . . . It is important that your movements should not be reported, and you will please avoid speaking or signaling any passing ship." Similar orders were sent to Captain Alexander McQueen of the *Agrippina,* although they ostensibly came from that ship's owners rather than Bulloch himself.[29]

Meanwhile, Semmes felt marooned in Nassau, unable to obtain passage back to Europe for several weeks. He finally arrived in Liverpool on the steamer *Bahama* a few days after the *Enrica* had sailed. He brought with him a new look. He had allowed his mustache to grow inordinately long and had twisted it in an upward curve ending in finely waxed points. This gave him a flamboyant appearance he did not previously have and made him a highly visible figure. But though the mustache, combined with his exploits, made him the darling of British society and the international press, the crew of the *Alabama* would be less impressed. The sailors came to call him "Old Beeswax." Though outwardly visible, he was very cautious in his actions. He quietly built up his staff of officers, mainly from the *Sumter,* to avoid conflicts with the Foreign Enlistment Act. He did recruit one British subject, however, Dr. David Llewellyn, as assistant surgeon for the new ship.[30]

He also made financial arrangements for his forthcoming assignment through the usual means of Fraser, Trenholm and Company. The *Alabama* would be well funded. Aside from what one of her officers, Lieutenant Arthur Sinclair, called "a considerable sum in gold . . . at all times kept in the strong box for emergencies," Semmes had the authority to draw on bills from Liverpool to meet his requirements. Sinclair noted, "Never during our cruise was there the slightest hesitancy on the part of merchants or others in accepting Semmes's 'sterling bills' on England, though amounting generally to about ten thousand dollars at each coaling port. . . . Indeed, the credit of the *Alabama* was, as they have it in commercial parlance, 'Al.' "[31]

Kell had no illusions about the coming cruise. On August 12, he wrote to his wife:

> I will try to write from unfrequented ports into which we go, but I can not even hope to hear from home again till the close of this dreadful war. We go on board ship in two hours, and sail early to-morrow morning to meet our new ship at the appointed rendezvous. She is said to be beautiful gunboat, and very fast. I hope before very long you will get good accounts of us and our work. She will be christened the *Alabama.* Young Armstrong is to be second lieutenant, tell his mother. I am glad of his promotion, as he is very efficient. God grant this war may close this winter, but should it continue longer we must be brave and bear up cheerfully till we have driven the invader from our soil and established our beloved Southland free and independent among the nations of the earth.[32]

The following day, August 13, the *Bahama* cleared Liverpool for the Azores, with Semmes, Kell, Bulloch, and other officers on board. As the tug that had towed her down the Mersey cast off, its crew gave the ship three cheers.[33]

3

The Alabama

THE *ENRICA* WAS RELEASED FROM QUARANTINE IN PRAYA ON the day Semmes left Liverpool to meet her. She had arrived at 7:00 A.M. August 9, after an uneventful voyage. There had been a few days of heavy weather, but aside from a stove-in gunport cover on the port bow, damage had not been noteworthy. A few ships were sighted but had passed without incident. The ship sailed well, and the engine functioned without any problems, prompting George Townley Fullam, who would later serve as her boarding officer, to remark, "She gave promise of being a good sea boat and also a swift one."[1]

Portuguese officials came on board the afternoon of the *Enrica*'s arrival and were told she was the *Barcelona,* bound from London to Havana for the Spanish government. With nothing to do but maintain the ship and wait, officers went ashore, where they found the local population friendly and fresh fruit and vegetables plentiful. Fullam observed the ancient Portuguese forts, built to defend the island, but "nearly useless thro' decay." On August 13, the American whaling schooner *Rising Sun* sailed in and anchored near the *Enrica.* The arrival of the American ship worried those on the *Enrica* because, "through the indiscretion of the Purser [Paymaster Clarence R. Yonge], our real character became known," Fullam wrote. No incident occurred, however, and when the *Rising Sun* sailed, her captain was apparently still unaware of the Confederate ship's mission.[2]

The *Agrippina* arrived on August 18 and at 6:00 A.M. the following day drew up alongside. By the end of twelve hours, all the guns, munitions, and purser's stores had been transferred to the *Enrica,* after which the supply ship hauled off and began cleaning up. Work resumed at 6:00 A.M. August 20. The crews were two hours into the job when a steamer was sighted standing in from the southeast. Everyone anxiously watched to see who the stranger might be. It was a common feeling among the crews that the United States "was in the habit of kicking all the small powers, that had not the means to kicking back," and that Portuguese neutrality would provide little protection if it were a U.S. warship determined to create an incident. Finally, she was identified as the *Bahama,* and everyone went back to work much relieved.[3]

On the *Bahama,* the sight of the *Enrica* created some anxious moments as well until she was identified. Looking his new command over as he came into the harbor, Semmes was "quite satisfied with her external appearance. She was, indeed, a beautiful thing to look upon. The store-ship was already alongside of her, and we could see that the busy work of transferring her cargo was going on."[4]

The *Bahama* carried another pair of thirty-two pounders for the *Enrica,* as well as additional stores. But the harbor of Porto Praya was exposed to the east, and a heavy wind from that direction made it dangerous for the ships to remain alongside each other. Semmes told Captain Butcher to take the *Enrica* to Angra, on the lee side of the island, where there was smooth water.[5] As the ships steamed around the island, a customs boat overhauled them, told him they were heading for the wrong anchorage, and ordered them back to Praya. The Confederate ships ignored the warning and continued to Angra, where the *Enrica* anchored at 5:00 P.M. The *Bahama* and *Agrippina* drew alongside. Semmes came on board the ship for the first time. He found the decks in "a very uninviting state of confusion" because there had been no time to stow cargo or mount the guns. The crew members, who had been selected at random from the docks and streets of Liverpool, were dirty and unkempt and did not strike Semmes as resembling navy seamen. Still, as he watched, he was impressed by the men and decided that with a good washing, clean shirts, and a little discipline, they would do well enough.[6]

In addition to the crew already on the *Enrica,* thirty-seven seamen had shipped on board the *Bahama.* Semmes showed them the new ship and told them their contracts had ended and they were free to do as they chose. Then he invited them to ship with him. He told them about the war, explained the purpose of the cruise, and outlined benefits such as prize money for ships taken. About half of them signed up that afternoon. Others held out, and he guessed they were waiting for better terms. Semmes moved his gear over and established himself in the cabin, where "I was to spend so many weary days, and watchful nights." To avoid another dispute with Portuguese customs, the ships moved out beyond a marine league the next morning and continued the cargo transfer outside Portuguese jurisdiction.[7]

"You can but faintly imagine the bustle and apparent confusion existing," Lieutenant Arthur Sinclair wrote. "The carpenter and mates assisted by the engineers were measuring and putting down the 'circles' [circular tracks] for the two pivot-guns. The boatswain and mates fitting train and side-tackles to the broadside guns. Gunner stowing the magazine, shot and shell lockers. Sailmaker looking after his spare sails, and seeing them safely stored in the sailroom. . . . Day and night on goes the work: each hour the 290 looking more like a man-of-war."[8]

At the end of the first day beyond the marine league, the *Enrica* and *Agrippina* steamed into the port of entry at East Angra, while the *Bahama* lay to at sea. As the ships passed the fort at the entrance to the harbor, officials began yelling something that no one on board could understand. Then the fort fired a warning shot, which the steamers ignored as they continued in and dropped anchor near a small Portuguese warship. About midnight, one of the officers calmly woke Semmes up and told him the warship was firing on them.

"The devil she is," Semmes said. "How many shots has she fired at us?"

"Three, sir," the officer replied.

"Have any of them struck us?"

"No, sir. None of them have struck us. They seem to be firing rather wild."

Semmes knew that even under the fiction of a merchant ship, the *Enrica* was too powerful for the little Portuguese ship to attack and decided it was a bluff. "Let him fire away. I expect he won't hurt you," he said, and rolled over and went back to sleep. Others, however, were less tranquil; outside the harbor, the *Bahama* immediately weighed anchor and began maneuvering to draw fire away from the *Enrica*. Early the next morning, it was learned that the gunfire had come from a mail steamer that had pulled in and expected to depart before daylight and was signaling passengers ashore to be ready to board.[9]

The *Enrica*'s crew began coaling at first light. Before long, a boat came out with two Portuguese customs authorities and soldiers. The officials came on board and demanded that the ships be registered before work continued. Semmes agreed, and coaling resumed. A short time later, the British consul came on board to explain that the Portuguese had thought the ships had come to take the island and were preparing their military forces to resist. Once they understood the true nature of the ships, they agreed to allow work to continue, provided the proper formalities were observed.[10]

While the *Enrica* coaled, the boatswain's mate went among the crew, trying to enlist as many as possible for the coming cruise. Arming the ship continued. The giant pivot guns were particularly dangerous to transfer from one ship to the other because each weighed several tons. Semmes was anxious to finish mounting the guns because the ship would have been virtually defenseless if a U.S. warship had come into port. On Saturday, three days after Semmes's arrival, the weather turned dark and rainy, but the crew worked on. Many had agreed to sign on; others still held back, waiting for better terms. It was obvious that they had not completely grasped the situation and believed this was a privateer rather than a naval vessel. By nightfall, the guns were all mounted, coal bunkers were almost full, and stores were distributed to their departments. There were still seven or eight tons of coal left to load, but Semmes wanted to get under way. The ship was ready.[11]

Sunday, August 24, 1862, was a beautiful day, and the Confederates took that as a good sign. Semmes ordered the ship prepared for sea. The coal left on deck was cleared and the ship was washed down. Decks were holystoned, awnings were set up and stretched tight, yards were squared, and rigging was hauled taut. At noon, the *Enrica* put to sea, accompanied by the *Bahama*. About four miles out, the ships hove to. All hands were summoned aft. The crew was neatly dressed. Officers wore their uniforms for the first time. They were gray, "with a redundancy of gold lace," and though Sinclair thought they were "quite dressy," he felt they were appallingly out of place at sea, considering that virtually every other navy on earth wore blue.[12]

Everyone uncovered his head as Ship's Clerk W. B. Smith read Semmes's commission from President Davis, followed by an order from Secretary Mallory appointing him commander of the Confederate States Steamer *Alabama*. While these were being read, two small balls were run up to the mastheads. When Smith finished, a bow gun fired, and the British flag came down. Halyards were jerked, and the balls unfurled into the Confederate ensign and the ship's pennant. A deafening cheer went up from the crew of the *Bahama*, which was returned by the officers and men of the former *Enrica*, now under her true name. The ship's band struck up "Dixie."[13]

When the ceremonies were over, Semmes mounted a gun carriage and repeated the speech he had previously made to the men of the *Bahama*. Again he discussed the war and the purpose of the cruise. He said that any man who wanted to return to Britain could leave on the *Bahama*. Passage would be free, and pay would continue until the ship reached Liverpool. Then he invited them to ship on the *Alabama*. Pay would be in gold. He promised them travel and adventure with shore leave in exotic ports around the world. Although their mission was commerce raiding and they were to avoid seeking a fight, he offered them an occasional battle if the odds were not too great.

Fullam called it "a most effective, spirited address" and said the crew gave three cheers. Semmes, however, later recalled being "very nervous about the success of this operation, as the management of the ship at sea absolutely depended on it." As he had feared, the holdouts wanted to negotiate. He was forced to increase the pay of seamen, petty officers, and firemen. Still, he considered himself lucky that they had not demanded a bounty as well. In all, eighty men signed on, twenty-five short of the number he had hoped for. This was the first and last time Semmes ever negotiated with any man in the crew. From then on, "I gave him a sharp order, and if the order was not obeyed in 'double-quick,' the delinquent found himself in limbo."[14]

The new men were almost exclusively British, and Sinclair noted:

These men have forfeited the protection of the English government by this act of enlistment, and must now look to the brave young banner floating over them to carry them through. No little struggle it is to men to make that plunge, knowing as they do the perfect security abandoned by this act of enlistment; and that they *have* enlisted, fully realizing the gravity of the situation, binds them to their officers with hooks of steel. Nothing now remains but to arrange financial matters for the brave fellows.[15]

Semmes worked late into the evening with the paymaster and clerk, preparing allotments for sailors' wives, drafts, and advance wages. He was gratified to see that a large number of men wanted half their pay sent home. Finally the financial arrangements were completed and turned over to Bulloch. At 11:00 P.M. Bulloch and Butcher returned to the *Bahama,* which cast off and headed back to Liverpool. The parting was particularly painful for Bulloch. He had put his heart into this ship, which was to have been his. Stepping over the side for the last time, he felt as though he was leaving part of himself behind. As the *Bahama* steamed away, he watched the lights of the *Alabama* and noticed how clear the sky was. Then a shooting star flashed across, and he knew Semmes and the *Alabama* would have "a glorious cruise." Back in Liverpool, Bulloch was amused to learn that the *Tuscarora* had poked around the harbors and bays of Great Britain and Ireland looking for the *Alabama* long after she had sailed for Praya. Then she had been refused permission to coal at Belfast and had found it necessary to go all the way to

Cadiz. In a letter to Mallory, Bulloch was openly contemptuous of the Union commander and closed by saying: "If Captain Craven continues to be curious in reference to the *Alabama*'s movements, he will, I think, very soon be gratified by frequent announcements of her locality."[16]

4

Flames in the Azores

CAPTAIN RAPHAEL SEMMES, CSN, WATCHED THE *BAHAMA* steam away, then turned his ship to the northeast, set fore-and-aft sails, and told the engineer to let the fires go down. The wind had picked up and the sea was rough. Exhausted, he went to his bunk and dropped off to sleep to the rolling of the ship and the smell of bilge water. The *Alabama* was alone.[1]

The ship was 940 tons, 210 feet long at the waterline, and 32 feet in breadth. When fully loaded and coaled, she drew about 15 feet of water.[2] Semmes loved her from the moment he saw her. "Her model was of the most perfect symmetry," he wrote, "and she sat upon the water with the lightness and grace of a swan." She was barque-rigged with long lower masts, allowing her to carry large fore-and-aft sails. Her topmasts were yellow pine, which would bend in a gale without breaking, and her standing rigging was iron wire. Four tubular boilers powered a pair of steam engines, with a condenser designed to distill fresh water for the crew from the seawater vapor. Unlike the *Sumter,* her sailing rig and engine could operate independently of each other. With an adequate supply of coal and her machinery in working order, she did not need sails. Conversely, if she went under sail, the propeller could be detached and drawn up into a well in fifteen minutes, eliminating any drag. She was unique for a warship of her time in that she carried a fully equipped machine shop and repair facilities that could handle almost any emergency. Reprovisioning herself from captured prizes, the *Alabama* could remain at sea a very long time.[3]

Although the *Alabama* carried enough coal for eighteen days of continuous steaming, Semmes preferred to make routine operations under sail. That way, if he had to chase a prize, he would have enough fuel to run her down with the engine if necessary. Likewise, too much use of power would have forced him into port to recoal more often and would have established a pattern for U.S. warships to follow. As Sinclair remarked, "We are bound for no port, and while coal lasts we are not apt to seek one."[4]

According to Semmes, her speed was always overrated. Although her specifications called for twelve knots, she ordinarily made ten, which was about average for a ship of her type. One time, under both sail and steam, she managed thirteen knots, somewhat less than the top speed of well-handled clipper ship operating under sail alone.[5]

She was armed with six thirty-two-pounders in broadside, three to a side, and two pivot guns on the centerline, which could be fired in either direction. The forward pivot gun was a hundred-pounder Blakely rifle of such poor quality metal that it was virtually useless because it overheated after the first few shots. The after pivot gun was an eight-inch smoothbore. Initially, eight thirty-two-pounders had been planned in broadside, but it was determined that they would make the ship top-heavy so the two extra guns were omitted. In battle, one of the existing thirty-two-pounders could be shifted from one side to the other.[6] Fully armed and fitted, the ship had cost the financially battered Confederate government $250,305.44, a respectable sum for a warship in those days. As a final touch, her wheel contained the ship's motto inlaid in gilt: *Aide-toi et Dieu t'aidera*—Help yourself and God will help you.[7]

Most of the master's mates and engineers in the steerage mess came from the *Sumter*. In the wardroom, however, despite Semmes's efforts, only one man, Kell, had served with him before as a line officer, although he did have Richard Armstrong and Joseph Wilson, who had been midshipmen on the *Sumter* and had since been promoted to lieutenants. Other *Sumter* men in the wardroom included Dr. Galt, the surgeon, Lieutenant Howell of the marines, and Chief Engineer

Miles J. Freeman, who had served as chief engineer on the *Sumter* before she had been taken into Confederate service. New additions included Lieutenants Sinclair and Low, Dr. Llewellyn, the assistant surgeon, and Sailing Master I. S. Bulloch, half-brother of the naval agent in Liverpool. There were also three midshipmen, E. M. Anderson, E. A. Maffitt, son of the captain of the *Florida,* and George T. Sinclair. Semmes considered them all fine officers with the single exception of Paymaster Clarence Yonge, who was ultimately discharged for "worthlessness."[8]

The captain was particularly pleased with his steward, A. G. Bartelli, an Italian whom he had enlisted from the *Bahama.* Bartelli was an alcoholic, whose ill treatment by the *Bahama's* captain, Eugene Tessier, had aroused Semmes's sympathy during the voyage to Praya. He felt that with proper handling, the little Italian could be reformed and offered him the steward's berth on the *Alabama.*

"There is one understanding, however, which you and I must have," Semmes warned him. "You must never touch a drop of liquor, on board the ship, on duty. When you go on shore, on liberty, if you choose to have a little frolic, that is your affair, provided, always, you come off sober. Is it a bargain?" Bartelli instantly agreed, and Semmes never regretted his choice. The steward kept his promise as long as he lived.[9]

On Monday, Semmes began the task of putting his ship to rights. No crew assignments had been made, and she was still disorganized and dirty below decks, with spare shot boxes and other articles getting in the way. She had been built "of rather green timber" and caulked during the winter, and the tropical sun was shrinking the wood and opening the seams, causing her to leak in her upper works. Because he would need several days to organize the ship, he left the sea lanes and went into little-traveled parts of the ocean so he could go about the job unmolested. Everything not yet stowed was put in place. Some minor changes were made in the battery for more efficient operation, and the guns were sealed with blank cartridges.[10]

As executive officer, Kell was responsible for getting the crew in shape. Sailors knew no loyalties in those days, and he found many nationalities among them. As one Confederate officer noted, "A jack tar is probably the only representative left of the old 'free lance,' who

Lieutenant John McIntosh Kell, CSN

served under any flag where he was sure of pay and booty." This was particularly true of a raider like the *Alabama,* which offered "a fair prospect of adventure and prize money." A large number of crewmen were "Yankee tars." Kell considered these misplaced Northerners to be among the best sailors, and they served the ship well. There were also highly disciplined Southern pilots from Savannah, Charleston, and New Orleans, who were made petty officers and "sustained their reputation nobly." Some members of the gun crews had been on warships before, and they trained the rest in naval procedure and discipline.[11]

Still, the crew left much to be desired, and Kell's duty, as he saw it, was to bring "our Liverpool packet material up to the standard of man-o'-war discipline." Trivial matters—such as crockery—caused incidents. In the 1860s, sailors on a warship customarily ate off the deck itself rather than at a table. Each man was entitled to a tin pot, pan, spoon, and sheath knife. The construction contract had called for "a ship of certain dimensions and power, furnished complete with everything for the voyage." Laird's had interpreted "complete" to mean four sets of crockery, for captain, wardroom, steerage, and crew. Given this luxury, the Liverpool wharf rats suddenly became very fastidious, and Kell was deluged with complaints about the mess cooks. One didn't wash the plates well enough. Another didn't polish the cups. He solved the problem by ordering all the crew's crockery on deck and heaving it over the side. Reduced to their customary tinware, the men settled down.[12]

During this shape-up time, several ships were sighted but, when overhauled, were found to be neutrals. Once his ship was in order, Semmes decided to hit the whaling grounds of the Azores. Time was short—it was already September, and the whales migrated south in October. At 5:15 A.M., September 5, a sail was sighted. The top-hamper appeared in unusually neat order for a merchant ship, which caused Semmes to suspect she might be a U.S. warship. The *Alabama* was luffed up to get the weather gauge and take advantage of the wind in case of a fight. The surgeons laid out their instruments and prepared to receive the wounded. But the strange ship outran the *Alabama* and was lost.

Semmes was not disappointed for long. A second ship was sighted lying to, with fore-topsail on the mast and quarterboats, which identified her as a whaler. She was in the midst of processing a large sperm whale hoisted partly out of the water. The *Alabama* ran up the British ensign, and the whaler responded with the U.S. flag. Semmes drew up near her and sent a boat over with a boarding party under Lieutenant Armstrong. As it drew up alongside the whaler, the British flag came down and the Confederate ensign went up. For the officers who had once served in the U.S. Navy, the sight of the American flag being lowered from the whaler's peak was an emotional moment. Remembering the many times they had stood at salute while sailors presented arms, the band played, and the colors were raised, Sinclair felt it was almost a desecration. But as more prizes fell into the *Alabama*'s power, more flags came down, and more ships were burned, it became a routine matter.[13]

The whaler proved to be the *Ocmulgee* from Edgartown, Massachusetts, under command of Abraham Osborn. The surprised Captain Osborn was brought over with the ship's papers. Armstrong and Kell, who were appointed to value the prize, appraised her at $50,000 and condemned her. The crew of thirty-seven men was transferred to the *Alabama*, where American-born prisoners were placed in irons in retaliation for the treatment of Paymaster Myers of the *Sumter*. Semmes also ordered the *Ocmulgee*'s fourth officer, S. F. Turner, confined because of drunkenness. The Confederate crew removed some rigging which the *Alabama* needed, along with beef, pork, and other stores. By the time the work was finished it was 9:00 P.M., and Semmes decided against burning her that night. Soaked as she was with oil, the burning whaler would be seen for miles and alert other ships in the vicinity. "I had now become too old a hunter to commit such an indiscretion," Semmes said. The *Alabama* lay to by the whaler that night and fired her at 9:00 A.M. the next day.[14]

On Sunday, September 7, Semmes mustered the crew for the first monthly reading of the Articles of War. The ship was gleaming. Decks were scrubbed, brass and ironwork polished, and sails trimmed. The Confederate flag at the masthead lent the authority of the government to the occasion, and the men were dressed in uniform, with jackets, trousers, and straw hats. Already Kell had brought several of the tougher seamen up on charges, and Semmes had placed them in confinement according to the seriousness of their offenses. He noticed during the reading that when certain offenses were mentioned, all eyes turned toward those who had committed them. The crew was also visibly impressed by the frequent mention of the death penalty and the fact that its enforcement rested solely with the captain and a court-martial board. If there had been any doubt about the nature of the cruise before, there was none now. This was not a privateering expedition; they were sailors on a government warship and subject to naval discipline. To reinforce the idea, officers always carried sidearms when on duty. Semmes was pleased at the result. The crewmen were not only better behaved, they were healthier.

They had had sufficient time to recover from the dives of Liverpool and showed more stamina than when they had signed on.[15]

That afternoon the *Alabama* neared a town on the island of Flores. The *Ocmulgee*'s crew was paroled and given three of the burned whaler's boats to row ashore. The prisoners were also allowed to take any of the *Ocmulgee*'s stores and other gear the Confederates did not need. Semmes reasoned that they could sell the boats and equipment to the local people for enough money to support themselves until they could contact the U.S. consul in Fayal. About half an hour after the whalers rowed away, a sail was sighted and the *Alabama* gave chase. The ship was soon identified as a fore-and-aft schooner, but she failed to respond when Semmes hoisted British colors. She looked suspicious and was trying to get within a marine league of the island, which would put her under Portuguese protection. There was little time to spare because she was now only five miles from land. Semmes ordered the *Alabama* across the schooner's bow and ran up the Confederate flag. On board the schooner, there was no mistaking the warship's intentions, especially when a shot crossed her bow. Still she pressed on, and Semmes threw a second shot, which whistled between the fore- and mainmasts, just over the heads of the people on board. She hove to and ran up the U.S. flag.[16]

The new prize was the *Starlight* of Boston, heading home from Fayal via Flores, where she was to land passengers. Once again, the American prisoners were placed in irons because of the Myers affair. When the *Starlight*'s captain protested that his rank should exempt him, Semmes replied, "Mr. Myers held a high position also, and was a gentleman, an officer of unblemished character and great worth, and should not have been treated like a felon."[17]

The American ship's passengers included several women. By now it was getting dark and too late to put them ashore. To calm the women, a light was hoisted from the peak of the *Alabama,* and the ships hove to for the night. The next morning, Low took one of the cutters alongside the *Starlight* to pick up passengers and their baggage and rowed them ashore at the town of Santa Cruz under a white flag. Local citizens crowded the landing; they had heard the guns firing the night before and seen the strange warship with its prizes lying offshore all night. Once the passengers were landed, the captain and crew were paroled, and Lieutenant Armstrong took them ashore. The governor came on board the *Alabama* and offered the Confederate crew the hospitality of the island, and Semmes apologized for any inconvenience to Portuguese subjects who had been passengers on the *Starlight*. Bartelli, the steward, stood by, filling glasses with champagne. Cigars were passed around, and Semmes bowed his guests off the ship.[18]

Back at sea, the *Alabama* overhauled the whaler *Ocean Rover* of New Bedford, which was heading home after forty months at sea with 1,110 barrels of oil.[19] The captain had decided to swing by the Azores to try to fill the few remaining empty barrels with oil from whales in the area, a fatal mistake for his ship.

When some of the Confederate crewmen mentioned that the captain and crew of the *Ocmulgee* had been allowed to row ashore, the captain of the *Ocean Rover* asked Semmes for permission to do likewise. The ships were several miles out, it was dark, and Semmes said it was too dangerous.

"Oh! That is nothing," the Yankee replied. "We whalers sometimes chase a whale, on the broad sea, until our ships are hull-down, and think nothing of it. It will relieve you of us the sooner, and be of some service to us besides."

Semmes agreed and allowed them to take personal effects and any other useful items the Confederates did not need. Two hours later, six boats from the *Ocean Rover* came alongside the *Alabama,* loaded almost to the gunwales, and Semmes thought these whalers had stripped everything movable from the ship, including a cat and a parrot.

"Captain, your boats appear to me, to be rather deeply laden," Semmes called. "Are you not afraid to trust them?"

"Oh no," the Yankee said. "They are as buoyant as ducks, and we shall not ship a drop of water."

Paroles were made out, and the boats pulled for shore. Semmes stood on the horseblock by the mizzenmast and watched them go. Presently, he heard a sailor in one of the boats start singing in "a powerful and musical voice," and the others picked up on the chorus. As he watched and listened, he little realized that several years later these acts of charity would be used against him with the claim that he had cast defenseless sailors adrift in the open sea.[20]

The *Alabama* now had two prizes, which Semmes planned to burn the following morning. But he was roused from his sleep shortly after midnight with news that a large ship had been sighted close by. He dressed and went on deck and saw her about a mile distant, heading toward the island. He tried to follow as unobtrusively as possible, but the stranger realized she was being chased and put on every sail she had. As he watched her, Semmes admired how well handled she was, with her white canvas against the night sky, her yards squared, and her lines taut. He followed her for about four hours and at dawn broke out the British flag. The stranger ignored it and continued to race toward the marine league of the island. Finally, the *Alabama* threw a shell close enough that the splash drenched those on the stern. The stranger ran up the U.S. flag and hove to. As Semmes sent a prize crew over, Bartelli came up to tell him his bath was ready. He bathed and dressed for breakfast while he waited for a report on the new prize.

The ship was the *Alert* of New London, only sixteen days out. She was equipped for a long voyage, part of which was to have included the extreme southern Indian Ocean, near Antarctica. This meant she was well supplied with winter clothing, which the crew of the *Alabama* needed. She also had several cases of tobacco, an item in short supply on the Confederate ship.

"I could see Jack's eyes brighten, as he rolled aft, and piled up on the quarter-deck, sundry heavy oaken boxes of good 'Virginia twist,'" Semmes wrote. The crew's morale improved noticeably as pipes glowed that night in the forecastle.[21]

The crew of the *Alert* was paroled and sent ashore, and the work of burning began—the *Starlight* at 9:00 A.M., *Ocean Rover* at 11:00 A.M., and *Alert* at 4:00 P.M., "so that we had three funeral pyres burning around us at the same moment." Another whaler was sighted, which responded to the *Alabama*'s British flag with the Portuguese. She had such an American look about her that Semmes sent a boat over to invite the captain on board. The ship's papers were legitimate, and the captain was Portuguese so Semmes thanked him for the visit and sent him on his way.[22]

At 5:00 P.M., another sail was sighted. This time the *Alabama* showed the U.S. flag. Once again, the stranger did not respond so a blank shot was fired. She was the schooner *Weather Gauge* of Province-town. As the prize crew was taking over, a large bark was sighted. Orders were sent to the *Weather Gauge* to meet the *Alabama* at the island of Corvo, and once again the chase was on. It lasted until 3:00 A.M., when the stranger was finally identified as the *Overman* from Denmark. Semmes was furious because there was no reason for a neutral ship to have fled his initial attempt at contact. Consequently, he insisted on full belligerent rights, and the Danes were forced to take in all sail while a boat was sent over to examine their papers. The time she would spend resetting sail would partially compensate him for the time he had wasted chasing her.[23] To confuse any enemy warships that might later board the *Overman,* he never revealed the *Alabama*'s true identity to the Danes, instead flying the U.S. flag and passing his ship off as the USS *Iroquois.*[24]

The *Alabama* met the *Weather Gauge* at Corvo, put her crew ashore, and burned her. While there, Semmes noticed another whaler, "a Yankee, no doubt," anchored close to shore under Portuguese protec-tion. Several more ships were captured and burned. In one case, Fullam described the procedure he generally used as boarding officer throughout the *Alabama*'s cruise:

> Fired a gun for her to heave to. Darkness prevented us know-ing who he was, so, I went on board to examine his papers, and which, if Yankee, I was to signal it and heave to until daylight. . . . Pulling under his stern, I saw it was the whaling ship "Benj. Tucker" of and from New Bedford. Gaining the quarter-deck, I was welcomed with outstretched hands. In answer to my questions, the Capt. told me her name, port of registry, &c. &c. all of which I was previously aware. I then told him that he was a prize to the C.S. Str. "Alabama," ordering him to put his clothes in one trunk, allowing the mates and men one bag each, all navigation books and instruments being left behind. At daylight sent the Capt. and crew with the ships papers and their luggage to the "Alabama." I then examined the ship, and finding some cases of stores, they were transferred to our ship. The preparations to fire her were soon made, so that after seeing her well fired we pushed off and regained our vessel.[25]

By the time the whaler *Elisha Dunbar* went up in flames on September 18, Kell noted with satisfaction that the *Alabama* had been at her career as a raider for only two weeks and had captured ten prizes.[26] The weather was deteriorating when the *Elisha Dunbar* was captured, and by the time she was destroyed, a gale was blowing. The sight of the burning ship in the storm prompted Semmes to some of his finest prose:

> The sea was in a tumult of rage, the winds howled, and floods of rain descended. Amid this turmoil of the elements, the *Dunbar,* all in flames, and with disordered gear and unfurled canvas, lay rolling and tossing upon the sea. Now an ignited sail would fly away from a yard, and scud off before the gale; and now the yard itself, released from the control of its braces, would swing about wildly, as in the madness of despair, and then drop into the sea. Finally the masts went by the board, and then the hull rocked to and fro for awhile, until it was filled with water, and fire nearly quenched, when it settled to the bottom of the great deep, a victim to the passions of man, and the fury of the elements.[27]

Inspired as he may have been, his immediate concern was bringing his own ship through the gale with minimal difficulties. He had confidence in the *Alabama* but was worried about the prisoners.

"The deck is more or less wet, and the prisoners must have an uncomfortable time of it, but I have nowhere else to put them," he wrote in his journal.[28]

The gale continued for another day, then passed, but before the ship was dry, another one blew up. At 11:00 A.M., the crew was mustered and took in sail, and the ship rode well. "Decks leaking for want of calking, but the ship otherwise tight," Semmes observed. Two days later, the gale blew out, and the remainder of the week was spent caulking and correcting defects in the ship which had been observed during the heavy seas and rain. The weather had blown the *Alabama* out of the shipping lanes, and few sails were sighted.[29]

The events of the past few weeks had a positive effect on the crew. The men were acting more and more like naval seamen. Still, they had a long way to go, and their captain was not yet ready to praise them.

"Mustered the crew and inspected the ship," Semmes wrote on Sunday, September 28. "We begin to look a little less like a troopship."[30]

5

Storm

*T*HE GALES THROUGH WHICH THE *ALABAMA* HAD PASSED WERE the early signs of the stormy season in the North Atlantic. September turned into October, the month when foul weather really set in. Yet Semmes chose that month to cruise in the North. His reasons were solid. The whaling season in the Azores was almost over. In the South, the cotton harvest was winding down and, normally, Northern ships would be crowding Southern ports to haul cotton to Europe. With that market closed, however, they packed Sandy Hook, the anchorage for New York, waiting to take on grain from the Midwest.[1]

The change of cruising grounds allowed the crew time to rest from the nerve-racking work of chasing, boarding, and burning prizes. With normal watches and no duties other than the routine maintenance and operation of the ship, they worked regular hours, stayed dry, and caught up on their sleep. Although boarding officers would try to secure the liquor stores on prizes immediately, the crew was generally allowed two servings of grog a day. As Semmes put it, "I was quite willing that Jack should drink, but I undertook to be the judge of how much he should drink."[2]

Sundays were reserved for cleaning the ship, particularly sleeping quarters and engine rooms. Unlike many people of the nineteenth century, Semmes associated filth with disease. He was a stickler for cleanliness and a firm believer in soap and water. The *Alabama*'s condensers provided fresh water in abundance, and he saw no reason not to use it. On Sunday inspection, officers and crew were expected to turn out in the uniform of the day, and that uniform was expected to be clean. Looking the men over, the master-at-arms would turn down collars and roll up the legs of trousers to make sure the crewmen had washed. Semmes was very proud that he never lost a man to disease on the *Sumter* or *Alabama*.[3]

Crew was mustered twice a day, at 9:00 A.M. and sunset. When weather allowed, the officers drilled them at the battery or with small arms. The more they worked, the less time they had to think. Old Beeswax did not like sailors who spent too much time thinking; the more they thought, the more they complained, and complainers disrupted the efficiency of the ship. For recreation, the *Alabama* was provided with violins, tambourines, and other traditional sailors' instruments. When the day was over, the crew would often gather on the forecastle deck, shove shot racks, rope, and other gear out of the way, and hold a dance. Those who had been designated as women would tie scarves around their waists. If there was no dance, they would gather around and listen to yarns from the older sailors. Meanwhile, the officers would relax and chat on the bridge. At 8:00 P.M., the bell was rung for the night watch, and the crew would rush to put everything back in order and get below. Then the ship settled down to quiet, broken only by the creaking of rigging, the sound of orders, the shifting of sails, and the call of the lookouts every half hour.[4]

At 8:00 A.M., September 30, the cry of "Sail ho!" came from the masthead, and the crew sprang into action. The ship turned out to be a French bark, but the men were glad of a little excitement after several days of routine cruising. That night the *Alabama* entered the Gulf Stream, where the warm water of the Gulf of Mexico rushes north and collides with the cold air of the North Atlantic winter and breeds storms. "A change of weather keenly felt, it being very cold," Fullam wrote. They were now only two hundred miles from the Grand Banks of Newfoundland and approaching the transatlantic shipping lanes.[5]

Two days later, another sail was sighted, but it had the advantage of the wind so there was no chase. A short time after that, two ships, both from New York, sailed straight into the *Alabama*'s grasp. The *Brilliant* carried American grain and flour for Liverpool. Semmes wrote in his memoirs that the cargo of the *Emily Farnum* was certified as British property, and for that reason she was bonded and released. The bond was the captain's pledge of honor that in return for the release of the ship, he would pay the specified amount to the Confederate government at the end of the war. But the Confederate government no longer existed when the war ended, and there is no record that any was ever paid. In his memoirs, written after the war, Semmes commented, "I have some of these debts of honor in my possession, now, which I will sell cheap."[6]

With the crew of the *Brilliant,* Semmes had more than fifty prisoners. He transferred them to the *Emily Farnum* and then burned the *Brilliant.* Describing the scene, and perhaps playing on the ship's name, Fullam wrote: "I never saw a vessel burn with such brilliancy, the flames completely enveloping the masts, hull and rigging in a few minutes, making a sight as grand as it was appalling."[7]

At 5:30 A.M. the next day the *Alabama* sighted another ship. In the ensuing chase, the two ships came near the *Brilliant,* which was still burning. After six hours, the stranger was overhauled and proved to be a Russian ship. Low, the boarding officer, asked the captain if he knew anything about the burning ship. He replied that he knew nothing of the circumstances but had sighted her during the night and had gone over to offer assistance. The Russians had found no men but had picked up a boat. When it was examined, it proved to be *Alabama*'s own captain's gig, which had been cast adrift after it was damaged by a muzzle blast from the eight-inch gun. As they talked, another sail was sighted ahead, but the captain assured Low it was also a Russian ship.[8]

Over the next several days the *Alabama* overhauled ships from Britain, France, Prussia, the various maritime cities of Germany, and other nations. On October 7, she stopped the *Wave Crest* out of New York with a cargo of American grain. Semmes allowed the gunners to use her for target practice before burning her. Just before dark, another sail was spotted. But this ship had seen the burning *Wave Crest* and had guessed the purpose of the strange warship coming down on her. The wind picked up, and the stranger put out her studding sails so that she was covered with a cloud of canvas. As he watched her through his night glasses, Semmes could not help but admire the skill with which her captain handled her. Finally, about midnight, the *Alabama* was close enough to fire a warning gun. The strange ship let go her sheets and let her sails flap as her crew scrambled up the masts to take them in.[9]

She proved to be the *Dunkirk* from New York with a cargo of American grain for Lisbon. She also carried Protestant religious tracts, printed in Portuguese by the New York Bible Society, for distribution among the Portuguese passengers and, presumably, for illegal distribution in Portugal itself. Semmes's Catholic sensibilities were outraged. It seemed to him that the Yankees were "determined to thrust their piety down the throats of the Portuguese, whether they would [want it] or not." Should the government of Portugal object, he reasoned that the United States would send "a gunboat or two" to settle the matter.[10]

One member of the *Dunkirk*'s crew was identified as George Forrest, a seaman who had deserted the *Sumter* at Gibraltar. He was clapped into irons to await trial.[11]

After burning the *Dunkirk*, the *Alabama* captured the sailing packet *Tonawanda* of Philadelphia, with seventy passengers, thirty of whom were women and children. Semmes faced a problem. The ship had a valuable cargo and was legally a candidate for burning, but what would he do with the passengers? The men could be placed with other prisoners, but there were too many women and children, and "it was not possible to convert the *Alabama* to a nursery, and set the stewards to serving pap to the babies." He placed a prize crew on board and ordered the *Tonawanda* to accompany the *Alabama* for a day or two in hopes of finding another, less valuable prize that could take the prisoners on board.[12]

George Forrest, the deserter captured with the *Dunkirk*, was court-martialed on October 10. Under the Articles of War, he could have been hanged. Instead, he was sentenced to serve the remainder of his enlistment without pay, after which he was to be dishonorably discharged from the Confederate navy.[13] The next day the *Alabama* overhauled and burned the *Manchester.* She had carried copies of the *New York Herald,* which were only five days old, and from them Semmes learned the positions and types of gunboats he might face. Of the total of 192 in the U.S. fleet, he estimated only 13 were superior to the *Alabama.* The side-wheelers were slow and "only tolerable." Two sets of propeller gunboats had been built since the war began, and the first was indifferent. The second group was "very fine and heavily armed."[14] One of this last group was named *Kearsarge.*

Semmes could no longer put off a decision about the *Tonawanda.* The weather was closing in, he had a hard time keeping her in sight, and she slowed down his hunting. He transferred all prisoners and passengers over to her, bonded her for $80,000, and released her.[15]

One person remained behind, however, David White, a black slave from Delaware, who was about seventeen years old. Under the laws of that state, he remained a slave until he was twenty-one and was therefore legally confiscated enemy property. He was assigned to serve as a steward in the wardroom, where he struck up a friendship with the officers and the other stewards. His name was entered on the rolls of the ship with pay as a mess steward. White became very attached to Dr. Galt and served him in the same capacity that Bartelli served Semmes. Although various U.S. consuls tried to entice him away in liberty ports, he always returned to the *Alabama* and died with the ship off Cherbourg.[16]

For the past two weeks the *Alabama* had been working her way toward New York, and Semmes planned to cruise along the coast of the United States and capture ships close to home. He even considered the possibility of sailing into Sandy Hook and burning ships at anchor there, right under the nose of the New York Board of Trade, an idea Kell wholeheartedly supported. Unfortunately for the plan, nature intervened. The weather had been worsening for several days, and on October 15, when the *Alabama* overhauled the *Lamplighter,* the boarding party had a hard time reaching her. By the time she was burned, the wind was blowing heavily. "A wilder scene I have never witnessed," Kell wrote. "The flames ran up the tarred rigging like demons to the mastheads, with burning lanyards flying to the gale!"[17]

That night the barometer continued to fall, and by morning Semmes realized the *Alabama* was caught in a hurricane. War and

The *Alabama* broaches in the hurricane in the Gulf Stream.
(from Semmes, *Memoirs of Service Afloat*)

prizes no longer mattered. The only concern was to save the ship. Topsails were close reefed to about one-third their original size and the main storm trysail was bent on and set. The quarterboats were swung in and lashed, all hands were called on deck, and all fires were extinguished except for the binnacle light. The ship was caught in several troughs and the water broke over her, flooding the deck knee deep. Kell rigged lifelines to keep the men from being washed overboard, but few ventured out unless they had to. The topgallant yards were sent down to expose as little to the wind as possible. Finally, the fore topsail was furled. The fore staysail had been torn to pieces. Semmes wondered whether to send men up to furl the main topsail or let it blow out as well. He had about decided that it was too dangerous when an iron bolt that held the main brace sheared, the main yard snapped like a matchstick, and the main topsail was ripped to shreds. The risk had to be taken or the wildly swinging yards would tear the masts and rigging apart. The men fought their way up the mast, secured the broken main yard, and lowered the remaining spars.

The captain of the forecastle went up and cut away the fore-topmast staysail. Otherwise the wind would have caught it and pushed the bow over into the deep trough of a wave, bringing the *Alabama* broadside to the sea and perhaps turning her over on her beam ends. A storm staysail was bent. The crew started to lower the main trysail, but it split.[18]

Now only the little storm staysail kept the *Alabama*'s heading straight. Wave after wave hit her and rolled her so far that Semmes was afraid she would go on her beam ends or that her masts would be carried off by the sea. The spray was blinding. The wind took a strip of the main topsail, the clewline, and the chain sheeting and twisted them all into one giant knot that could only be undone with a knife. One quarterboat was torn from its davits and smashed to pieces. The barometer continued to fall until it reached 28.64. Then, suddenly, all was quiet. They were in the eye of the storm.[19]

"Mr. Kell," Semmes said, "in a few minutes we will get the wind with renewed violence in the opposite direction." Kell knew what to do. The yards were braced and the storm staysail was shifted to receive the wind in the opposite direction. The calm lasted half an hour, followed by two more hours of battering by wind and waves. Finally, the hurricane passed. That afternoon the men were sent aloft to lower the ruined main yard. Semmes now had to capture another ship so he could repair the damage and secure new boats.[20]

The weather did not completely clear for several days. Finally, the crew was able to turn out for repairs. Sails were loosed and dried and wet clothing hung out. The main yard was repaired well enough for temporary use and hoisted into place. The arms chests, located on the afterdeck, had been saturated with water and the small arms were starting to rust so they had to be taken out, cleaned, and oiled. More bad weather set in, and tons of water poured onto the deck. "Verily, we seem to be in the very caldron in which all the storms of the North Atlantic are brewed," Semmes wrote in the ship's journal on October 22. The prisoners, previously confined to a tent on deck, were sent down to the forward fireroom to protect them from the weather.[21]

The ship's journal was beginning to read like a legal text. Because of Confederate depredations, Northern shippers had begun to consign their cargoes to neutral accounts. Here, Semmes's legal training came into play. Examining each bill of lading, he cited case law which showed that neutrality was not clearly established or would not become legally binding until actual delivery of the cargo. Hence the ships and cargo were condemned as American property and burned.

These efforts at subterfuge always irritated him. Either the cargo was American or it was not. "The old man rarely displayed temper, except when tangled ownership of cargo clouded ship's papers, and set him over-hauling his law library for 'precedents,'" Sinclair said. "The skipper might look out for a blast, did Semmes, in his search unearth a trick or subterfuge in 'certificates.' Then, there's many a 'd———n your eyes.'"[22]

While the *Alabama* operated in the shipping lanes, fires were kept going constantly under the boilers so she could get up steam if a U.S. warship appeared. On October 29, Semmes bonded the American brigantine *Baron de Castine,* sending her away with his prisoners and a message to the New York Chamber of Commerce that he would be off New York by the time the message arrived. Soon, however, coal ran low, and any plans he might have had for burning ships at Sandy Hook had to be abandoned. The *Alabama* headed south to rendezvous with the *Agrippina* and recoal. En route, she overhauled and burned the whaler *Levi Starbuck* and the American East Indiaman *Thomas B. Wales.*[23]

The *Thomas B. Wales* was a windfall. She carried seventeen hundred bags of saltpeter, which Northern munitions factories would have turned into gunpowder. She also carried jute, which the North was using as a substitute for Southern cotton. Her main yard had the same dimensions as the broken one on the *Alabama* and was carried over to the Confederate ship. A substantial amount of other rigging was taken to replace that lost in the storm, prompting Semmes to call the prize "a sort of shipyard." Nine recruits were also signed up from the crew of the *Wales.* Together with those from other prizes, the *Alabama* now had 110 men, only 10 short of her full complement.[24]

Perhaps the luckiest break for Semmes personally was that among the passengers was George H. Fairchild, a U.S. government official stationed in Mauritius, who was returning home to New England with his family and a female friend. Fairchild had no particular prejudices against Southerners, and Semmes liked him. The officers turned their staterooms over to the family and took the children under their wing. Mrs. Fairchild and her friend were upset over the loss of their fine East Indian furniture when the *Wales* was burned but eventually got over it.[25]

Semmes enjoyed the Fairchilds' stay. He had a canary on board, taken from a previous prize. Early in the morning, he would lie half-awake, listening to the bird chirping and the sound of the children running and playing on the deck overhead and would imagine himself back home with his own family. Then Bartelli would give his bunk a shake and announce the time, bringing him back to reality.[26]

After the war, when the federal government was investigating charges of cruelty to prisoners, Fairchild remembered his kind treatment on the *Alabama* and testified on Semmes's behalf. Semmes always believed this helped save him from prison and possibly even from the hangman; he never forgot it.[27]

6

Lincoln's Dilemma

*I*N WASHINGTON, GIDEON WELLES WAS NOT SITTING IDLY BY while the U.S. merchant fleet was being sent to the bottom by Confederate commerce raiders. The modern fleet of steam sloops, which Semmes had noted, had been built largely to protect against such an eventuality. Once they were ready, Welles dispatched as many of them as possible to hunt down the Southern ships. Yet to his credit, Welles refused to be stampeded. Although he acknowledged that the depredations of the *Alabama* were "enormous," the blockade was his main priority and would remain so until the end of the war. Any reassignment that would seriously weaken the net along the Confederate coast was out of the question, no matter how many Union ships were sunk on the high seas.[1]

As usual, Lincoln backed Welles even though the *Alabama* worried him greatly. According to Carl Sandburg, the president went so far as to host a séance, partly in jest, in which he asked the spirit world how to catch the Confederate raider. Welles was present, along with Secretary of War Edwin M. Stanton and a reporter for the *Boston Gazette,* who wrote that the *Alabama*'s image appeared in the mirror over the mantelpiece. Two ships were burning, and she was preparing to chase a third. Then the image changed to show the *Alabama* under the guns of a British fort. Lincoln, who believed in spiritualism more than he cared to admit, took this to mean that public opinion might ultimately force the British government to seize the *Alabama*. Nevertheless, he told Welles to continue construction of gunboats and monitors according to the current plan. After some further communication from Beyond, Welles commented that he had plans of his own for the *Alabama*.[2]

The president might relax in the atmosphere of a séance, but the problem remained very real, and it affected his administration in odd ways. Once Captain David D. Porter came storming to Washington because he had been relieved of his command and ordered to build gunboats on the western rivers. He felt the assignment was political retribution (it probably was—he had quarreled with Welles) and proposed to resign his commission and ask the New York merchants to outfit a privateer with which he planned to hunt and destroy the *Alabama*. Lincoln calmed him down and appointed him commander of the Mississippi Squadron,[3] which ultimately led to the fall of Vicksburg, assuring Porter's place in history.

Lincoln got some relief when the Russian fleet visited in 1863. Though the Russians had not come purely for goodwill, the visit was a much-needed boost for morale. The United States had become increasingly isolated from most of the major powers, and even the tsar was a welcome ally. The general feeling was summed up by Welles, who wrote, "God bless the Russians." By the time the fleet sailed, the American people were assured that although Great Britain and France might regard the *Alabama* as a legitimate naval vessel, Russia intended to treat her as a pirate.[4]

From the time the *Alabama* burned her first ship until she was finally sunk, she represented one more headache to the overburdened Lincoln. Northern newspapers, shippers, and shipowners cried for action. From overseas came ominous reports of more Confederate ships being acquired or under construction in Great Britain and France with apparent indifference to American protests.

Adams was making little headway in London. As early as November 1862, he filed claims with Lord Russell for compensation for the *Alabama*'s depredations and demanded assurances that the British government would take measures to prevent the building of more ships of her type. But he did not press the point too hard. Russell and Palmerston were already irritated with his protests, and he did not want to alienate them entirely. Russell, however, had mixed emotions. The *Alabama*'s escape was a genuine embarrassment, both to himself and to the government, but he did not see any need to revise the Foreign Enlistment Act or its method of enforcement. Hence the British could easily provide such ships in the future.[5]

While the North worried about the Confederate threat on the high seas, the *Alabama* continued south toward its rendezvous with the *Agrippina*. Several foreign ships were overhauled, and one would not heave to until a blank shot had been fired. She was bound from Demarara to Cork and some of the crew had yellow fever. Her mate had died a day or two before, and the captain and a sailor were ill.[6]

The weather became warm, and the crew was set to painting the ship. By Sunday, November 16, the woolen clothes were uncomfortable. The crew was mustered at 11:00 A.M. and the ship was inspected. She had fresh paint inside and out. The masts had been scraped and the rigging retarred. Guns had been coated, all the brightwork polished, decks holystoned white, and awnings spread. After the crew was dismissed, the men lay about the decks and relaxed. Semmes was now completely satisfied with them. Far from the Liverpool wharf rats who had signed on, he noted in the journal, "I have never seen a better disposed or more orderly crew. They have come very kindly into the traces."[7]

At 4:00 A.M. Tuesday, the *Alabama* sighted Martinique. The propeller was lowered and the engineers got up steam. At dawn she began steaming toward Fort-de-France, her first port since leaving the Azores two months before. As soon as she arrived, Kell was sent to call on the French admiral and present his compliments. That officer responded with kind regards but suggested that the *Alabama* be brought under the guns of the fort. The *Agrippina* had arrived eight days earlier. Although she was supposed to represent herself as an ordinary merchant ship on routine business, Captain McQueen had gotten drunk and spread the word of his actual mission so it was expected that a U.S. warship could arrive at any time in search of the *Alabama*. Semmes summoned McQueen and told him to get under way after dark for a rendezvous at Blanquilla, Venezuela.[8]

Within an hour or two of anchoring, the Fairchild party from the *Thomas B. Wales* and the various prisoners were landed. Bumboats came alongside, loaded with fruit, tobacco, orange juice, and souvenirs to trade with the crew. They also brought liquor, which was smuggled aboard despite the vigilance of the petty officers—or, as Semmes suspected, with their consent. The afternoon was spent entertaining French sightseers from shore. Martinique had been flooded with newspapers from the North and statements about "Semmes the pirate" from the U.S. State Department; many of the visitors were surprised to find "a rather stylish-looking ship of war, with polite young officers to receive them, at the gangway, and show them round the ship, instead of the disorderly privateer, or pirate, they expected to find." When the officers pointed out Semmes, they eyed him especially closely. Having come to see "a Captain Kidd, or Blue Beard," they met instead a naval officer in a slightly faded uniform with a graying mustache.[9]

Shortly after sunset, when the visitors had departed, Semmes went below to have some tea and sample the fruit Bartelli had procured from the bumboats. Suddenly there was a commotion overhead. Many of the crew had gotten drunk on the liquor supplied by the boats, and now, goaded by the deserter, Forrest, and some other troublemakers, they were creating a disturbance. When Kell went forward to quiet them down, one sailor threw a belaying pin at him. Fortunately, the man was too drunk to aim well and missed, but several others threatened Kell. Semmes came out on deck and found chaos.

"Mr. Kell," he snapped, "give the order to beat to quarters." The fifer and drummer sounded "At quarters," and the men fell in by their guns mechanically from constant drill. Some were so drunk they reeled and staggered at their positions. As Semmes had anticipated, the scene was more ludicrous than dangerous; a drunken crew with only sheath knives and belaying pins faced thirty well-armed officers, who were ordered to cut down any man who hesitated to obey an order. Semmes, Kell, and the officer of the deck went among them, inspecting each one. Whenever a drunk was found, he was placed under arrest, ironed, and gagged. The inspection ended with twenty men in custody. Semmes had them marched over to the gangway, and three quartermasters began dousing them with buckets of water. Soon they were choking and gasping for breath through their gags. The punishment took two hours with officers and crew standing at attention the whole time. Occasionally Semmes heard an amused snicker from the sober crewmen.

When the last one was done, Semmes turned and said, "Mr. Kell, give the orders to beat the retreat." The malefactors were sent below to change and sleep it off. Forrest was triced up—tied spread eagle—in the mizzen rigging, two hours on and two hours off. There were no deaths or injuries, and the crew never went out of control again. From then on they had a saying: "Old Beeswax is hell when he waters a poor fellow's grog."[10]

While Semmes was drenching his crew, the *Agrippina* cleared harbor. This was fortunate because word of McQueen's boasting had reached U.S. naval authorities. Early the next morning, a large warship came into the harbor and hoisted the United States flag. Semmes ordered the *Alabama* cleared for action. The ship's funds were sent ashore for deposit as a precaution against capture. But the local merchants demanded a 5 percent fee so the money was returned to the ship until the merchants offered to transmit it to Liverpool at a lower rate.[11]

Soon the enemy ship was recognized as the *San Jacinto,* and it recognized the *Alabama* as well. Given the option of remaining in port for at least twenty-four hours after the *Alabama*'s departure or putting to sea beyond France's three-mile limit, her captain took the latter course, steamed out, and assumed a blockade position. Having identified his adversary, Semmes never considered engaging her except as a last resort. The weight of her gunfire was twice that of the *Alabama,* and she had double the Confederate ship's crew. Supplies were taken on board, and the *Alabama* prepared to get under way. She took on a pilot at 7:30 P.M. and left under steam, her crew at battle stations just in case. Once clear of the harbor, she never caught sight of the slow, lumbering old *San Jacinto.*[12]

The following morning, the propeller was hoisted and the *Alabama* returned to sail. A day later she sighted the *Agrippina* at Blanquilla. About the same time, however, an American whaling schooner was spotted close to shore, where a tent and boilers had been set up on the beach to try out a whale recently taken. Semmes ordered the U.S. flag raised, and soon a boat brought out the Yankee captain, who offered to pilot the ship into the anchorage. The offer was accepted and the *Alabama* dropped anchor near the shore. The captain was shown through the ship and was especially pleased at the guns. This, he said, was the very ship to "give the pirate Semmes fits." The "pirate Semmes" then identified himself and informed the captain he was on board the *Alabama,* and the man "stood aghast."[13]

Semmes was sorely tempted to burn the whaler because only a few shepherds would notice the violation of Venezuelan neutrality. But his legal side took hold, and he informed the captain that out of respect for Venezuelan sovereignty the schooner was safe. For the security of his own ship, however, Semmes required the Yankee captain and mate to spend every night on board the *Alabama* as hostages until coaling was completed.[14] Soon, the *Agrippina* was warped alongside, and the backbreaking, dirty job of coaling began.

While the *Alabama* was filling her bunkers, the mate of the Yankee ship spotted a whale offshore. All the boats pulled out and the chase began. The Confederates watched, fascinated, as the whalers caught up with the animal and began sinking their harpoons. After several hours, the whale was dead and the carcass was towed ashore to be tried out.[15]

Coaling took several days. Maintenance that could not be handled at sea was undertaken. The old, storm-damaged main yard was finally lowered and replaced with the one taken from the *Thomas B. Wales.* Liberty parties were organized so that the men who were off duty could go ashore. Officers fished, and the crew enjoyed swimming. Seabirds were in abundance, and some of the men went hunting. Others raided local banana fields, causing their owners to complain to Semmes about crop losses. He made good on them from the ship's stores, and everyone was satisfied.[16]

It was time, also, to address some problems. George Forrest was court-martialed as a mutineer for his part in the disturbance at Martinique and was sentenced to forfeit all prize money due him and discharge from the service. All hands were mustered, the sentence was read, and Forrest was landed ashore. Recording the incident in the ship's journal, Semmes wrote: "One has all sorts of characters to deal with in a ship's crew, and a vigorous arm is necessary. The boys (picked up in the streets of Liverpool) are most incorrigible young rascals. We are now in commission, however, three months, and I am beginning to bring 'order out of chaos.'" Three other crewmen were invalided off because of illness and exchanged for new recruits from the *Agrippina*.[17]

When the coaling was about finished, a British ship appeared. Semmes signaled her and got the latest newspapers. From them he learned that Galveston, Texas, had been captured, and General Nathaniel P. Banks was preparing to use it as a base for the invasion of that state. Semmes's service on the Gulf Coast had familiarized him with the layout of Galveston Harbor. He knew the bay was too shallow for the large number of transports needed to land Banks's thirty-thousand-man invasion force and most of the ships would have to anchor in the open sea.

"Much disorder, and confusion would necessarily attend the landing of so many troops, encumbered by horses, artillery, baggage-wagons, and stores," he said. "My design was to surprise this fleet by a night-attack, and if possible destroy it, or at least greatly cripple it." The Northern press had reported the *Alabama* off Brazil and headed toward the East Indies. "The surprise would probably be complete, in the dead of night, when the said gun-boats of the enemy would be sleeping in comparative security, with but little, if any steam in their boilers. Half an hour would suffice for my purpose of setting fire to the fleet, and it would take the gun-boats half an hour to get up steam, and their anchors and pursue me." The newspapers provided Semmes with a timetable for the invasion. The *Alabama* had almost six weeks to prowl the Caribbean looking for prizes.[18]

The *Agrippina* cast off with orders to rendezvous for the next coaling in Arcas Cays. The *Alabama* also sailed after Semmes cautioned the captain of the whaling schooner to stay clear in the future; he might not be so lucky the second time.[19]

Semmes now turned his attention to the ship's armament. He was completely dissatisfied with the big Blakley rifle, which constituted half of the ship's main battery. "Indeed, the gun is too light for its caliber," he wrote. To compensate for the deficiency of the rifle, he shifted his armament so that one of the midships thirty-two-pounders could be used on either side in empty ports near the bridge. The broadside facing the enemy would then have six guns: four thirty-two-pounders and the two heavy swivels. In his journal he wrote: "I regard my crew now as in fair fighting trim, though for want of surplus shot I have not given them as much target practice as I could desire. I am looking for a California steamer, and whilst I am looking for her perhaps I may find a fight."[20]

California steamers were the American equivalent of the Spanish galleons of old. They made regular runs from Aspinwall in Panama to the East Coast carrying the gold of California that was vital to the U.S. economy. The seizure of one of these ships would be a terrible blow to the federal government, particularly because it was hard-pressed for cash to support the war. There was another reason: the treasure carried on a single California steamer would provide the funds necessary to purchase several more ships of the *Alabama*'s class and drive United States commerce completely off the seas.[21]

With these possibilities in mind, he headed for the shipping lanes. At 9:00 A.M. on November 29, the Confederates entered the Mona Passage, between Puerto Rico and Hispaniola, and soon encountered a bark. Semmes ran up the U.S. flag, and the stranger responded with the British colors, dipped in salute. But the salute was for the United States rather than the Confederacy, and the *Alabama* did not respond.[22] The next morning, a Spanish schooner twenty days out of Boston was boarded, and Semmes got the latest newspapers. They were filled with reports of the preparation for Banks's expedition to Texas and how it had revitalized the New England economy. The Spaniard was told to report that he had been boarded by the USS *Iroquois* and sent on his way.[23]

Soon after, the lookout gave the cry, "Sail ho!" The rig was definitely American, and after several hours' chase, the ship proved to be the *Parker Cook* of Boston. This was a lucky find. The *Alabama* was running low on provisions and the crew removed pork, cheese, crackers, and other stores. At 10:00 P.M., the *Parker Cook* was burned, illuminating the nearby shore of Hispaniola.[24]

On this occasion, as on all others, the prize ship's chronometer was removed before she was burned. Semmes saved chronometers because they commanded a high price in relation to their size and weight. To be maintained in proper working order, they had to be wound each day. But as the number grew, the routine winding became "quite a task." By the time the *Alabama* landed at Cherbourg, the collection, including those carried over from the *Sumter,* had grown to seventy-five, and the daily winding had been abandoned as too time-consuming.[25]

After the *Parker Cook* was burned, the *Alabama* hove to for the night. Semmes got to sleep about midnight but was shaken loose two hours later and told that a large ship was standing down on them. He ordered the main topsail set, dressed, and hurried out on deck. The night was dark and the ship could not be seen clearly until she passed. The *Alabama* wore round. Studding sails were set, and she followed the stranger, which ultimately proved to be a Spaniard. Over the next several days, Semmes got very little rest because the shipping lanes were crowded. It seemed that every time he managed to get to bed, another ship was reported. They were all either neutral or could not be identified. One French bark failed to respond when a blank cartridge was fired and did not heave to and show colors until the *Alabama* fired a live round. When the boarding officer demanded to know why the captain did not respond to the blank, the angry Frenchman replied, "I and my government are not fighting anybody! There is no war going on with my people." France was then invading Mexico, and Kell found this information "astonishing."[26]

By December 5 Semmes began to despair of finding his quarry. "If the California steamers still take this route," he wrote in the journal, "the steamer of the 1st must have been delayed, otherwise she should have passed us last night." He was answered about noon, when the *Alabama* captured the schooner *Union* from Baltimore. The ship's cargo proved to be legitimately British so she was bonded for $1,500. Prisoners from the *Parker Cook* were transferred over, and the captain was told to lay alongside until sunset. "Our hopes of capturing a California steamer were considerably dampened by the intelligence given us by the master of this schooner that the California steamers no longer ran this route, but that the outward bound took the Mona Passage and the homeward bound took the Florida Gulf Passage. Still I [will] wait a day longer, to make sure that I have not been deceived."[27]

On Sunday, December 7, the *Alabama* was cruising along the coast of Cuba. Semmes mustered the crew at 11:00 A.M. and read the

Articles of War. At 1:00 P.M., Bartelli was serving coffee when the lookout shouted, "S-a-i-l h-o!"

"Where away?" the officer of the deck asked.

"Broad on the port bow, sir!"

"What does she look like?"

"She is a large steamer, brig-rigged, sir!"

"All hands work ship!" Kell shouted through his speaking trumpet.[28]

The propeller was lowered, fires spread under the boilers, and the new six-gun broadside run out. After a short chase, the *Alabama* hoisted U.S. colors and the stranger responded. "We scrutinized her closely," Kell wrote. "She had no guns, so must be a packet ship. All her awnings were set, and under those on the upper deck were a crowd of passengers, male and female, and as we drew nearer we could see that there were officers in uniforms and soldiers in groups. The scene was stirring and beautiful."[29]

Semmes ordered a blank shot and ran up the Confederate ensign. Aboard the steamer there was no question as to who they had encountered. One passenger, George Willis Read, came up to see what was going on. Noticing the flag, he said, "I knew it was the 290 at first sight." The steamer ran on toward Cuba to try to reach the marine league. The *Alabama*'s steam was not up sufficiently to make a long chase so two live rounds were fired. One struck the American ship's foremast. "The Capt. stopped the engine, and lowered our flag in double quick time, I assure you," Read commented.[30]

A boarding party brought the captain to the *Alabama* with the ship's papers, which showed her to be the California steamer *Ariel*, owned by Cornelius Vanderbilt. She was outward bound from New York and so did not carry the gold Semmes wanted so badly. She did have 500 passengers in addition to 140 marines and naval officers en route to assignments with the Pacific Squadron. The marines had been drawn up and armed to resist boarding, but their officers saw that the *Alabama* had full broadside trained on the steamer and decided such an attempt would be suicidal. They were disarmed and paroled immediately. Two hundred new Enfield rifles and $45,000 cash were condemned and removed.[31]

Low, the boarding officer, was struck by the reaction of the male passengers. As soon as the Confederates appeared on the ship, they hid their watches and went through their trunks, trying to stash anything valuable. "I believe they think us no better than their Northern horde of thieves plundering dwelling houses and robbing defenseless women and children," he told Kell. In fact, the passengers were surprised at the cordial treatment they received from the Confederates. Low talked to one of the U.S. Navy officers, who told him he would inform the federal government that accusations of Confederate brutality were groundless, and he offered to speak for all the passengers on board.[32]

The captain of the *Ariel* told Semmes that the homeward-bound California steamer would come through the following day. The *Alabama*'s engineers were sent aboard to remove the *Ariel*'s valves so that she could not escape and ordered the prize crew back to the *Alabama*. The wind rose during the afternoon, however, and the *Ariel,* designed primarily for steam, had difficulty maneuvering. As Read noted, "Our prospects were anything but pleasing, I assure you. Jeff Davis was cursed by many not much given to that way of blessing, during the three hours we drifted and tumbled about in the old ship."[33] Semmes had the valves returned, replaced the prize crew, and ordered the Union ship to keep company. Then both ships began steaming toward Jamaica, along the route he thought the homeward-bound steamer would take. He planned to land the prisoners in Kingston and have the *Ariel* condemned.[34]

By Tuesday morning the second steamer had not been sighted. About 8:00 P.M., the *Alabama* began chasing a ship and had overhauled her and lowered a boat when one of the engine valve castings broke. The stranger began moving away, and the *Alabama* was not able to chase under sail. Finally the wind fell and the boat returned. The boarding officer said he had managed to hail the ship, which turned out to be German, out of Kingston. Her captain reported that yellow fever was raging there. Semmes doubted that he would be permitted to land prisoners there, and even if he could, he was certain that many of the women and children among the *Ariel*'s passengers would become victims of the disease. Because the *Alabama* was unable to keep up with the prize as long as her engine was down, he decided to release the *Ariel* on bond.[35]

Repairs to the engine took several days. Semmes was down with fever and chills, and the ship needed work. No new ships were sighted, and he did not want to see any except the homeward-bound steamer. Galveston now had his full attention, and his whereabouts had to be kept secret if his plan was to succeed. "God willing, I hope to strike a blow of some importance and make my retreat safely out of the Gulf," he wrote. He contemplated putting into the Caymans to get fresh fruit for the crew but decided against it for security reasons. The time was spent cleaning the ship and drilling the crew at quarters and with small arms. On December 21 the *Alabama* rounded Cape Catoche and entered the Gulf of Mexico. A large steamer was sighted, which Semmes reckoned to be a French warship from Veracruz. Two days later, the *Alabama* met the *Agrippina,* and that evening the two ships anchored in the Arcas Cays.[36]

The Arcas are almost like a Pacific atoll, enclosing a shallow lagoon connected to the sea. At high tide, fish would swim in and be trapped inside when the tide fell. On Christmas Day, Sinclair and several others took the dinghy in to spear fish, while Chief Engineer Freeman waded in the lagoon about one hundred yards from shore. Suddenly the men in the dinghy spotted the dorsal fin of a shark. The animal was swimming along leisurely, apparently sated from the abundance of fish. "We at once put our worthy engineer on his guard," Sinclair recalled. "The shark was between Freeman and the boat; so there was nothing to do on his part but make for shore—and such fun! I say fun, for the shark had no idea of attacking him." Freeman half-waded, half-swam, stumbling and falling as he made his way through the shallow water to the beach. Michael Mars, coxswain of the boat, jumped into the water and ripped the shark's stomach open with his knife. The shark thrashed about, and Mars was ordered back into the boat. "But his Irish blood was up and the fight was continued until the shark was vanquished." They made the shark fast to the boat and towed it ashore.[37]

Others spent the day in their own pursuits. Kell wrote to his wife, giving her the coordinates for the Arcas so she could look on a map and find where he had spent Christmas. Fullam, a native Englishman who was not inspired by the tropics, wished "for a good old English Christmas with its merry associations and innocent pleasures."[38] Semmes allowed the crew to go ashore and then went himself. It was the first time he had touched land since leaving Liverpool on August 13.

"It is indeed very grateful to the senses to ramble about over even so confined a space as the Arcas, after tossing about at sea in a continual state of excitement for months," Semmes noted. "My thoughts naturally turn on this quiet Christmas day, in this lonely island, to my dear family. I can only hope, and trust them to the protection of a merciful Providence. . . . Our poor people have been terribly pressed in this wicked and ruthless war, and they have borne privations and sufferings which nothing but an intense patriotism could have sustained. They will live in history as a people worthy to be free." That night he ordered an extra ration of grog for the crew.[39]

Battle

Ews of the *Ariel*'s capture arrived in Washington on December 28, and Welles braced himself for more abuse of the Navy Department. "I am exceedingly glad it was an outward and not a homeward bound vessel," he wrote in his diary. "It is annoying when we want all our force on blockade duty to be compelled to detach so many of our best craft on the fruitless errand of searching the wide ocean for this wolf from Liverpool."[1]

There was a positive side, however, not for Welles specifically but for the Northern cause as a whole. Already the nation was astir with the prospect of emancipation, which Lincoln planned to proclaim with the new year. Although applicable only in those parts of the Confederacy which the United States could conquer and secure, it gave a new sense of purpose for the North for which the abstract cause of preserving the Union had not been enough.

The implications of emancipation were not lost to the Southerners. Even the steerage officers of the *Alabama* were fully aware of the situation through captured newspapers, and they planted a tasteless statement of defiance in the sands of the Arcas Cays. It was a tombstone, made from a board about four feet long by two feet wide, on which was carved:

In Memory of Abraham Lincoln, President of the late United States, who died of Nigger on the brain. 1st January 1863. 290

Attached, in a weatherproof container, was a paper with a message in Spanish, asking, "Will the finder kindly favor me, by forwarding this tablet to the U.S. Consul at the first port he touches at[?]"[2]

On January 1, Welles went to the White House to wish Lincoln a happy new year and noted with satisfaction that the Emancipation Proclamation had been published in the *Washington Star*.[3] The same day, Semmes wrote in the *Alabama*'s journal:

> The first day of the new year; what will it bring forth? The Almighty, for a wise purpose, hides future events from the eyes of mortals, and all we can do is to perform well our parts and trust the rest to His guidance. Success, as a general rule, attends to him who is vigilant and active, and who is careful to obey all the laws of nature. It is useful to look back on this first day of [the] new year and see how we have spent the past; what errors we have committed and of what faults we have been guilty, that we may avoid the one and reform the other.[4]

For the North, 1863 was a year of victory on land and of Russian support at sea. For the South, it was a year for the raiders. The *Alabama, Florida,* and *Georgia* were at sea that year, and other Confederate ships were either under construction or negotiation. Welles might ask blessings on the Russians, but as the year began his West India Squadron had the immediate problem of the Confederates.

The squadron, organized specifically to track down the *Alabama* and *Florida,* was under the command of Acting Rear Admiral Charles Wilkes, who had clearly remained in the service beyond any usefulness. He had embarrassed the federal government with Great Britain by overhauling the British mail steamer *Trent* and forceably removing the Confederate commissioners John Slidell and James Mason. Even so, Welles had confidence in him and had given him command of the West India Squadron at the request of Lincoln and Secretary of State William Seward. It was a choice they would soon regret.[5]

Wilkes's flagship, the USS *Wachusett,* had put into Grand Cayman in late December, missing the *Agrippina* by three days. There he learned of the attack on the *Ariel,* guessed Semmes's plan to capture the homeward-bound California steamer, and set out to intercept him. But the *Wachusett* and her escort, the *Sonoma,* were damaged in a gale and lost time making repairs. Finally, Wilkes spotted a steamer that resembled the *Alabama,* and the excited federal crew cleared for action. Upon capture, however, she turned out to be the Confederate merchant steamer *Virginia.*[6]

Wilkes's problems were twofold. He was expected to search for the Confederate cruisers as well as intercept blockade runners bound for the Confederacy. He had only five ships available and advised Welles that unless he received more, he could do one job or the other but not both.[7] Consequently, he gave his captains discretionary authority to choose their own priorities, and as time passed, Welles began to believe that the admiral was less interested in capturing the *Alabama* than in the prize money to be gained from capturing blockade runners.[8]

Wilkes was not the only federal officer looking for the *Alabama.* The USS *Vanderbilt,* a giant passenger steamer which shipping magnate Cornelius Vanderbilt had donated to the federal government as a cruiser, was searching the Atlantic. Her commanding officer, Acting Lieutenant C. H. Baldwin, had taken her from Fayal to Barbados, where he learned of the *Alabama*'s visit to Martinique six weeks earlier. Baldwin, a "hard case" who had worked his way up from the ranks and seriously wanted to end the Confederate ship's career, reasoned that Semmes had plenty of time to learn about Wilkes's squadron and would have left the Indies in favor of his old cruising grounds in the Atlantic. Accordingly, he took the *Vanderbilt* north, then turned back around between Bermuda and Cape Hatteras, where a shortage of fuel forced him into Hampton Roads to recoal.[9]

While federal officers searched and fretted, the *Alabama* headed north toward Texas. The reports that General Banks was bound for Galveston were erroneous. In fact, Banks was en route to New Orleans to assist in opening the Mississippi and securing the area from the Red River to Mobile.[10] Galveston had been captured in October 1862, but the South retook it on January 1. Rather than sailing in on troop transports as he supposed, Semmes was heading toward a blockading squadron of five U.S. warships.[11] Ignorant of this situation, he was confident as he began his entry for Sunday, January 11:

"My crew are a fine-looking body of men, have been well drilled, and are not averse, I think, to a trial of skill and force with the enemy."[12]

By noon that day the *Alabama* was within thirty miles of Galveston. Semmes planned to stand off and perhaps anchor in the Gulf until moonrise, which he estimated would be about 11:30 P.M. Then he would run in and attack the transports.[13] Galveston Island was so low and flat, however, that ships along the coast were visible before the island itself came into sight. For that reason and what Semmes called "the carelessness in the lookout at the masthead," the *Alabama* came within plain sight of the federal ships before it spotted them. There were at least three steamers, one of which, a heavy warship, turned out to be the USS *Brooklyn,* flagship of Commodore H. H. Bell. No transports could be seen. Suddenly a shell exploded over the city.

"Ah, ha!" Semmes remarked to the officer of the deck. "There has been a change of programme here. The enemy would not be firing into his own people, and we must have recaptured Galveston, since our last advices."

"So it would seem," the officer replied.[14]

Semmes tacked immediately, hoping that he could pull away without being spotted. It was too late. At 3:00 P.M. Commodore Bell signaled Lieutenant Homer C. Blake, in the USS *Hatteras,* "to chase a sail to the southward and eastward." Blake got under way immediately and headed at full speed in the direction ordered. Shortly thereafter the *Hatteras* spotted the sail, and Blake signaled to the *Brooklyn* that it was a steamer.[15]

On the *Alabama,* Semmes pondered his next move. He had not come across the Gulf of Mexico to fight several federal warships, but he had promised his crew on the Arcas that they would see action. About that time, the lookout spotted the *Hatteras.* "The *Alabama* had given chase pretty often, but this was the first time she had been chased," Semmes wrote. "It was just the thing I wanted, however, for I at once conceived the design of drawing this single ship of the enemy far enough away from the remainder of her fleet, to enable me to decide a battle with her before her consorts could come to her relief." He ordered up steam and lowered the propeller, then wore ship under sail as though he were fleeing. Every so often, he would order a few turns of the engines to keep the *Alabama* just ahead and draw the *Hatteras* farther away from support.[16]

Blake was no fool. Knowing his own ship was slow, he realized that he was gaining on this strange steamer too rapidly. He suspected a trap and ordered the *Hatteras* cleared for action. He doubtless realized there would be no contest. The *Hatteras* was an iron-hulled side-wheel passenger steamer that had been bought by the federal navy in 1861. Her broadside consisted of two thirty-two-pounders, a thirty-pound rifled Parrott gun, and a twenty-pound rifle against the *Alabama*'s formidable battery. Still, he wanted "everything in readiness for a determined attack and a vigorous defense." By 7:00 P.M. it was dark. The *Hatteras* was within four miles. The stranger had hove to and was lying broadside, waiting. From her general appearance and maneuvering, Blake began to suspect he had come onto the *Alabama*. He decided to close in as much as possible to get maximum benefit from his limited armament.[17]

The ships were now so close that the men on each could hear conversations on the other. The *Alabama*'s crew was excited. The men were at their guns, lock strings in hand, waiting for the command to open fire. In the darkness they could not tell what kind of ship they were facing except that it was a side-wheeler. Then a call came out from the Union ship.

"What ship is that?"

"Her Britannic Majesty's Steamer *Petrel*," came the reply, after which the Confederates asked the identity of the Union ship several times.[18]

A pause ensued, and it seemed to Sinclair that the American officers were consulting. Meanwhile, Semmes was trying to ease the *Alabama* into a raking position, but each time, Blake maneuvered to keep his port battery facing the Confederate ship. In the darkness, Semmes was not completely certain this was the Union ship that had been chasing him, and he told Kell to continue with his inquiry. Finally, Blake identified the *Hatteras* as a United States warship and shouted that he intended to send over a boarding party. A boat was lowered and started toward the *Alabama*.

Although the Confederates could not understand all of Blake's statement, they did catch "United States something or other."

Battle between the *Alabama* and *Hatteras*
(from Semmes, *Memoirs of Service Afloat*)

Semmes was satisfied that he faced a Union warship.[19] He turned to Kell.

"Are you ready for action?"

"The men are only waiting for the word," Kell replied.

"Don't strike them in disguise," Semmes ordered, "tell them who we are, and give the broadside at the name." Word was passed to the gun divisions "that the signal to fire would be 'Alabama.'"

Kell took the speaking trumpet and shouted, "This is the Confederate States Steamer *Alabama*—fire!"[20]

The starboard battery cut loose with a broadside. The *Hatteras* replied immediately with her port battery. Blake knew his ship was vulnerable and believed his only chance was to ram and board the *Alabama*. He turned the *Hatteras* and headed straight toward the Confederate ship. But his bottom was foul, slowing down the ship, and the *Alabama* avoided him easily.

The *Hatteras*'s boarding boat had hardly pulled away when the shooting started. It was soon left behind as both ships moved ahead at full speed. Acting Master L. H. Partridge, who commanded the boarding party, thought he should try to get back to the *Hatteras* and ordered the crew to row toward her. By now the warships were so close to each other he could hear musket fire over the noise of the cannons.[21]

The months of drilling on the *Alabama* paid off. The Confederate crew was highly disciplined and worked the guns with precision. "The coolness displayed by them could not be surpassed by any old veterans," Fullam remarked. One of the boatswains, having read a New York newspaper that called the crew "the scum of England," shouted, "That's from the scum of England. . . . That's a British pill for you to swallow," as the *Alabama*'s shots hit the *Hatteras*.[22]

Blake managed to bring the *Hatteras* within thirty yards of the *Alabama*, but his ship was a wreck. Most of his shots were too high and either went into the Confederate upperworks or passed through the rigging. The *Alabama*'s guns were heavily depressed and hit the *Hatteras* in the hull and along the waterline. The Confederates could feel the concussion as their shots slammed into the Union ship. Fullam noticed that when shells exploded along the *Hatteras*'s hull, "her whole side was lit up and showing rents of five or six feet in length." A shell hit amidships and set the hold on fire. Another crashed through the sick bay and exploded in the adjoining compartment, setting it on fire. Finally, a Confederate shell smashed the exposed engine cylinder, filling the ship with steam and knocking out all power.

Blake hoped to disable the *Alabama* and at the same time attract the attention of the fleet off Galveston, but it was useless. Water was pouring in, and the ship was sinking rapidly. Meanwhile, the *Alabama* had pulled away, off the port bow, beyond the range of the Union guns, and was preparing to rake the decks. This would have been a slaughter, and Blake saw no point in it. The fire was nearing the magazines, and his ship was in danger of blowing up. He ordered the magazines flooded, fired a lee gun, and hoisted a light over his deck. He was finished.[23]

Fearing a ruse, the *Alabama*'s crew reloaded and trained the guns on the Union ship. Then Semmes ordered her in close. Blake shouted that he had surrendered and needed help. The *Alabama* immediately secured her guns and lowered her quarterboats, while the Union crew lowered its own boats and prepared to abandon ship. Left behind in the *Hatteras*'s boarding boat, Acting Master Partridge saw the *Alabama* draw up alongside his own ship and could hear cheering. He realized the *Hatteras* had been captured and started the boat back toward the fleet off Galveston, arriving the next morning.[24]

The *Hatteras* was listing badly now and in danger of sinking with many men still on board. Blake ordered the port battery jettisoned to stabilize the ship. This bought time, and everyone still alive was removed from the ship. Ten minutes after she was abandoned, the *Hatteras* went down bow first, her pennant still flying from the masthead. The battle lasted thirteen minutes. Blake lost two men killed and five wounded. On the *Alabama*, Dr. Galt and Dr. Llewellyn turned the sick bay over to the *Hatteras*'s surgeon for treatment of the wounded. Two Confederate crewmen were listed as "slightly wounded."[25]

The Galveston blockading squadron was not idle during the fight. The gun flashes had been seen, and the *Brooklyn, Sciota,* and *Cayuga* got under way immediately. Commodore Bell had no doubt that the *Hatteras* was engaging the *Alabama*. The three ships separated and swept the general area, hoping that one would find the combatants. Finally, at 11:00 A.M. the following day, the *Brooklyn* discovered "two masts of a sunken vessel standing out of water." A United States naval pennant was still flying from the main truck. Among the floating wreckage were the hurricane deck and wheelhouse. Bell recognized these as being from the *Hatteras* because they showed traces of damage from a collision with the *Brooklyn* a short time previously. Three of the *Hatteras*'s boats were found a few miles to the north, where they had drifted after being cast off by the *Alabama*.

Arriving back on station off Galveston at 3:00 P.M., Bell dispatched the gunboat *Clifton* to occupied New Orleans with a report for Admiral David G. Farragut. Acting Master Partridge was also on board to give an eyewitness account of the fight. In his report, Bell said the *Alabama* "has probably destroyed numerous vessels in the track between Key West and New Orleans, and doubtless intends to sweep away the blockading vessels of inferior force along the whole extent of the Gulf coast, trusting to his celerity of movement." To counter this, he recommended that three or four fast cruisers be placed in the Yucatan Channel to intercept because the federal gunboats were no match for the Confederate ship.[26]

The loss of the *Hatteras* was a profound shock to the navy, the second within two weeks. The powerful federal steamer *Harriet Lane* had been captured when the Confederates retook Galveston, and Bell considered her "capable of doing nearly as much injury to our commerce on the ocean as any vessels the rebels have afloat." With the loss of the *Hatteras,* Admiral Farragut had to write Welles of "still another disaster off Galveston." Farragut's chances of catching the *Alabama* were slim to none. He had few ships to spare, particularly because the *Florida* had put into port at Mobile, and he hoped to keep her bottled up there. Even if he could spare ships, the only ones powerful enough to fight the *Alabama* were the *Oneida* and *Cuyler,* and he worried about the latter's machinery, which was exposed in the same manner as that of the *Hatteras.* Still, he sent those ships to reinforce the Atlantic Squadron, hoping they might catch the *Alabama* as she left the Gulf.[27]

Semmes did not intend to be caught. The Confederates realized the Gulf of Mexico was a trap with only two ways in or out: the Yucatan Channel leading to the Caribbean and the Florida Straits to the Atlantic. They knew the federal squadron off Galveston would be rushing to support the *Hatteras* and had no idea of its strength or capabilities. After the Union crew was taken on board, she sped away under sail and steam. Aside from escaping from the Gulf, the Confederates wanted to land their prisoners as soon as possible. Altogether there were 101 federal sailors and 17 officers on board, and although they were under parole, it would have been a pretty even match had Lieutenant Blake and his officers decided to take the ship. Watching over them put a strain on the *Alabama*'s officers and crew, who remained armed even when they slept.[28]

The federal officers were berthed with the *Alabama*'s, according to rank, and given freedom of the ship, while the men were placed in irons.[29] Semmes shared his quarters with Blake. The next morning, Kell was on deck supervising damage repair, when Blake, who had known him before the war, came up and saluted.

"How do you do, Mr. Kell?" he asked. "Fortune favors the brave, sir."

Thanking him, Kell replied, "We take advantage of all fortune's favors."[30]

Sinclair struck up a friendship with Acting Master Henry O. Porter, the *Hatteras*'s executive officer. Porter knew Sinclair's father, and the two walked the decks, stood watch together, and talked about old times. *Hatteras* crewmen were also allowed to share in the ship's daily grog ration, which had been abolished in the U.S. Navy the year before. Two days after the fight, the *Alabama* overhauled the *Agrippina,* which dipped her colors in salute. The Confederates returned the salute as a perfunctory gesture and did not attempt to communicate. Semmes did not want his federal prisoners to identify the ship.[31]

After a stormy passage, the *Alabama* anchored at Port Royal, Jamaica, shortly after 7:00 P.M., January 20. The following morning, Semmes called on the naval commander and received permission from the governor to land his prisoners. Over the next few days, Semmes took a much-needed rest ashore and visited friends, while Kell supervised repairs and recoaling. Lieutenant Howell, the lone marine on board, had the responsibility of keeping order on the ship. Despite his vigilance, many a drunken sailor spent the night in the brig. Other officers were forced to divide their time between their various shipboard duties and entertaining the numerous visitors who came to see the now famous ship.[32]

Semmes returned to the ship on the evening of January 24 to find that most of the crew were drunk ashore. Worse, Paymaster Clarence Yonge had gone ashore, started drinking with paroled *Hatteras* men, and been in "traitorous communication with the United States consul." Kell sent an armed party, which returned him to the ship under arrest. Semmes ordered him dismissed from the service and drummed off the ship. Dr. Galt was named acting paymaster.[33]

The following day was spent getting the *Alabama* ready for sea. Semmes paid a final courtesy call on British naval authorities and settled the ship's bills ashore. The Jamaican police returned most of the crew, and those who needed it were put away to sober up. Three crewmen jumped overboard in broad daylight, swam to a passing dugout, grabbed the paddles from the confused local boatmen, and started paddling ashore, chased by the *Alabama*'s cutter. Realizing they needed to lighten ship, the deserters heaved one of the boatmen over the side. The cutter lost time when it stopped to pick the man up so the other boatman went into the water. Finally, however, they were run down and brought back on board.[34]

By 5:00 P.M., January 25, the work had been completed and fires were lit under the *Alabama*'s boilers. At 8:30 P.M., she steamed out of the harbor and put to sea.

For Lieutenant Blake, the stay in Jamaica was less pleasant. He reported to the consulate and sent his reports as soon as he was released. Throughout his narrative, he referred to the *Alabama* as a "piratical craft," which Semmes later read and considered an affront to the hospitality Blake had received on board. Blake also complained about the treatment of his officers and crew in Jamaica, which he considered "an unfriendly shore." Aside from general criticism, he was offended because the band of the HMS *Greyhound* had played "Dixie" on the night of the *Alabama*'s arrival. Blake lodged a protest with British naval authorities, and the band was ordered to play "Yankee Doodle." When the time arrived, the flagship, HMS *Jason*, led off with "God Save the Queen," after which the HMS *Challenger*'s band played concert music. The *Greyhound*'s band concluded the evening by carefully playing "Dixie," after which it crashed into "Yankee Doodle" with the instruments deliberately out of harmony.[35]

Petty affronts aside, the officers and crew of the *Hatteras* were in serious straits. They had no money and no clothing other than what they were wearing when they had abandoned ship, and in the nineteenth century such things were considered a sailor's personal misfortune. U.S. Vice-consul John Camp arranged for them to draw on the Navy Department for funds and saw to their needs while in Jamaica. Camp also arranged for Blake to charter the American ship *Bordino* [*Borodino?*], which took the *Hatteras*'s people to Key West, where they were outfitted with new clothing and caught passage to New York.[36]

A court of inquiry convened at New York Navy Yard to investigate the loss of the *Hatteras*. When it concluded, Welles wrote Blake that the court found he had handled the ship "in an efficient and praiseworthy manner," and his "conduct thereafter was altogether commendable and proper." The secretary also said the court ruled that "the conduct of the officers and crew of the *Hatteras* was good, and every effort was made by them to defend and preserve the vessel in this very unequal contest."[37]

8

The Glory Days

*B*ACK AT SEA, ONE OF THE FIRST ORDERS OF BUSINESS WAS disciplinary action against the crew for various infractions in Jamaica. Semmes called them "a beautiful set of fellows . . . now all sober, but the effects of their late debauches were visible upon the persons of all of them. Soiled clothing, blackened eyes, and broken noses, frowsy, uncombed hair, and matted and disordered beard, with reddened eyes that looked as if sleep had long been a stranger to them. . . . And so I listened to their penitential excuses, one by one, and restored them to duty, retaining one or two of the greatest culprits for trial by court-martial, as an example to the rest."[1]

He then turned his attention to the sailors who had seized the dugout and who were now charged with attempted desertion and attempted murder of the two native boatmen. They vehemently denied the accusations, saying the natives were good swimmers and that they had known the cutter would pick them up. It had never occurred to them to desert, they said, because they considered them-selves "part owners" of the *Alabama*. "We only wanted to say good-by to the girls," one protested. "The girls," coupled with an admission that they had been drunk, aroused Semmes's sympathy, and he let them off. Privately, he tended to blame the Jamaicans, who kept the men plied with liquor during their stay. He was amused to learn that once the *Hatteras* prisoners had been landed, they had gone drinking with the crew of the *Alabama* and the well-heeled Confederates covered the tab for their penniless American counterparts.[2]

No sooner were the cases concluded than a sail was sighted, which proved to be the bark *Golden Rule,* bound from New York to Aspinwall, Panama. Her cargo included masts, spars, and a complete set of rigging for the USS *Bainbridge,* which was laid up in Panama after being dismasted in a gale. The ship was burned, assuring that the *Bainbridge* would remain out of action for months to come, and nine prisoners were taken. A day later, the *Chastelaine* of Boston followed the *Golden Rule* to the bottom. On January 28, the *Alabama* reached Santo Domingo, which Semmes had visited in 1846 as first lieutenant of the USS *Porpoise.* The same pilot came on board to take in the *Alabama,* and despite the passage of years, they recognized each other. The pilot arranged permission for shore leave and to land prisoners. The *Alabama* took on fresh provisions and fruit and the following morning got under way again.[3]

As Semmes burned his way through the Caribbean, Lieutenant Baldwin in the *Vanderbilt* was running down leads. More imaginative than Wilkes and unconcerned about prize money, Baldwin had decided to follow the *Alabama* long enough to determine her route, then try to head her off in one of the passages or sea lanes which he knew the Confederate ship would have to take. Years later, Sinclair of the *Alabama* praised Baldwin, "whose unerring judgment led him, as the hound after the fox, to follow us from point to point, without a loss of the scent at any time, until he had tracked us from the West India Islands to the Brazil thoroughfare, thence to the Cape of Good Hope."[4]

Initially, Baldwin's tracking took him to Jamaica, where Vice-Consul Camp told him about the *Alabama's* stay and the loss of the *Hatteras.* Camp also advised Baldwin that several Confederate crewmen had offered to desert and had told Camp "that some forty or fifty more would also desert." But the vice-consul, who was only temporarily serving in that capacity after the death of the consul, did not consider the matter important and felt that he was not authorized "to interfere." Baldwin disagreed, saying that Camp could have quietly covered the desertions without becoming personally involved.

His business with the vice-consul completed, Baldwin called on the port authorities, who told him he must sail in twenty-four hours. He would be allowed to take only enough coal to get him to the nearest U.S. port, "and this immediately after the 290 [*Alabama*] had been allowed to take in 160 tons of coal," he complained.

Word of the destruction of the *Golden Rule* had reached Jamaica so Baldwin took the *Vanderbilt* up the Windward Passage and around Hispaniola and Puerto Rico, overhauling several ships but obtaining no information. Finally, his coal almost exhausted, he put in at Saint Thomas to recoal and scale his badly fouled boilers.

"We have a great many reports of the *Alabama* and her recent doings, many of them quite contradictory, probably set afloat by those of the various islands opposed to our cause, of whom I regret to say there are many, principally, however, British subjects, who, as a class, are bitterly opposed to us," Baldwin wrote to Welles. As for his own plans, he said, "This ship is better to lie at some central point, coaled and ready to act on the instant when reliable information is received, than to cruise." Otherwise, the *Vanderbilt*'s coal consumption was such that valuable time would be wasted recoaling. "The Department may rest assured I shall not trifle away an hour," he concluded.[5]

The *Alabama* entered Mona Passage, between Hispaniola and Puerto Rico, at 8:30 P.M. the day she sailed from Santo Domingo. At 10:00 P.M., she hove to for three hours to tighten the bolts on her engine cylinders, then got under way again. Semmes was zigzagging in and out of the Caribbean, hoping to mop up a few more Union ships before heading on to Brazil. Generally, the days passed uneventfully. The *Alabama* overhauled a Spanish schooner and gave her the longitude and sighted a square-rigger, which was too far astern to chase. On Sunday, February 1, the crew was mustered for the monthly reading of the Articles of War and to hear the sentences of the court-martial.[6]

The following day a fire alarm was given. Semmes ordered the crew beat to quarters, but the fire was extinguished before everyone was in place. Investigation showed that the captain of the hold had gone into the spirit room to pump off the liquor ration and had violated standing orders by using an open flame for light.

The fumes from the liquor casks had ignited. Semmes ordered the man confined in double irons and demoted from his position as petty officer.[7]

On February 3 the *Alabama* overhauled the U.S. schooner *Palmetto*, reprovisioned from her stores, and burned her. As always, officers kept an eye on the crew to make certain they did not do any personal looting. There were two reasons: all items confiscated from an enemy ship were credited as part of the prize money due every officer and man, and the men always had to remember that they were not pirates or privateers but the crew of a government warship and subject to naval discipline. As Sinclair noted, "Nothing so demoralizes a crew as being allowed to plunder *ad libitum*." So, as confiscated stores were carried over from the *Palmetto* and other condemned ships, "the distrustful Kell" stood on a gun carriage. Any hammock, net, or locker that looked suspicious was ordered opened, and if plunder was found, it went over the side.[8]

The cruise continued with little break in the routine. The *Alabama* entered the "road of the ocean," a passage charted by oceanographer Matthew Fontaine Maury, which, Sinclair noted, "all vessels *must* follow, cruisers or no cruisers. Navigators have only the choice of some sixty miles of width at one point off the Brazil coast. Neglect warning, stray from the mile-stones, and head on baffling winds and currents will waft you hither and thither, any way but the one wished."[9] In this heavily traveled passage, the lookout spotted as many as seven sails at once.

"They were all European bound, and were jogging along, in company, following Maury's blazes, like so many passengers on a highway," Semmes remarked. "The *Alabama* stood like a toll-gate before them, and though we could not take toll of them, as they were all neutral, we made each traveller show us his passport, as he came up."[10]

From old newspapers on some of the foreign ships, Semmes learned that the *Vanderbilt* and *Sacramento* were looking for the *Alabama*. A passing British ship provided more ominous news—now that the Emancipation Proclamation was official, British abolition societies were stirring up support for the North in the United Kingdom.[11]

On February 15 he noted the second anniversary of his resignation from the U.S. Navy. "I have more and more reason, as time rolls on, to be gratified at my prompt determination to quit the service of a corrupt and fanatical majority, which even then had overridden the Constitution and shown itself in so aggressive and unscrupulous a form as to alarm us," he noted in the ship's journal. He went on to rail against Union "knaves and swindlers" and the United States as a whole, with "its Beechers in the pulpit and its Lincoln in the chair of Washington, its Sumners and Lovejoys in Congress."[12]

Two more ships were captured and burned on February 21. After that, no more U.S. vessels were sighted until March 1, when the *Alabama* overhauled the *Bethiah Thayer* of Maine. Because she was loaded with guano belonging to the Peruvian government, she was bonded, but a day later, another Union ship, the *John A. Parke*, was burned. From the *Parke*, Semmes was gratified to learn that the *Florida* had escaped from Mobile and was now at sea. More than a week passed before the *Panjaub*, a U.S. ship with British cargo, was bonded and received the crew of the *John A. Parke*. Newspapers on the *Panjaub* informed Semmes that Yankee ships were now avoiding the usual trade routes, which accounted for the lack of sightings. Again, a week passed before overhauling another American ship, which was bonded with British cargo, and burning a whaling schooner.[13]

Not only were U.S. ships avoiding the usual sea lanes, but they continued to resort to subterfuge. The *John A. Parke* had carried false papers listing her cargo as British-owned, when, in fact, it was American. On March 25, the *Alabama* overhauled two ships, the *Charles Hill* and the *Nora*, both of Boston and both carrying false papers representing their cargoes as British. Both ships were condemned, and cargo and coal were transferred to the *Alabama*, a process that lasted most of the following day. Despite Kell's vigilance, several of the crewmen managed to smuggle liquor on board from the prizes and got drunk. Semmes noted that the "rascals . . . are sometimes my best men, who can be trusted with everything but whisky." But he managed to enlist six additional seamen from among the prisoners. The two ships were finally fired at 9:00 P.M., March 26, and on the following morning were still in sight, "advertising our whereabouts for 30 miles around in a column of smoke."[14]

On April 4 the *Alabama* overhauled the *Louise Hatch,* a U.S. ship with coal listed as French, consigned from Cardiff to Ceylon. Semmes conducted a condemnation hearing and determined that there was no documentation to back the claim. Therefore, he ruled "that this cargo, being on board an American ship, is American, shipped on speculation to the far East by the owner or his agent in Cardiff," and was therefore condemned. As it happened, the *Alabama* was running low on coal, and the *Louise Hatch* was ordered to accompany her until it was convenient to transfer the cargo. Bad weather delayed coaling for several days, and when it finally commenced, the task proved impractical at sea so Semmes waited until he reached the Brazilian island of Fernando de Noronha. They anchored there at 2:30 P.M., April 10, and began to transfer the coal that night.[15]

The decision to take coal from the *Louise Hatch* proved to be wise. Semmes had intended to rendezvous with the *Agrippina* at Fernando de Noronha, where he knew Bulloch was sending her with the next load of coal and provisions. But the *Agrippina* failed to appear and was never again seen by the *Alabama.* Semmes and Kell always believed that Captain McQueen sold the cargo elsewhere, lined his own pockets with the proceeds, and returned to Bulloch in England with "a cock-and-a-bull story, to account for his failure." Almost four decades later, when Kell wrote his memoirs, he still referred to McQueen as "the old Scotch sinner," and that has been the verdict ever since.[16] This judgment is unfair because McQueen tried his best to fulfill his obligations. As Bulloch commented: "The *Agrippina* was not a clipper. She made a long passage from the Arcas Islands to England, and sprang her foremast in a gale before getting into the Channel. She was refitted and despatched as quickly as possible, but this time the arrangements failed."[17]

McQueen was still en route to the rendezvous when the *Alabama* lay at Fernando de Noronha, a volcanic island long familiar as a landmark for passing mariners but rarely visited. At the time, Brazil used it as a penal colony. It was far enough from the Brazilian coast that the governor, supported by a battalion of troops, administered it to suit himself. "Very few of the prisoners are kept in close confinement," Semmes noted. "The island itself is prison enough, and there are no possible means of escape from it. The prisoners are, therefore, permitted to run at large, and mitigate the horrors of their lot by manual labor on the farms, or engage in the mechanic arts."[18]

Semmes sent a letter to the governor explaining the purpose of his visit and requesting permission to coal from the *Louise Hatch,* which he carefully noted was a prize of war. Dr. Galt was sent ashore to inquire about purchasing supplies. The governor responded by sending two representatives to welcome the *Alabama* to the island and to arrange for supplies. Over champagne and cigars, Semmes was surprised to learn that one of the representatives was a German convict, serving a six-year sentence for forgery in Brazil. Semmes shrugged it off, but several of the Confederate officers were uneasy, and Bartelli was offended that someone of his captain's station should be greeted by a convict. He immediately returned the remaining cigars and champagne to their lockers to indicate that he was above serving such riffraff. Later during the *Alabama*'s visit, the governor called, and Sinclair observed that his "garish uniform, with lace galore, seemed fully up to Bartelli's idea of the proprieties."[19]

The various courtesies included a breakfast hosted by the governor and his wife. Once again, the German convict was present, along with his daughter, about seventeen years old, who accompanied him on his exile, and the local priest. The governor took pains to explain that the German was a cut above the common class of criminal, describing him as "a very clever old gentleman, and . . . he has a very pretty daughter." In addition to the provisions purchased for the ship, the governor sent gifts to all the messes and gave the crew the freedom of the island, although the lack of saloons and dance halls did not encourage them to take advantage of the offer. This was a relief to Kell, who "enjoyed a quiet life at the island," free from having to control drunken sailors.[20]

Throughout this time, the slow work of coaling continued. Coal was transferred by boat because Fernando de Noronha's anchorage was an open roadstead, and the *Alabama* and *Louise Hatch* could not be moored together without damage. Semmes, yet unaware of Captain McQueen's difficulties, still awaited the arrival of the *Agrippina.*[21] About 1:00 A.M. the first day, a strange steamer came round the point. The crew was beat to quarters, guns were run out, fires raised, and the anchor chain readied for slipping. But the strange ship steamed on, and the crew was piped down.[22]

Coaling was finished on April 15. About 11:00 A.M. that day, two whaleboats from American ships standing offshore pulled into the anchorage. The crews wanted permission to make repairs and reprovision their ships. Recognizing the American lines of the *Louise Hatch,* they pulled alongside, where George Fullam, the prizemaster, told them the warship at anchor was the USS *Iroquois.* The boatmen, however, noticed a Confederate boat's ensign aboard the ship and began pulling away. It took the *Alabama* more than an hour to get up steam and get under way, and had the American ships headed toward the island and come within the marine league they would have been safe. Instead, they ran to sea and were overhauled in international waters about midafternoon. This time, Semmes did not bother with disguise; the *Alabama* ran up the Confederate ensign and the two ships responded with American flags. One was the bark *Lafayette,* the second prize of that name, and the other the hermaphrodite brig *Kate Cory.* The *Lafayette* was burned at sea and the *Kate Cory* brought back to the anchorage.[23]

Semmes had originally intended to place all prisoners on the *Kate Cory* and bond her, but the governor gave permission to land them on Fernando de Noronha. The next morning, as a column of smoke still hung over the burning *Lafayette,* Semmes formally notified the governor that the ships had been captured beyond the marine league and, as previously arranged, requested permission to land the prisoners. On April 17, the *Louise Hatch* and *Kate Cory* were taken beyond the league and burned.

"Received four recruits from the *Louise Hatch* and more volunteered, but I am full," Semmes noted in the *Alabama*'s journal. The next several days were rainy, and the *Alabama* remained at anchor waiting for the *Agrippina.* Semmes noted in the journal: "The island, after the rain, is blooming in freshness and verdure, and as my eye roams over its green slopes and vales, looking so peaceful and inviting, I long for the repose and quiet of peace in my own land. I do not think it can be far off."[24]

His ship was beginning to worry him. The steam tubes were leaking badly. Even a small amount of pressure dumped large amounts of water into the hold, and Semmes knew that as time went on the problem would grow worse. He realized the *Alabama* needed an overhaul.[25]

Despite her engine problems, the *Alabama* steamed out of Fernando de Noronha on the morning of April 22 after leaving word for the *Agrippina* to rendezvous in Bahia. Semmes was optimistic: "The *Alabama,* with full coal-bunkers and a refreshed crew, was again in pursuit of the enemy's commerce. I had at last accomplished my cherished design—which had been frustrated in the *Sumter*—of a cruise on the coast of Brazil."[26]

During the following days, she made several captures: the whaler *Nye* of New Bedford overhauled and burned on April 24; the ship *Dorcas Prince* of New York burned on April 26; the *Union Jack* of Boston and *Sea Lark* of New York burned on May 3. Having had no news for more than seventy days, Semmes was pleased to find recent newspapers on the last two captures. The war news from home, however, was grim. As he noted in the journal, "The Yankee papers appear to be jubilant at the state of affairs, especially at the prospect of our being starved."[27]

One of the passengers on the Shanghai-bound *Union Jack* was the Reverend Franklin Wright, described as "late editor of a religious paper and consul to Foo-Chow by recent appointment." Semmes confiscated his consular seal and official papers to delay his accreditation to Chinese officials. Wright estimated his losses to the U.S. Department of State at $10,015, causing Semmes to remark, "I had no idea that a New England parson carried so much plunder about with him."[28]

The *Alabama* was now heavily loaded with prisoners, including women, who had recovered from the initial shock of capture and now wandered all over the ship, sleeping on the wardroom floor and generally getting in the way. One complained to Sinclair that her opera glasses had been confiscated as a navigational instrument. Sinclair referred her to Semmes, who ordered the glasses returned. Although Sinclair admitted enjoying their company, he said, "I often had the thought present itself, in this situation, what would become of these women if we should get alongside of an enemy's cruiser."[29]

During this time, a large warship was sighted to the windward, but from the rake of her masts and her double funnels, the *Alabama*'s officers recognized her as the *Florida*. She was too far to the windward for an attempt to contact and was soon lost over the horizon. After the war, Sinclair learned that the *Florida* had also seen the *Alabama* but did not recognize her.[30]

The *Alabama* anchored in Bahia at 5:00 P.M. May 11 and began arrangements to land the prisoners. The only other warship in the harbor was from Portugal, and there were no Americans among the merchantmen. The crew was given liberty, and an English merchant hosted a dance for the officers. The captain of the British bark *Castor* called on the *Alabama* and told Semmes he had been dispatched to Bahia to provide coal and provisions for the CSS *Georgia*. Still there was no word of the *Agrippina*, and Semmes, still unaware of McQueen's situation, began "to fear that some disaster has befallen her."[31]

At first light on May 13, a strange warship was sighted anchored about half a mile from the *Alabama*. Uncertain of her identity, the Confederates nevertheless made colors as usual at 8:00 A.M. "To our great surprise and delight, she, too, hoisted the Confederate flag," Semmes wrote. Recognition signals were exchanged, and the *Alabama* sent a boat to the other ship, which proved to be the *Georgia*, under Lieutenant Commander W. L. Maury. On board were Lieutenants R. T. Chapman and W. E. Evans, who had served in the *Sumter*. As visits were exchanged, a telegram came stating that the *Florida* had arrived at Pernambuco to land prisoners and take on coal.[32]

"We can straighten up now and put on airs, boast of the 'Confederate squadron of the South American station,' and await the arrival of any vessel of the enemy's navy in perfect security," Sinclair wrote. "The Alabama is supposed to be dodging the United States cruisers; yet now the Georgia is in port with us, and the Florida within telegraphic communication and two days steaming, it would be tough luck for the enemy should one of his cruisers happen to stumble in. We cannot avoid the feeling of pride and satisfaction that our struggling little Confederacy has actually been able to overmatch the enemy in cruisers, at least for the time being, and put them on the defensive so far as the Brazilian coast goes."[33]

Sinclair was right. These were the glory days of the Confederate navy. Never before and never again was so much Southern sea power concentrated in a single area. To those present, it seemed as though the Confederate States might, after all, establish themselves as an independent power.

9

The Tuscaloosa *and Cape Town*

*F*OR MOST PEOPLE ON THE *ALABAMA*, THE STAY IN BAHIA
was quiet, drawing little comment from Kell or Sinclair. The
sailors, as usual, got out of hand on shore, and the Brazilian police were
requested to jail them until they sobered up. There were sightseeing
excursions to the venerable old colonial buildings, visitors were entertained on board, and there were pleasant exchanges with the officers
of the *Georgia*.[1]

Semmes, however, was embroiled in a diplomatic dispute with
the president of Pernambuco State, under whose jurisdiction Bahia
and Fernando de Noronha fell. The day after the *Alabama*'s arrival
in Bahia, the president sent a messenger with a late copy of the
Diario de Bahia demanding that he leave Fernando de Noronha within
twenty-four hours of receipt, which, presumably, meant Bahia as
well.

It appeared that some of the Yankee prisoners had arrived in
Pernambuco claiming that they had been attacked in Brazilian
waters at Fernando de Noronha. In reply, Semmes told the president
that he had paid careful attention to Brazilian neutrality, "and
this consideration, along with the fact, that I had the heaviest
guns in the harbor, induced me to be rather careless, I am afraid,
in the choice of phraseology. . . . I simply charged that the whole
proclamation was a budget of lies, and claimed that I had been

insulted by the Government of Brazil, by the lies having been put into an official shape by it, without first communicating with me." Satisfied, the president said the *Alabama* could receive the hospitality of the port of Bahia, but he preferred that she leave in "three or four days."[2]

The arrival of the *Georgia* created a new complication. The president was afraid two Confederate ships might compromise his neutrality and the emperor in Rio de Janeiro would demand explanations. This fear was carefully cultivated by the U.S. consul, and soon a representative in civilian clothes appeared on the *Alabama* and asked to see Semmes's commission. Semmes answered that he could present his commission only on written demand from an accredited officer of equal rank but added that he would be willing to present it personally to the president. A meeting was arranged at which Semmes told the president that he sought only the same rights that would be extended to a United States warship. He also pointed out that Brazil, one of the last Western nations officially to sanction Negro slavery, had a vested interest in the victory of the slaveholding South. The president replied that the *Georgia* and *Alabama* would have to coal from boats because port regulations prohibited the *Castor* from mooring alongside. He also repeated his desire that the Confederate ships leave as soon as possible.[3]

The next morning, however, the *Castor* was ordered to suspend operations and haul off because the United States consul had charged that she was transferring munitions. As Semmes pondered these new developments, officials were sent to the *Alabama* and *Georgia* with orders that both ships put to sea within twenty-four hours. Semmes responded by accusing the government of creating the delays and, to emphasize the point, sent another party of sailors ashore for liberty. The war of nerves continued for another three days. In a second meeting, the president repeated the charge that the *Castor* was transferring munitions and that the *Alabama* had enlisted one of the paroled prisoners after landing him in Brazilian territory. Semmes said that several had volunteered, but he did not receive any of them because he had a full crew. That afternoon, he sent a letter to the president formally demanding the right to coal from the *Castor*. Finally, on May 20, the *Alabama* steamed out of Bahia with full bunkers, having remained in port for nine days.[4]

On June 1 the *Agrippina* finally arrived to find two federal warships, the *Onward* and the *Mohican,* in port. The U.S. consul had already notified their commanders to watch for the *Castor* and was suspicious of the *Agrippina* as well. Upon learning that the *Onward* was eyeing him especially carefully, Captain McQueen consulted the British consul, who advised him that the *Agrippina* would probably be overhauled upon leaving port and risked being sent to the United States for condemnation. McQueen spent some time in Bahia, trying to figure out a way to follow Semmes's instructions and deliver his coal. Finally, he went to the British consul again and was advised to sell the coal and take freight for Great Britain. He did so and was given a consular certificate stating that Bahia was under blockade and that he had acted in the best interests of the owners.[5]

In the meantime, the *Alabama* overhauled and burned several U.S. ships as she entered new hunting grounds of the South Atlantic. One night the lookout spotted "an exceedingly rakish-looking ship, whose canvas showed white under the rays of the moon, and which was carrying a press of sail." The Confederates crowded on sail, too, but the other ship maintained its lead. Semmes stood on the horseblock all night, excitedly thinking that here, at last, was a worthy opponent. It became a matter of pride to see which ship was faster, and he pushed the *Alabama* as hard as she would take. Little by little, the Confederates gained on the unknown ship. At daybreak, Semmes, exhausted, went below to rest as the chase continued. Finally, the *Alabama* drew close enough to throw a blank shot, and the stranger backed her sails. Too tired to go out on deck, Semmes waited below until an officer reported that she was the Dutch ship *Arnhem,* bound for Rotterdam. "I must have looked a little sour at the breakfast table, that morning, as Bartelli was evidently a little nervous and fidgety," Semmes remarked.[6]

Forty-eight hours later, he received compensation for his loss of sleep when a night chase lasting more than five hours overhauled the *Jabez Snow* of Rockport, Maine. The *Alabama* fired two shots before the New Englander hove to and showed her colors. A Confederate junior lieutenant was turned out of his stateroom so a woman listed as a "chambermaid," whom Semmes suspected of being the Maine captain's mistress, could have some privacy. After removal of some cordage and provisions needed by the *Alabama,* the *Jabez Snow* was burned.[7]

The weather being good, the quartermaster aired the ship's signal flags, running them up along with all the captured American flags. In addition to chronometers, Semmes collected captured flags and miscellaneous navigational gear "much as persons are in the accumulation of postage-stamps and other odds and ends." Sinclair commented, "We might have supplied the entire United States navy, without exaggeration; and as for quadrants and sextants, even Jack can be seen forward at mid-day, instrument in hand, 'taking the sun' for the benefit of the forecastle."[8]

Soon another sail was spotted in the predawn hours, and the chase began. The ship, which was originally approaching the *Alabama,* turned about and crowded on sail. The wind was strong and the ship was fast; Semmes ordered the big trysails set to move the *Alabama* faster. At dawn, as if in defiance, the other ship showed the United States flag and sailed on. Semmes was in a foul mood and ordered the Confederate flag run up and a blank cartridge fired. When the stranger failed to respond, a second shot was fired. Finally, at 10:30 A.M., the *Alabama* was close enough to pivot out the big rifled gun and fire. The noise of the shell whistling toward him was enough for the American captain, and he came to.

The ship was the *Amazonia* of Boston, bound for Montevideo. At the bottom of her hold, stowed under her other cargo, were items the *Alabama* sorely needed, such as soap and candles. Describing the scene, Sinclair wrote: "Overboard go pianos, pier-glasses, cases of fine boots and shoes, etc., articles of high value, for what? Why, to get a few boxes of soap, of more value to us at present than all the pianos in Boston."[9]

Once the transfer of cargo was completed, the *Amazonia* was burned. Again, the *Alabama* was crowded with prisoners so the following day Semmes overhauled a British ship bound for Rio de Janeiro. In exchange for two weeks' provisions and the gift of a chronometer, the captain agreed to take the prisoners on board. That night, the light of a burning ship was seen in the distance, and the *Alabama* raced to the scene.

"It disappeared suddenly," Semmes recorded, "having been sunk, no doubt, but as I supposed it might possibly be an accidental fire (we were 45 miles from where we had burned the *Amazonia* thirty-six hours before) I ran within 5 or 6 miles of the supposed spot of disappearance and hove to until daylight, that we might pick up any boat, etc." He never discovered the cause of the mysterious fire, but there was a strong northerly current, and he speculated that it might have been the last of the *Amazonia,* pushed some twenty-five or thirty miles in that direction.[10]

Semmes hit a windfall on June 5, when he overhauled the *Talisman,* bound for China, where the Taiping Rebellion was under way. The cargo included four rifled brass twelve-pounder guns mounted on ship carriages, powder and shot, and two steam boilers and other equipment to fit out a gunboat for the Chinese strife. Remarking on the New England trade in narcotics and Bibles in China, Semmes said, "I am afraid I spoiled a 'good thing.' With a Yankee Mandarin on board, and a good supply of opium, and tracts, what a smashing business this little cruiser might have done."[11]

The *Alabama* took provisions, as well as two of the twelve-pounders, which Sinclair declared "battery enough to tackle the heaviest merchant-ship, even with a crew inferior in numbers." Soon these American-shipped guns would be turned against the United States. That night, the *Talisman,* "a beautiful craft of 1,100 tons," was burned.[12]

Most American ships were now using false papers. Generally Semmes saw through the ruse, but on June 6, he came upon one that stumped him. The ship was obviously an American design, and no secret was made that she had been built in Maine. But the papers, all appearing completely legal, listed her as having been sold to English owners and carrying foreign cargo. Semmes was convinced that "if this ship could have been sent before a prize court it might have turned out that the transfer was only nominal and the property really American." But, he said, "I could not destroy upon a mere presumption growing out of the fact of transfer during war," and she was allowed to sail.[13]

June is winter in the South Atlantic, and the weather turned ugly. The *Alabama* approached Abrolhos Shoals, which Semmes called "a sort of Brazilian Cape Hatteras for bad weather" and the danger they posed for ships. A sail was spotted, but the rough seas precluded a chase. After several days, the weather cleared but soon turned bad again. One day the *Alabama* made a top speed of only eight knots under sail. When the weather finally did permit a chase, it was obvious that the impact of the Confederate cruisers was felt in the North; several American ships were overhauled, now legally registered in foreign countries. "Here was a humiliating spectacle for the 'old flag,'" Semmes wrote, "as no doubt the motive of the sale was the insecurity of the property under it."[14]

While Semmes took satisfaction in the havoc he had created, it was a frustrating time for Captain Baldwin in the *Vanderbilt*. He had guessed that the *Alabama* would be cruising the coast of Brazil and, accordingly, Welles had ordered him to Fernando de Noronha to head her off. At that point, however, fate intervened in the person of Admiral Wilkes. According to Welles, Wilkes, "finding *Vanderbilt* a commodious ship with extensive and comfortable accommodations, deliberately annexed her to his squadron and detained her in the West Indies as his flagship, hunting prizes." Now the *Vanderbilt* was wandering back and forth through the Caribbean as Wilkes followed numerous leads, invariably wrong. The nearest Confederate cruiser was on the opposite side of the equator.[15]

Welles was furious. "I, of course, shall be abused for the escape of the Alabama and her destruction of property by those who know nothing of the misconduct of Wilkes," he groused. Discussing the problem with Secretary of State Seward, Welles said Wilkes "is always disinclined to obey orders which he receives if they do not comport with his own notions. His special mission, in his present command, had been to capture the Alabama. In this he had totally failed, while zealous to catch blockade-runners and get prize money. Had he not been in the West Indies, we might have captured her, but he had seized the Vanderbilt, which had specific orders and destination and gone off with her prize-hunting, thereby defeating our plans."[16]

Although the *Trent* Affair with Great Britain had embarrassed the United States, Wilkes's action had been popular in the North, and he had been praised as a hero. Now Seward pointed out that his removal from the West Indies command would make him a martyr and bring further embarrassment to both the State and Navy departments. Yet Seward said he would run that risk if Welles were willing. Welles replied that "any abuse of me in the discharge of my duty and when I knew I was right would never influence my course." To Seward's suggestion that Wilkes be recalled for his failure to capture the *Alabama,* Welles said, "I care to assign no reasons,—none but the true ones, and it is not politic to state them."[17]

Within two weeks of that conversation, however, Welles decided that Wilkes had to go: "He has accomplished nothing, but has sadly interrupted and defeated the plans of the Department. The country, ignorant of these facts and faults, will disapprove his removal and assail the Department for the mischief of the Alabama, whereas, had he been earlier removed, the latter would not have happened."[18]

With Wilkes out of the way, Baldwin headed for Brazil and learned of the Confederate visits to Fernando de Noronha, Bahia, and Pernambuco. Overhauling ships at sea, he obtained information about both the *Alabama* and *Georgia* and formed a pretty good idea of their tracks. But he was running low on coal and had to put into Rio de Janeiro, where the United States government had laid in a supply. There he had trouble getting Brazilian authorities to release the coal, even though it was government-owned, and Baldwin indicated that in the future the navy might better set up coaling stations in Pernambuco, Bahia, and Fernando de Noronha, where the officials were more friendly. In a report to Welles on July 23, he said he would be laid up in Rio de Janeiro for another week or so for work on his boilers but would get under way again once it was completed. "Of course I can not say positively in what direction I propose moving," he wrote, "this will depend on the information I may receive."[19]

Baldwin hardly suspected that he had yet another Confederate warship to contend with. On June 20 the *Alabama* had captured a ship that Semmes deemed too useful to burn. She was the *Conrad* of Philadelphia and, calling her "a tidy little bark, of about three hundred and fifty tons, with good sailing qualities," he decided to commission her as an auxiliary cruiser. The twelve-pounders captured from the *Talisman* were placed on board, along with twenty rifles and half a dozen revolvers and ammunition.[20]

"Never, perhaps, was a ship of war fitted out so promptly before," Semmes wrote. "The *Conrad* was a commissioned ship, with armament, crew, and provisions on board, flying her pennant, and with sailing orders signed, sealed, and delivered. . . . I called the new cruiser, the *Tuscaloosa,* after the pretty little town of that name, on the Black Warrior River in the State of Alabama. It was meet that a child of the *Alabama* should be named after one of the towns of the State."[21]

On June 21 the *Tuscaloosa* was formally commissioned with a salute gun, the hoisting of the flag, and cheers. Lieutenant Low commanded her, and three other officers and fourteen men were transferred from the *Alabama.* Then the ships separated, the *Tuscaloosa* preparing to meet the enemy on her own, with orders to rendezvous with the *Alabama* in Cape Town.

"May the *Tuscaloosa* prove a scourge to Yankee commerce!" Semmes wrote in the *Alabama*'s journal. He had little time to reflect on the new ship, however, for in less than two hours, the *Alabama* overhauled the British bark *Mary Kendall* and transferred the prisoners from the former *Conrad* for the trip to Rio de Janeiro.[22] Initially Semmes planned to sail on to Cape Town, but on June 27 he learned that much of the ship's bread had been eaten by weevils.

"We were actually by this time in search of food," Kell wrote. Only by capturing a well-provisioned American ship could the *Alabama* continue without returning to Brazil. After several days of unsuccessful cruising, Semmes decided to put in at Rio to reprovision. More bad weather was encountered, and the ship rolled badly, much to Semmes's discomfort: "The fact is, I am getting too old to relish the rough usage of the sea. Youth sometimes loves to be rocked by a gale, but when we have passed the middle stage of life we love quiet and repose."[23]

Now luck intervened on the *Alabama*'s behalf. She captured and burned the American ship *Anna F. Schmidt,* taking about thirty days' supply of bread and other provisions so that the trip to Rio was no longer necessary.

On July 3, 1863, as the fate of the Confederacy hung in the balance at a little Pennsylvania town called Gettysburg, the Confederate States Steamer *Alabama* came about and headed toward South Africa. Soon after, the *Express* of Boston provided additional provisions before she was burned. Two weeks later, a British ship was overhauled, and the prisoners were transferred. For the most part, the trip across the South Atlantic was monotonous. The *Alabama* spent the better part of one Sunday chasing three ships, all of which proved to be foreigners, and wasting the time that Semmes had planned to devote to reading his Bible. Finally, at 10:30 A.M., July 28, the *Alabama* sighted the heights around Cape Town, and at 1:45 P.M. the following day, anchored in Hontjes Bay.[24]

Hontjes Bay is part of the vast, protected anchorage of Saldanha Bay, about fifty or sixty miles northwest of Cape Town. It was isolated, with only a few scattered farmhouses in the hills and fishing huts along the shore, and Semmes had chosen it to avoid any federal warships that might be waiting in the Cape of Good Hope. Sailors were sent out with a seine and soon returned with large amounts of fresh fish. Others were set to work overhauling the ship's machinery, repairing rigging, caulking, painting, and handling other maintenance chores. The crew received liberty ashore and proceeded to live down to its usual standards, obtaining liquor somewhere and getting so drunk that one of them pulled a revolver on the master's mate. Semmes revoked the liberty privileges.[25]

The morning after anchoring, Semmes landed to take a sighting to check his chronometers. It was the first time he had ever set foot in Africa, and he spent the next several days strolling around the countryside, meeting local farmers. A schooner came in from Cape Town with letters from merchants who offered to supply the *Alabama* with coal and provisions. He sent back a letter to Sir Philip Wodehouse, governor of Cape Colony, informing him of the *Alabama*'s arrival and requesting the courtesies of the colony. Visitors were starting to arrive from the surrounding area, and Sinclair remarked on "long wagon trains" that "followed each other in quick succession, coming from interior points to view the remarkable ship, visitors tumbling on board in an ever-flowing stream. They were in family parties, from the venerable grandfather and grandmother to the little

Captain Semmes and Lieutenant Kell on the deck
of the *Alabama* at Cape Town

tot carried in the arms." Semmes was impressed by the "plump,
ruddy Dutch girls, whose large, rough hands and awkward bows, or
courtesies, showed them to be honest lasses from the neighboring
farms, accustomed to milking the cows and churning the butter."
The farmers invited the officers to come hunting with them in the
interior, and several accepted.[26]

Sinclair, Third Assistant Engineer S. W. Cummings, and Master
Irvine S. Bulloch spent August 3 duck hunting. Cummings was
getting into the boat to return to the ship when the hammer of his
gun caught in the thwart and it discharged. Cummings slumped
over without a sound, a load of scattershot in and around his heart.
Sinclair and Bulloch called for help from native laborers working in
a nearby field, but the natives panicked and fled so they went on to
the *Alabama*. A silent crowd lined the rail as they came to the
gangway. Sinclair was summoned to the cabin to report on the
incident. "Semmes was deeply affected, trembling with emotion, and

brushing away a tear creeping slowly down his weather-beaten cheek, he said, 'That will do, sir; good night.' "[27]

Arrangements were made to bury Cummings in the family cemetery of a local farmer. The next day, colors were lowered to half-staff; all six boats were put over the side, colors likewise at half-staff. The boats formed in line with all officers and crewmen who could be spared from duty and pulled ashore, oars dipping at the funeral stroke. At the cemetery, Kell read the Protestant Episcopal service. "This young gentleman had been very popular, with both officers and crew, and his sudden death cast a gloom over the ship," Semmes wrote. A collection was taken and a marble tombstone ordered from Cape Town. Officers of the British Royal Navy later delivered it and set it in place.[28]

On August 5 the *Alabama* got up steam and pulled out of Saldanha Bay, bound for Cape Town. At 10:30 A.M., the *Tuscaloosa* was sighted, and a boat brought Lieutenant Low on board. He reported that he had captured the American ship *Santee* with a load of British-owned rice and had bonded her for $150,000. Semmes ordered him to proceed on to Simon's Bay for supplies. Two hours later, the *Alabama* spotted a sail and the chase began. She proved to be the *Sea Bride* of Boston. Both ships hove to, while bearings were taken of the headlands and lights of the cape.

"We anticipate a controversy over the distance of the barque from the land at the time of capture, and are preparing for it," Sinclair explained. Distance was calculated at about six miles and therefore legal. A prize crew was placed on board and the *Sea Bride* ordered to stand off until further notice. The *Alabama* steamed into Cape Town harbor and anchored.[29]

10

Hound and Hare with the Vanderbilt

*D*ESPITE SEMMES'S MISGIVINGS, THE CAPTURE OF THE *SEA Bride* excited less controversy than the arrival of the *Tuscaloosa*. The question arose as to whether she was a legally commissioned warship or a prize of war. If the latter, she was prohibited from entering a British port because neither side could take prizes into a neutral zone. While Semmes insisted that the *Tuscaloosa* was a commissioned warship, Rear Admiral Sir Baldwin Walker, commander of the British squadron at the cape, disagreed. In a letter to Governor Wodehouse, Walker said: "To bring a captured vessel under the denomination of a vessel-of-war, she must be fitted for warlike purposes, and not merely have a few men and a few small guns put on board her (in fact, nothing but a prize-crew), in order to disguise her real character as a prize. Now, this vessel has her original cargo of wool still on board." Therefore, Walker said the designation of the *Tuscaloosa* as a naval tender of the *Alabama* could be regarded as nothing more than a ruse to allow a prize to enter a neutral port, there to dispose of her cargo at leisure.[1]

The governor was unconvinced and allowed the *Tuscaloosa* to remain, but he was concerned about the *Sea Bride*. The U.S. consul protested the capture, which he felt was a violation of British waters. Wodehouse, in turn, telegraphed Admiral Walker in Simon's Bay, ordering him to look into the matter. That night, Walker sent the

HMS *Valorous* around to Cape Town, and the next day her commanding officer and Semmes exchanged visits. Semmes also exchanged
letters on the subject with Wodehouse, and the governor was satisfied
that there had been no violation.[2]

Semmes had planned to take his ship to the more protected anchorage of Simon's Bay, but a gale set in, forcing him to remain in Cape
Town. Several ships were wrecked, and Semmes worried about the
Sea Bride, anchored in international waters, because he was arranging
to sell her to a South African shipper. He signaled her that if she
could not hold her anchorage, she should head for Saldanha Bay,
where the *Alabama* would meet her on August 15.[3]

Despite the bad weather, the *Alabama* was crowded with visitors.
The capture of the *Sea Bride* had been witnessed by a crowd on shore,
and as soon as the *Alabama* anchored, people rushed to hire boats to
visit her.[4] The local population, sympathetic to the Confederacy, kept
Semmes busy shaking hands and signing autographs.

"Army officers and their wives, all the city officials and their
families called, and we numbered visitors from every class and station
in life," Kell wrote. Sinclair found himself and the other officers
besieged with so many questions that he wished he had printed
information sheets.[5]

Bartelli was in his natural element as he handled the various
dignitaries who came to see the captain. Watching him, Sinclair
commented: "Bartelli is a scientist in his way, knows all the grades
of grandeeism, and just when to pop the champagne. It is amusing
to watch the air of consequence that sits upon the countenance of
our captain's steward . . . he is a born diplomat in disposing of such
as in his opinion are not an honor or ornamentation to the cabin.
Bartelli, however, never offends."[6]

One of the visitors was Captain Edward Cooper of the bark *Urania*
out of New York, the only American ship then in port. As Semmes
was busy at the time, he ordered Bulloch to give Cooper a tour of
the ship, and the Yankee captain "saw the great armament necessary
to capture unarmed traders." After twenty minutes, Cooper was taken
to see Semmes and said the *Urania* was chartered to Britons and, to
the best of his knowledge, all cargo transactions were British. Under
such circumstances, he asked if the ship would be burned or bonded

should the *Alabama* capture her on the high seas. Semmes replied that an admiralty court convened aboard ship ruled on all prizes and that if his papers were in order, the *Urania* would be bonded and released, despite American ownership. After a pleasant visit, Cooper asked one final question as he prepared to leave. He had heard that Semmes had become angry on seeing the U.S. flag run up from the *Urania* and had threatened to hang the man responsible.

"You have no right to any other flag, sir!" Semmes replied, adding that he had all the more respect for Cooper for flying it, inasmuch as he was the only American captain in a port that was obviously pro-Confederate. In fact, it did require nerve for Cooper to fly the U.S. flag in Cape Town, as he told the owners of the *Urania:* "The excitement on shore and Southern sympathy was at first so great that, fearing personal injury, I armed myself, but other than a few wordy insults from individuals to whom my person was known, but who themselves were strangers for me, I was not molested."[7]

On August 9 the *Alabama* steamed out of Cape Town and around the Cape of Good Hope to Simon's Bay. En route, she overhauled the *Martha Wenzell* of Boston, but on taking bearings, found she was within the marine league. The American captain returned to his ship, and the *Alabama* continued to Simon's Bay, where more visitors crowded on board. The next day, Semmes called on Admiral Walker and his family in Simon's Town and later had dinner on the Chinese gunboat *Kwan-tung*. The next several days were spent exchanging courtesies and maintaining the ship. As usual, the crew made a name for itself ashore, and several were put in irons. Quartermaster Thomas Weir, two stewards, and two dinghy boys deserted, although the stewards and boys were caught and brought back on board.

The *Tuscaloosa* sailed on August 14 and picked up the *Sea Bride* in Saldanha Bay. The following day the *Alabama* steamed out and spent the next two weeks cruising the coast, after which Semmes met the *Tuscaloosa* and *Sea Bride* at Angra Pequenha, beyond British jurisdiction. The prize had been delivered to her new owner for £3,500 and arrangements made to sell her cargo on consignment.[8]

The *Alabama* and *Tuscaloosa* again separated. Low was ordered to cruise the coast of Brazil, rendezvousing with the *Alabama* at the cape at a later date. During the first half of September, the *Alabama*

USS *Vanderbilt*

cruised along the coast of South Africa, meeting only neutral ships. "No sail in sight!" Semmes noted in the journal for Sunday, September 13. "Mustered the crew. How tiresome is the routine of cruising becoming!"[9]

While Semmes searched for prizes, the *Vanderbilt* had put in at Cape Town and was now in the immediate vicinity. But for Semmes's phenomenal luck, the *Vanderbilt* might have caught him in the harbor, for Baldwin had intended to arrive much earlier. The *Vanderbilt* put in at St. Helena, in the South Atlantic, on August 15. The boilers and tubes were so corroded that Baldwin dared not have them scaled. This impeded the efficiency of the engines, which, together with the poor quality of coal obtained in Rio, increased the ship's consumption by ten tons a day. The fuel situation was aggravated because Baldwin had set aside one hundred tons of coal in bags piled up around the exposed machinery to protect it from shells in case of a fight. The day before he arrived in St. Helena, another ship had come in with a cargo of about four hundred tons of coal, which the owners offered at the inflated price of $31.50 per ton. He declined because, under the Proclamation of Neutrality, he would be prohibited from coaling again at a British port for three months, and he did not think four hundred tons was enough to make the restriction worthwhile.

In St. Helena, Baldwin learned that the *Alabama* was cruising the Cape of Good Hope and that Semmes had applied to Governor Wodehouse "to come in and go on the dock there to clean his bottom; that it was reported the governor would only consent to his coming in for twenty-four hours." That information, combined with other sightings of the Confederate ship around the cape over a period of time, convinced Baldwin that he could still catch her in the vicinity, and, despite his engine problems, he sailed on August 17.[10] He had been under way for twelve hours when he realized that adverse winds would hinder him so that he would barely have enough coal to reach the cape. Consequently, he put back in at St. Helena and applied for permission to coal. Permission was granted, and he managed to load four hundred tons before the time limit expired.

"Now that I have taken coal in at an English port, I fear I shall have great difficulty in getting permission to take what I shall require, or indeed any, at the Cape of Good Hope," Baldwin wrote to Welles. "However, as it seems to me of very great importance to get this ship in that neighborhood with the least possible delay, I must take the chances of the future." He also cautioned Welles that he would be unable to follow the *Alabama* beyond the area of the cape because the *Vanderbilt's* coal consumption was too great and her boilers could not function much longer without an overhaul.[11]

The *Vanderbilt* steamed out of St. Helena at sunset on August 20 and, because of adverse winds and boiler problems, took ten days to reach Simon's Bay. The pilot told Baldwin that the *Georgia* had departed the previous evening so he turned around and put to sea again, hoping to intercept her or the *Alabama* in the heavily traveled sea lanes off Cape Agulhas. Instead, he encountered the Dutch bark *Johanna Elizabeth,* which had been badly damaged in a storm and appeared unlikely to reach port. Baldwin made the agonizing decision "on the score of humanity" to tow her to the nearest port, ninety miles distant, which cost him a full day of hunting. "During the two succeeding days I spoke some ten or twelve vessels from various directions, but could gain no trace of the whereabouts of the *Georgia* or other privateers," he reported. Finally, he had to abandon the search and put in at Simon's Bay, where, despite the restrictions, he received permission to coal. Although an inspection showed his engines and boilers in even worse condition than he had suspected, Baldwin planned to continue the search as long as possible.[12] Over dinner, he told Admiral Walker that if he encountered the *Alabama*, he did not intend to fight her with gunfire but would instead run her down with the immense, iron-hulled *Vanderbilt* and cut her in half.[13]

Baldwin may have come closer to cutting the *Alabama* in two than either he or Semmes ever suspected. During one night of thick weather, the *Alabama*'s watch officer heard four bells strike on another ship close by. Through the night glasses he could make out "a very large steamer, looming high out of the water." The *Alabama* lay so low in the water that the big steamer did not see her, and the watch officer ordered silence on deck. Semmes was summoned, but by the time he came on deck the steamer was no longer visible. Sinclair always believed she was the *Vanderbilt;* Semmes assumed she was "probably the English mail steamer, due about this time and bound for the cape."[14]

The *Alabama* anchored in Simon's Bay on September 16, missing the *Vanderbilt* by five days. During the first visit, the news from home had been good; General Robert E. Lee had crossed Maryland and invaded Pennsylvania. Now Semmes learned that Lee had retreated across the Potomac into Virginia; Vicksburg and Port Hudson had fallen; and William S. Rosencrans's federal troops were marching south, deep into Louisiana. "Our poor people seem to be terribly pressed by the Northern hordes of Goths and Vandals, but we shall fight it out to the end, and the end will be what an all-wise Providence shall decree," he wrote.[15]

Although Semmes thought the *Vanderbilt* had spent more time in port than was permissible under the neutrality proclamation, he raised no objections. "The more time Baldwin spent in port, the better I liked it," he wrote. Indeed, he wondered why U.S. consuls so often insisted that the *Alabama* be sent to sea immediately "when nearly every day that the *Alabama* was at sea, cost them a ship."[16]

Semmes may have been able to overlook violations, but U.S. consul Walter Graham charged that the *Sea Bride* and her cargo had been sold at an island dependency of Cape Colony rather than Angra Pequenha and so had violated neutrality. Semmes countered that the *Sea Bride* had put into Saldanha Bay, in British territory, "through stress of weather," had subsequently been escorted outside local waters by the *Tuscaloosa,* and had proceeded to Angra, where the transaction had been completed.[17]

Once these diplomatic problems were straightened out, Semmes and Kell again had dinner with Admiral and Mrs. Walker, where the admiral informed them of Baldwin's plans to ram the *Alabama.* Semmes replied that the *Vanderbilt* was four times larger than the *Alabama* and had the advantage of speed, but because of its size the federal ship required a much larger turning circle. Such a situation, he said, resembled a hound chasing a hare; the hare would make a sudden sharp turn and the hound would stumble over himself. Semmes no doubt also realized that a shot from the *Alabama* into one of the *Vanderbilt's* paddle boxes would smash the paddle wheel and seriously cripple her. Walker, however, was unconvinced. Referring to the *Vanderbilt's* near miss with the *Georgia,* he reminded Semmes that the *Alabama's* arrival was the second time the *Vanderbilt* had barely missed catching a Confederate ship in port; the third time, the Confederates might not be so lucky.[18]

Despite his bravado, Semmes was seriously concerned about the *Vanderbilt.* The federal ship had exhausted the coal supply in Simon's Town, requiring him to order from Cape Town and await delivery. He also learned that Baldwin was again cruising off Cape Agulhas and might hear of the *Alabama's* presence in Simon's Bay and attempt to blockade him. This would detain Semmes even longer while he waited for the moon to turn so he could make a dash for sea in total darkness. Having nothing to do but wait, he relaxed ashore, attended mass, and visited the Constantia Vineyard, where he was given a cask of wine. His journal entry for September 18 states: "Took a long stroll up the hills, permitting the men to visit the shore on liberty, and they are behaving badly, as usual."[19]

One of the cases of misbehavior involved Chief Boatswain's Mate Brent Johnson, who got drunk and pulled a knife on an officer trying to control him. Johnson was court-martialed and sentenced to forfeiture of all pay and prize money due him, three months' confinement in irons, and dismissal in disgrace from the ship. Semmes upheld the sentence, saying that "the plea of drunkenness should not protect any offender from punishment; [Semmes] believing that intoxication was a crime in itself." Semmes let Johnson spend a month in confinement, then, in view of his past good conduct and services, released him with a reduction to seaman. He also promised to present Johnson's case before Congress so that the forfeited pay and prize money might be restored.[20]

After the *Alabama* had spent three days in port, a steamer arrived from Cape Town with coal, and she began loading. By the time the job was finished, the crew, including petty officers, was seriously out of control. Semmes was presented with bills, some exorbitant and totally without merit; fourteen men had deserted and British authorities refused to force their return. He partially offset this loss with eleven men found in Simon's Town. To avoid violating the Foreign Enlistment Act, they came on as passengers, then signed articles once the *Alabama* had cleared British waters. Two of these men, Maximilian, Baron von Meulnier, and Julius Schroeder, were members of the Prussian aristocracy and former naval officers. They had been stranded at the cape by a shipwreck and signed on the *Alabama* as master's mates. They remained with the ship until the end.[21]

To avoid a possible confrontation with the *Vanderbilt,* the *Alabama* steamed out into the face of a gale at 11:30 P.M. September 24. Finally, about 3:00 A.M., Semmes went to bed to try to catch some rest before beginning the arduous work of prize-hunting again. Later in the morning, steam was reduced and the ship was put under sail. On September 27, Semmes's fifty-fifth birthday, he reflected: "How time flies as we advance toward old age. . . . My life has been one of great vicissitude, but not of calamity or great suffering, and I have reason to be thankful to a kind Providence for the many favors I have received. I have enjoyed life to a reasonable extent, and I trust I shall have fortitude to meet with Christian calmness any fate that may be in store for me, and to undergo the great change, which awaits us all, with composure and a firm reliance on the justice and goodness of God."[22]

The *Alabama* was in the Indian Ocean now, bound for the Sunda Strait between Java and Sumatra, to show the Confederate flag in the East Indies. Baldwin had guessed Semmes's intentions and had turned the *Vanderbilt* east also. A boiler gave out during heavy weather so he put in at Port Louis, Mauritius. Because of recent federal victories in the South, Baldwin found the British governor very cooperative, which was "—to our experience—a new state of things." He received permission to repair and recoal and was invited to the governor's country home.

Despite the deteriorating boilers, Baldwin planned to continue pursuing the *Alabama* and hoped to catch her in the Sunda Strait. But as the engineers worked on the boilers, they found a two-foot crack in the starboard paddle wheel shaft and had to build a heavy timber platform to hold it should it break. It was obvious that the *Vanderbilt* could no longer chase the *Alabama*. Baldwin decided to take her to the Seychelles, in case the *Georgia* tried to attack the American whalers working in those waters, then cruise south along the east coast of Madagascar, stop again in Cape Town, and head home.

In a letter to Welles, he explained:

In my present crippled condition, I shall have to go along slow and nurse the shaft as much as possible, unless occasion should present, when I am willing to take any risk for corresponding chances of success.

I beg to remind the Department that all our repairs in this part of the world have to be done entirely by our own people, it being impossible to obtain any mechanics or boiler makers in these ports.[23]

The chase was over. Baldwin had given it his best, but the hare had outlasted the hound. It was not a total waste, however, because the *Vanderbilt* overhauled the British bark *Saxon* off Angra Pequenha, loaded with cargo from the *Sea Bride*. The cargo was condemned as stolen United States property and a prize crew put aboard to take the *Saxon* to New York. Unfortunately, one of the boarding party's weapons accidentally discharged, killing the chief mate of the *Saxon*.[24] This was embarrassing because the only deaths caused by the *Alabama* were in combat; no one ever died in any of her boardings.

11

"My Ship Is Weary"

ONCE THE *ALABAMA* WAS AT SEA, THE EFFECTS OF THE DE-
serted crewmen were divided among the crew, and the "passengers" who came aboard in the cape signed on. They were in for a
rough voyage because the *Alabama* was sailing south for the "Roaring
Forties," the strong, continuous west winds around the fortieth paral-
lel, which sailing ships took for a fast trip. The southern ocean in
these latitudes is among the wildest on earth, and Semmes noted
that "the waves rose into long, sweeping swells, much more huge
and majestic than one meets with in any other ocean." Huge swells
passed under the *Alabama*'s high stern, lifting her up to the crest of
the wave and pushing her forward "at a speed that would cause the
sailor to hold his breath."[1]

On October 3 the *Alabama* overhauled the Shanghai-bound British
steamer *Mona,* whose captain reported that three New York steamers
were scheduled to arrive in Shanghai about the same time as his
ship. Semmes continued into almost constant gales over the next
several weeks. Although the *Alabama* moved swiftly, she had been
at sea for more than a year now, and the strain was starting to show.
She leaked at her seams, gradually at first and then more, until all
the bedding in the wardroom was wet and water had dripped on
Semmes's bookcases. The islands of St. Peter and St. Paul were passed;
Semmes had hoped to cruise there for several days, but bad weather

prevented it. On October 16, the anniversary of the hurricane off the Grand Banks the year before, the *Alabama* encountered a heavy gale, which smashed her best quarterboat.[2]

Eventually the weather abated and the crew set about cleaning up. The ship was painted, the brass work polished, and the battery, magazine, and shell rooms put in order. No other ships had been sighted for nineteen days, although Semmes hoped to see some within the next four or five. A sail was spotted on October 23, but the *Alabama* did not chase her because too much time would have been lost. "Being only about 700 miles from the Strait of Sunda, I am anxious to hurry on and see what the 'fortune of war' has in store for me," Semmes explained. Another concern was the shortage of food. Dr. Galt reported that although he had contracted for a three-month supply of coffee and butter, the ship had been shorted and the supply exhausted after only twenty-seven days. Four days later the stock of beans was gone.[3]

On October 26 the *Alabama* encountered her first ship from the Sunda Strait, a British bark, which reported that the USS *Wyoming* was cruising the strait between Anjer and Krakatoa. Two days later the captain of a Dutch ship reported that he had been boarded by a boat from the *Wyoming* off Anjer. It was obvious to Semmes that if he tried to sail through the strait he would find the enemy ship. In preparation, he had all but one gun shifted to the same broadside. The ship had no problem with the realignment of weight, and Semmes decided that in battle he would move the guns accordingly. "The *Wyoming* being a good match for this ship, I have resolved to give her battle," he wrote.[4]

Although the *Alabama* was rapidly deteriorating, Semmes's confidence was well founded. The *Wyoming,* a 997-ton screw sloop armed with seven guns, was commanded by Mexican war veteran David M. McDougal, with a battle-seasoned crew. Four months earlier, when a Japanese warlord attacked an American ship in the Inland Sea, McDougal had retaliated by assaulting a Japanese fort and sinking two armed ships. In that fight, however, she suffered eleven direct hits and lost five killed and six wounded. McDougal would have preferred to return home for repairs and new men before engaging the *Alabama,* but he nevertheless obeyed a directive from Welles and began patrolling the Sunda Strait.[5]

A large number of ships were sighted as the *Alabama* approached
the strait, but all were neutral, causing Sinclair to wonder what had
become of the great American China clippers. From a Dutch captain
Semmes learned that the *Wyoming* had put in at Batavia and was
now back cruising the strait; the possibility of a fight seemed more
likely than ever now. A British captain told him the American *Winged
Racer* had sailed near him earlier. A short time later the *Alabama* got
up steam and chased two ships, hoping one of them would be the
Winged Racer, but both ran up British colors. A third ship, however,
was the American bark *Amanda,* Semmes's first prize since leaving
the Cape of Good Hope. The ship was condemned and burned.

Semmes based the condemnation on the usual absence of a sworn
oath of neutrality to accompany consular certification of cargo. This
time, however, he committed a grave tactical error. The *Amanda*'s
cargo was, in fact, legally British. In deference to Semmes, as Charles
Grayson Summersell has noted in his commentary on Fullam's journal, "the nature of a ship's register was such" that it was easier to
determine the nationality of the ship itself than the nationality of
the cargo. Still, the destruction of the *Amanda* and its cargo cost the
Confederacy valuable support among the erstwhile friendly British
shipowners.[6]

The *Alabama* anchored for two days by Flat Point, on the north
side of the Sunda Strait, where Semmes hoped to procure fresh vegetables. The crew had existed for several weeks on a salt diet, and he
was worried about their health. But he found the natives too poor
even to have fresh vegetables and so weighed anchor to enter the
strait. The ship took a narrow and unfrequented channel and, soon
after exiting, overhauled a clipper which proved to be the *Winged
Racer.* She carried sugar, coffee, and tobacco, all of which were needed
on board the *Alabama.* Semmes ordered both ships anchored, and
the Confederates spent the better part of the night reprovisioning.
A Malay boat came alongside and sold them poultry, fresh fruit, and
vegetables. The boat was out of Anjer and reported that the *Wyoming*
had been there two days previously. At their own request, the crews
of the *Amanda* and *Winged Racer* were allowed to row ashore. The
Malays, not realizing the *Winged Racer* was a prize of war, were
moored to her, and when they saw the flames leap up, they cut lines
and pulled at oars as fast as they could move.[7]

The next day the *Alabama* overhauled another ship, raised the U.S. flag, and the stranger responded in kind. Semmes ordered a gun fired and showed the *Alabama*'s true colors. But instead of the traditional Stars and Bars, this time she flew the newly designated Confederate flag, with the Southern Cross in the corner on a solid white field. The American ship was the *Contest* and determined to live up to her name. Her captain loosened the topgallant and topmast studding sails, and she pulled away. Semmes ordered a shot fired from the big rifled gun, but it fell astern, and the Yankee skipper ignored it. The chase continued for over an hour, the men of the *Alabama* crowding the rail to watch. Semmes ordered full steam and moved guns and men aft to trim the ship. At one point, frustrated with the chase, Semmes called down to the engine room, demanding to know why he wasn't getting enough steam. "The tea-kettle will stand no more," Second Assistant Engineer Matthew O'Brien replied. "If we attempt it we shall scatter the pieces for the chase to pick up." Finally, the *Alabama* was close enough to throw a shell between the *Contest's* masts, and she hove to. Semmes ordered both ships anchored in the shallow, open sea and took what was needed off her. By nightfall, the work was finished and he sent a firing party over to burn her. Even then, the *Contest* seemed to put up a fight. She dragged her anchor and started to pull away. A rain squall was setting in, and the firing officer, afraid that he would lose sight of the *Alabama* in the dark, ordered his crew back into the boat and returned. The *Alabama* got up steam and again had to chase down the *Contest* before burning her. "We had never captured so beautiful a vessel," Sinclair wrote. "She was a revelation of symmetry, a very racehorse. A sacrilege, almost a desecration, to destroy so perfect a specimen of man's handi-work."[8]

The chase after the *Contest* showed that the *Alabama* was wearing out. The copper plating on her bottom was coming loose and curling, and her boilers were so corroded with salt that it was dangerous to use full steam. Adding to the problems, the crew was becoming discontented. They had behaved as well as could be expected for a year since the drinking incident in Martinique. Now, however, more than twenty men were seriously ill from the long privation at sea, and morale was low. When on November 13 Semmes ordered cigars from the *Winged Racer* divided between officers and crew, the crew threw theirs overboard so contemptuously that the ringleaders were arrested. Three were later court-martialed as an example to the rest. One of the guilty sailors was Michael Mars, the *Alabama*'s resident maverick, who was sentenced to one month's forfeiture of pay, three months' police duty cleaning ship, and to be triced in the rigging three hours daily for a week.[9]

At 3:30 P.M. on November 19, the *Alabama* overhauled the British ship *Avalanche*. Semmes ran up the Dutch flag and sent Baron von Meulnier as boarding officer with instructions to tell the British captain that she was a Netherlands warship. "Oh! that won't do," the amused Englishman replied. "I was on board of her in Liverpool when she was launched." The British captain told Semmes that several U.S. ships were laid up in Singapore and that there was "a general stagnation of American trade." He provided newspapers only forty days old, telling of recent Confederate victories, good news after hearing of the loss of the Mississippi in Cape Town. Over the next couple of days, other ships reported Americans laid up at Bangkok and Manila for fear of being captured.[10]

On November 22, Semmes made a remarkable entry in the ship's journal: "At 9:30 A.M. passed a couple of ships, neither looking American. Showed English colors to the nearest, which was returned with the same."[11]

The fact was that the *Alabama,* which could once run down ships in any weather, was no longer in condition for the chase. Semmes was low on coal and the ship could not take hard use under sail so he left his course only when a ship appeared "decidedly American." The problem became even more obvious the next morning, when a stiff breeze blew in from north-northeast, which reduced the speed under sail and steam to six knots and consumed what little coal remained at an alarming rate. Finally, Semmes ordered the fires down and tried to move under sail alone. Most of the area was uncharted, with dangerous banks and reefs and unknown, variable currents, necessitating frequent soundings of the bottom. It was the monsoon season, and bad weather prevented regular sightings to determine position. "Drifting, we don't know where," Semmes commented in the journal. The kedge anchor was thrown out to slow the rate of drift.[12]

The uncertainty was hard on Semmes, who got very little sleep during this time. "He must have a rugged constitution and iron nerves to pull through as he does," Sinclair remarked. "At all hours of the day and night he may be seen bent over his chart in the cabin, or on deck conning the soundings. A heavy responsibility; for the lives of all are in his hands, to say nothing of the inestimable value of the charge he is piloting through this labyrinth."[13] As time would show, however, Semmes was as worn out as his ship.

At last, the *Alabama* put in at the Pulo Condore group, in the China Sea south of the Mekong River, which, Semmes was surprised to learn, had recently been taken over by the French. A French naval officer came on board to welcome the Confederates but told them that because of a native revolt there was little fresh produce available. The governor of the islands, a conscientious naval officer about twenty-five years old, offered them such hospitality as he and his garrison could provide. The governor was amazed that the Confederates were unaware of the French takeover because France had notified all the major powers. Semmes replied jovially that he had hoped to claim the island in the name of the Confederacy, but "I had found the French ahead of me."[14]

Semmes received permission to stay as long as was necessary, and Kell set about repairing what he could on the ship. The most serious problem was the bottom. With the protective copper plating pulling loose, the ship was not only slowed but the bottom was exposed to damage from worms. Kell designed a caisson that could be lowered over the side and pumped out, allowing the carpenter to work underwater. While bottom work was under way, the decks were littered with tools, tar, and paint that threatened to ruin the officers' uniforms as they waited to go ashore and call on the governor. They boarded the boats, and the crew, decked out in tropical whites, pulled them ashore.[15]

During the visit Semmes noticed that Cochin Chinese prisoners of war were being used as slave laborers and remarked that the French system was worse than the Southern because the Cochins "were quasi white people, whereas we enslaved only the African." "Oh! our slavery is not universal," the governor replied; "we only enslave the bad subjects of our society."[16]

Despite the French claim that little produce was available, the governor sent so much to the *Alabama* that Semmes feared "my generous friend has been robbing himself." Confederate hunting parties explored the entire main island, bringing back everything from apes to monitor lizards. The daredevil Michael Mars, who had taken on the shark in the Arcas Cays the previous Christmas, amused himself by catching venomous snakes by the tail and snapping them to break their necks.[17]

French newspapers arrived, informing the Confederates that the western European powers had backed down from a dispute with the Russians over the Polish insurrection and that Russia was suppressing the uprising. Although the impact of the *Amanda*'s burning had yet to be felt in London, the British government, preoccupied with the Polish problem and pressured by public opinion favoring the North's crusade for emancipation, had become increasingly cool to the Confederate cause, and Commissioner Mason had been recalled from London. In the Far East, however, French sympathy was still with the Confederacy, and Semmes learned that the *Alabama* was expected in Saigon even though he gave no indication he intended to visit.[18]

While the *Alabama* was undergoing repairs at Pulo Condore, McDougal in the *Wyoming* was still searching the area around the Sunda Strait. That he had missed the *Alabama* when she passed through was not owing to negligence on his part. For weeks there had been rumors of a vast Confederate naval and maritime presence in the Indian Ocean and China Sea. American authorities had diligently tracked these rumors down only to find that they were false. Thus neither McDougal nor the U.S. consuls in Batavia and Singapore believed that a real emergency existed, and McDougal was becoming increasingly concerned about the Japanese battle damage to the *Wyoming*. Nevertheless, on hearing that a Confederate supply depot had been established on Christmas Island, he steamed down to investigate, missing the *Alabama* when she passed through the strait. Having followed a false lead once again, he resumed his station in the strait. When it became obvious that the *Alabama* was not in the area, McDougal steamed toward Singapore to follow yet another lead.[19]

At Pulo Condore it took two weeks to put the *Alabama* in condition to sail again. When she left on December 15, Semmes wrote:

Well, we are on the seas once more, with our head turned westward, or homeward. Shall we ever reach that dear home, which we left nearly three years ago, and which we have yearned after so frequently since? Will it be battle, or shipwreck, or both, or neither? and when we reach the North Atlantic, will it still be war, or peace? When will the demonlike passions of the North be stilled? These are solemn and interesting questions for us, and an all wise Providence has kindly hidden the answers behind the curtain of fate.[20]

There was no longer any reason to cruise the East Indies because U.S. shipping had been reduced to a negligible amount and it was too risky to chase prizes. Semmes determined to try the Cape of Good Hope once more, then perhaps cruise the coast of Brazil and recoal at Barbados. After that, the *Alabama* would need a complete overhaul, such as could be provided only in a European dry dock.[21]

On December 22 the *Alabama* moored to the Peninsular & Oriental Docks in Singapore, where company officials allowed the Confederates to recoal at a reasonable price from their own store. A horde of people of all races and nationalities swarmed on board to see the ship, and guards had to be placed by the officers' quarters to keep the crowds out. "Our decks are begrimed with coal-dust; the song of the Malay coal-passers mingling with the cries of the fruit-vender," Sinclair wrote. At times the crowd was so thick that the officers had trouble leaving and boarding the ship. Finally, they found out the cause; the natives, vaguely aware of Southern slavery, had heard a rumor that the *Alabama* kept several Negro giants chained in the hold, whom they unleashed in battle. They waited for hours hoping to catch sight of these monsters.[22]

While they were in port, the mercantile firm of Cumming, Beaver & Company was contracted to supply the ship, and local representatives saw to all the details and provided excursions and entertainment for the officers. During the visit, Semmes learned that the *Wyoming* had been in port twenty days before, but there had been no word of her since. Twenty-two American merchant ships were laid up in Singapore, and none could get a cargo for fear of destruction by Confederate raiders.[23]

Despite the curiosity about the ship and the arrangements provided by Peninsular & Oriental and Cumming, Beaver, the *Alabama* was more tolerated than welcomed. News of the *Amanda*'s destruction had reached the city, and British shippers were affronted.[24] The problem was aggravated by the conduct of the ship's company. The crew behaved as usual ashore, but this time the officers got into trouble as well. Several from the *Alabama,* playing billiards in a local hotel, were invited for drinks by some of the stranded American captains. The Confederates accepted. Sinclair claimed that during the course of the evening, the Americans became so abusive that a fight broke out. Backed by the muscle power of the *Alabama*'s engineers, the Confederates emerged victorious but barely managed to beat the police back to the ship.[25]

The *Alabama* sailed on Christmas Eve and at 1:00 P.M. that day overhauled the *Martaban,* which showed British colors. The ship had such an American look about her, however, and the papers appeared so irregular that Fullam, the boarding officer and himself an Englishman, requested that Semmes personally inspect the ship. For the only time in his career, Semmes rowed over and boarded a prize. In her commander, Captain Samuel B. Pike, he saw "Puritan, *May-Flower,* Plymouth Rock . . . all written upon the well-known features." Examining the papers, Semmes determined that both registry and cargo were false.

"You hadn't ought to burn this ship," Pike protested.

The New England phrase "hadn't ought" was his ship's death sentence; Semmes condemned her.[26]

The captain was furious.

"You dare not do it, sir," he shouted at Semmes and, pointing to the British ensign flying over his ship, added, "That flag won't stand for it!"

"Keep cool, captain," Semmes replied. "The weather is warm, and as for the flag, I shall not ask it whether it will stand it or not— the flag that *ought* to be at your peak, will have to stand it, though."

According to Semmes, Pike subsequently gave a deposition that the ship was actually the *Texan Star,* U.S. registry, and that he had falsified a sale to Britain after hearing that the *Alabama* was in the area. Evidence supported this assertion, and when the *Alabama* claims were finally adjudicated nearly a decade later, the court ruled that the ship was legally American.[27] On the surface, however, there was enough legality in the transfer to raise British ire, and the destruction of the *Martaban/Texan Star,* hard on the heels of the *Amanda,* further alienated the British shpping community at a time when the Confederacy desperately needed friends.[28]

The next day the *Alabama* was decked out in flags and signals in honor of Christmas. Visits were exchanged with the British authorities at Malacca, and Captain Pike and the crew of the *Martaban/Texan Star* were allowed to row ashore before the *Alabama* got under way again. Two more American ships were seized and condemned during the remaining week of 1863. In January the *Alabama* sailed across the Bay of Bengal, doubled Ceylon, seized and burned the *Emma Jane* of Bath, Maine, and, on January 16, anchored at the Portuguese enclave of Anjenga near Travancore in India.[29]

An officer was sent ashore to arrange landing of the prisoners, but when some time passed without his return and gunfire was heard ashore, Semmes suspected trouble with the natives and sent Kell with a landing party. As it turned out, the Portuguese magistrate was attending a religious festival, which accounted for the delay, and the noise was from celebrants firing into the air. In his own Episcopalian fashion, Kell remarked on the "priest-ridden superstitions and idolatry" of the Spaniards and Portuguese. Presumably he never shared these thoughts with Semmes; Old Beeswax, as fiercely Catholic as any of the locals, would not have appreciated hearing such sentiments from a subordinate officer.[30]

After landing prisoners, the *Alabama* put to sea again. Despite her wear, she made good headway, putting in at the Comoros for more provisions, then heading southwest across the Indian Ocean. The main concern was the day-to-day operation of the ship, but on February 28, the cry, "Man overboard!" sounded on the *Alabama* for the first time. Seaman Henry Godson, convalescing from illness, had been ordered on deck by the surgeon for sunshine and fresh air and had fallen overboard. Lieutenant Joseph Wilson, officer of the deck, ordered the ship hove to, a life ring cut away, and a boat lowered. Michael Mars, ever ready to risk his neck, threw a grating over the side, jumped in after it, and shoved it under the exhausted invalid.

"But for the gallant and timely assistance of Mars, Godson must have become food for fishes," Fullam observed. During the next monthly reading of the Articles of War, Semmes read a general order to the crew, praising Mars as an example for the others. Mars called the tribute "a bloody fuss over nothing."[31]

A gale set in, and although the seas were not overly turbulent, the *Alabama*'s leaking decks were continually flooded. "My ship is weary, too, as well as her commander," Semmes wrote. At 8:00 A.M. on March 11, the *Alabama* rounded the Cape of Good Hope. After cruising the area for nine days in an unsuccessful search for prizes, she anchored once again in Table Bay at Cape Town.[32]

12

Cherbourg

A T CAPE TOWN, SEMMES FOUND THE *TUSCALOOSA* ATTACHED
on orders from Governor Wodehouse and Admiral Walker.
Low had entered port for repairs on December 26. The following
day, the ship was seized and a lieutenant and twenty-five armed
sailors and marines sent on board to secure her. The pretext was
that she had never been properly adjudicated and condemned in an
admiralty court in the Confederate States, and therefore, her entry
into British waters was a violation of neutrality. Low countered that
she had been allowed in port as a legal warship the previous August
and at that time he had received the impression that she could return
as such.[1]

Low went to Britain to represent the case, and on March 4 Wodehouse was ordered to "restore the *Tuscaloosa* to the lieutenant of the
Confederate States who lately commanded her, or, if he should have
left the cape, then to retain her until she can be handed over to some
person who may have the authority from Captain Semmes, of the
Alabama, or from the Government of the Confederate States to receive
her."[2] No one at the cape was yet aware of the order, and Semmes
entered a protest with Admiral Walker. Beyond that, there was
nothing he could do except vent his anger on the British. He wrote
in the ship's journal: "England is too rich to be generous. . . . She
is afraid of losing the Canadas and her money bags afloat on the

ocean. All her human sympathies being thus dried up, she is ready to make friends with the stronger party."[3]

The British government and its colonial officers may have been lukewarm to the Confederate cause, but the *Alabama* still had a special place in the hearts of the colonists. Once again, the ship was crowded with sightseers and well-wishers, including military and colonial officials en route to places recently visited by the *Alabama* in the Far East. Although the visits interfered with maintenance of the now aging ship, the Confederates were glad to have them. Newspapers arrived, but the outlook at home was grim, and Kell felt that "defeat seemed to stare our struggling people in the face, and with the failing finances and shut-in ports ruin seemed inevitable!" Detached as they were from events at home and, as Sinclair put it, "not blinded by the desperation of a forlorn hope," the men of the *Alabama* realized the Confederacy was finished.[4]

While the *Alabama* was reprovisioning and coaling in Cape Town, the *Urania* sailed in from Boston. Remembering the conversation with Captain Cooper on the *Urania*'s display of the U.S. flag during the previous visit, Semmes noticed that this time she was flying the British.[5]

The *Alabama* steamed out of Cape Town for the last time at 10:00 A.M. on March 25, to cheers from boatmen and sailors in the harbor. As she left, the American steamer *Quang Tung* entered, the two ships passing so close that the Confederate and U.S. flags almost snapped against each other, the crews lining the rails and staring at each other in silence. Semmes wished he had sailed half an hour earlier because he would have caught her in international waters.[6]

Once clear of the harbor, Semmes ordered the fires down and put the ship under sail. It was obvious that the *Alabama* was in no condition to follow his original plan to cruise the Western Hemisphere again. Additionally, Semmes's health was failing and the officers were worn out. He would now take the *Alabama* out toward the hump of Brazil to catch the prevailing winds, then swing northeast to Britain or France, where she could get a complete overhaul. The cruise had been long, and it was increasingly certain that it would not affect the final outcome of the war. Still, Semmes could not be ashamed of his ship or her mission: "We had destroyed, or driven for protection under the English flag, in round numbers, one half of the enemy's ships engaged in the English trade. We did even greater damage to the enemy's trade with other powers. We broke up almost entirely his trade with Brazil, and the other South American States, greatly crippled his Pacific trade, and as for his East India trade, it is only necessary to refer . . . to the spectacle presented at Singapore."[7]

The *Alabama* had to be nursed during the voyage, and on inspecting the ship one Sunday, Semmes noted: "Many of the beams of the ship are splitting and giving way, owing to the greenness of the timber of which she was built."[8]

Several days were spent in the vicinity of St. Helena in hope of finding a prize, but none were sighted. On April 17 the *Alabama* overhauled an Italian bark, which reported that three U.S. ships were laid up in Buenos Aires, unable to obtain cargo. Later in the day, the captain of a French ship carrying guano from Callao said that there were no American ships loading guano in the Chincha Islands. Semmes reflected that the previous July, when he burned the guano ship *Express,* seventy to eighty American ships had been in the islands.[9] Finally, on April 23, the lookout reported a ship that appeared to be American-rigged. She was the *Rockingham,* out of Callao with a load of guano. Once the crew was transferred to the *Alabama,* the gunners used her as a target "with reasonable success," and she was burned.[10]

On Wednesday, April 27, 1864, the *Alabama* captured her last prize, the clipper *Tycoon,* from New York to San Francisco. At 3:00 A.M. the following day, transfer of prisoners and provisions was completed and the ship was burned. One of the *Tycoon*'s crewmen, Edward Burrell, signed articles to serve on the *Alabama,* the last man to do so.[11]

From the prizes and neutral ships the *Alabama* obtained newspapers, which, Kell said, "made us sick at heart. There was gloom and disaster on every hand, and our poor Southland in her single-handed fight against the world was giving out! We passed through the Azores, bringing vividly to mind the opening of our career, when the beautiful *290,* fresh from her builder's hands, was christened and received her armament, and full of life and spirit was ready for the fray! Now worn and jaded officers, men and ship—what a contrast!"[12]

The ship was indeed worn out. Semmes noted: "Our bottom is in such a state that everything passes us. We are like a crippled hunter limping home from a long chase."[13]

A gale set in on May 25 and lasted for several days. The copper sheathing stripped off the bottom at an alarming rate, the ship was flooded, and the decks were leaking badly.[14] An even greater problem arose in the ship's armament. Semmes was suspicious of the shells and ordered several tried. When they failed to explode, he had new fuses placed in every shell in the ship. He blamed the problem on the magazines, which were often damp with excess steam from the condensers. An inspection of the magazines showed the powder stored in barrels to be defective, and it was thrown over the side. Powder was also stored in copper canisters, and they still appeared to be in good condition. Despite these efforts, when he found it necessary to fire over a British ship that would not heave to for inspection, the shell failed to explode.[15]

At 2:00 A.M. on Friday, June 10, in the bad weather that often besets the English Channel, the Alabama was put under steam. As she passed the Lizard, she picked up a French pilot, who would take her into Cherbourg. Semmes noted: "I felt a great relief to have him on board, as I was quite under the weather with cold and fever, and was but ill qualified physically for exposure to the weather, and watching throughout the night. And thus, thanks to an all-wise Providence, we have brought the cruise of the Alabama to a successful termination."[16]

Damage to American commerce aside, the search for the Alabama had occupied twenty-five federal warships, drawing them away from other duties. It had also cost the United States government over $7 million,[17] approximately twenty-eight times the cost of the Alabama's construction. Now her work was done. At 12:30 P.M. on June 11, she entered Cherbourg, where Semmes arranged to send the prisoners ashore that night.[18]

By Semmes's estimate, the ship needed at least two months in dry dock, and the officers and men needed time ashore. As for himself, he felt that the cruises of the Alabama and Sumter had aged him greatly. The exhaustion was aggravated by depression over the grim news from home and fears for the future. He needed a rest, and upon learning that Flag Officer Samuel Barron, senior Confederate naval officer in Europe, was in Paris, wrote to him asking to be relieved. Barron agreed and assigned Captain Thomas J. Page to command the *Alabama*.[19] It was a command Page would never hold.

The arrival of the *Alabama* put the French government in an embarrassing position. They, like the British, realized that the war in North America was drawing to a close and the United States would emerge victorious. Given Lincoln's position on secession, there would be no Confederate government to contend with once the conflict ended. From the French point of view, there were too many Confederate warships in port. The *Georgia,* which was deemed unfit for further service, was in Calais, where the Confederate authorities planned to transfer her armament to the *Rappahannock,* recently arrived from Great Britain. As Barron worked on these arrangements, U.S. minister William L. Dayton threatened the French government with claims for compensation for any losses that might be incurred from Confederate raiders originating in France. The USS *Kearsarge* was on station in the channel, blockading against both the *Rappahannock* and *Georgia,* as well as against Confederate ships under construction in French yards. The French, already questioning whether the *Rappahannock* was in violation of their neutrality, were in no mood to receive the *Alabama.* As John Slidell, Confederate commissioner to France, noted, "the frequent visits of our ships to French ports and especially to those devoted to the military marine [Cherbourg was a naval base], were not agreeable to the [French] Government."[20]

News of the *Alabama*'s arrival was immediately telegraphed to Paris and soon spread throughout Europe. The *Kearsarge* was at anchor in the Scheldt at Flushing, where Union sailors were painting the ship and enjoying the friendly hospitality of the Dutch. On Sunday, June 12, Captain John A. Winslow went ashore and was given a cable from Minister Dayton in Paris. As he returned to his gig, the American sailors were surprised to see the Dutch lining the docks and cheering. Coming aboard, Winslow ordered a gun fired, signaling officers and men ashore to return to the ship, and soon the *Kearsarge* was steaming down the Scheldt. Winslow ordered the crew mustered and addressed them: "My lads, I am happy to congratulate you that the *Alabama* has arrived at Cherbourg and your duty will here after be off that port. She is a ship that is noted for her speed and cleverness in eluding our cruisers—and if we take her it will be rendering our country a great service. She has a great reputation in England." He then ordered the crew piped down, but it was useless; the men were cheering wildly. Several jumped on the pivot gun and others on the hatch, leading three cheers for the *Kearsarge* and three more for Winslow. "The old man was much pleased to see us manifest our love for him in this way," noted Charles Fisher, a mulatto who served in various capacities on the ship.[21]

Semmes, in the meantime, had requested permission to put the ship into dry dock and was informed by the port admiral that all docks and arsenals in Cherbourg were for the exclusive use of the government. He told Semmes he should have put the *Alabama* into Le Havre, where she could have entered a private dry dock. Nevertheless, he agreed to refer the matter to Paris, although permission could be granted only by Napoleon III, then vacationing in Biarritz.[22]

On Monday, Semmes learned that the *Kearsarge* was en route, and he kept the crew on board for exercise at general quarters. At 11:00 A.M. on Tuesday, the *Kearsarge* appeared off the breakwater.[23] Seeing the Confederate flag flying over the *Alabama,* the federal surgeon Dr. John M. Browne wrote: "Officers and men gathered in groups on deck, and looked intently at the 'daring rover' that had been able for two years to escape numerous foes and to inflict immense damage on our commerce. She was a beautiful specimen of naval architecture."[24]

The *Kearsarge* steamed around the harbor, sent a boat ashore to ask permission to take on the prisoners landed by the *Alabama,* then put out to sea again without anchoring.[25] A short time later, Semmes summoned Kell to his cabin and said:

I have sent for you to discuss the advisability of fighting the
Kearsarge. As you know, the arrival of the *Alabama* has been
telegraphed to all parts of Europe. Within a few days,
Cherbourg will be effectually blockaded by Yankee cruisers.
It is uncertain whether or not we shall be permitted to repair
the *Alabama* here, and in the meantime, the delay is to our
advantage. I think we may whip the *Kearsarge,* the two

Captain John Ancrum Winslow, USN

vessels being of wood and carrying about the same number of men and guns. Besides, Mr. Kell, although the Confederate States government has ordered me to avoid engagements with the enemy's cruisers, I am tired of running from that flaunting rag![26]

They discussed the difference in armament, and Kell mentioned the *Alabama*'s defective powder. Privately, Kell had reservations, but "I saw his mind was fully made up, so I simply stated these facts for myself," Kell said. "I had always felt ready for a fight, and I also knew that the brave young officers of the ship would not object, and the men would be not only willing, but anxious, to meet the enemy!"[27]

Semmes now wrote to Auguste Bonfils, the local Confederate commercial agent, one of the most remarkable letters in the annals of naval warfare:

C.S.S. *Alabama*
Cherbourg, June 14, 1864

Sir:

I hear that you were informed by the U.S. consul that the *Kearsarge* was to come to this port solely for the prisoners

USS *Kearsarge* in 1864
(from Ellicott, *John Ancrum Winslow*)

Captain Winslow and his officers on the deck of the *Kearsarge*

landed by me, and that she was to depart in twenty-four
hours. I desire to say to the U.S. consul that my intention is
to fight the *Kearsarge* as soon as I can make the necessary
arrangements. I hope these will not detain me more than
until to-morrow evening, or after the morrow morning at
furthest. I beg she will not depart before I am ready to
go out.

    I have the honor to be, very respectfully, your obedient
servant,

                                        R. Semmes,
                                        Captain[28]

Neither the U.S. consul nor Captain Winslow acknowledged the
challenge because any official communication would have implied
recognition of the *Alabama* as a legally belligerent warship. Welles
had specifically ordered Winslow to avoid communication with
the Confederate ship. But though he may not have acknowledged
Semmes's challenge, Winslow was determined to end the *Alabama*'s
career. He therefore arranged with the consul to station lookouts on
the bluffs overlooking Cherbourg Harbor, who would fire signal
rockets if Semmes tried to escape under the cover of darkness; it
never occurred to the federals that the Confederates would attempt
to fight.[29]

Semmes now canceled his request for a dry dock, instead ordering
one hundred tons of coal. According to Confederate sources, the crew
was sent aloft to bring down the topgallant and mizzen yards as the
Alabama prepared for action.[30]

    The news of the challenge swept through Europe. In Paris, Meulnier
and Schroeder, having been paid off and discharged, were en route
home to Germany. Learning that Semmes planned to fight, they
boarded a train back to Cherbourg to resume their places on the
ship.[31] Authorities in Cherbourg were astounded at Semmes's an-
nouncement and unanimously believed the *Alabama* should not fight.
Bonfils passed their concerns on to Slidell, adding that he personally
felt the *Alabama* should go into dry dock, get an overhaul, and
continue her mission of commerce raiding rather than risk a battle
he called "entirely unequal." Slidell replied that Semmes was the

best judge of how to handle his ship. But he thought the position of the French government had forced Semmes's hand.[32]

Semmes did not consider the contest unequal. In the penultimate entry in his journal, he wrote: "My crew seem to be in the right spirit, a quiet spirit of determination pervading both officers and men. The combat will no doubt be contested and obstinate, but the two ships are so equally matched that I do not feel at liberty to decline it. God defend the right, and have mercy upon the souls of those who fall, as many of us must."[33]

Bonfils was more realistic in his assessment than Semmes. As Kell noted, the *Kearsarge* was "just out of dock and in thorough order." Although she carried one less gun than the *Alabama,* her two eleven-inch pivot guns gave her more broadside weight. Her midship section was protected by chain armor, which had been planked over, a fact of which Sinclair said Semmes was fully aware but of which Semmes later denied any knowledge. The two greatest factors, however, were the crews and the powder. Semmes's crew consisted primarily of mercenaries, on board for excitement and prize money rather than patriotic motives; and although Semmes represented a de facto government and had the theoretical authority of that government behind him, he never had the real power to force the men into total submission. They were trained as well as could be expected, but that training was limited by the amount of control Semmes could exercise and by the *Alabama*'s inability to resupply her stores of powder in neutral ports. Gunnery practice had always been restricted to occasional use of a prize as a target, and the powder was defective. By contrast, the *Kearsarge*'s crew was superbly trained, well disciplined, and highly motivated; Winslow's authority was backed by the entire federal fleet. The *Kearsarge* could resupply her powder in the United States at will, allowing gunnery practice on a regular basis with good powder.[34]

Optimism aside, why, then, did Semmes fight? As Slidell indicated to Bonfils, there was no other choice. On Wednesday, June 15, the minister of the marine and colonies notified the marine prefect of Cherbourg of the government's position on the two combatants. The U.S. prisoners from the *Alabama*'s last prizes, who had been landed in Cherbourg, could not be allowed to board the *Kearsarge* because

Semmes had protested that this would augment the *Kearsarge*'s crew. The real point of the message, however, was that the *Alabama* would not be allowed to refit in a government dock and could make repairs only in a private dock so she could put to sea again.

"You will observe to the captain of the *Alabama* that he has not been forced to enter into Cherbourg by any accidents of the sea, and that he could altogether as well have touched at ports of Spain, of Portugal, of England, of Belgium, and of Holland," the minister wrote.[35]

Another factor, suggested by Warren Spencer in *The Confederate Navy in Europe,* is that Semmes had no alternatives except to fight or remain in port. As Semmes himself had indicated to Kell, the *Kearsarge* was watching the harbor and could be reinforced at any time. The *Alabama* was no longer in any condition to wait for a moonless night, then try to run a blockade at high speed. Semmes had developed a strong emotional attachment to the ship, which had been his home and battlefield for almost two years. He knew from the newspapers that the Southern cause was living on borrowed time; therefore, the *Alabama* no longer had any reason to exist. Rather than have her enter history as a "commerce raider" and a "pirate," he intended that she be remembered for what she was—a fighting ship.[36]

Captain Winslow learned of Semmes's intention to fight on Wednesday, when he called on the admiral in Cherbourg. He and Semmes had served together and knew each other reasonably well. Yet, because of the Northern impression that the *Alabama* would go to any length to avoid combat, Winslow at first doubted that the challenge was real. When he realized Semmes was serious, he returned to the *Kearsarge,* summoned his officers, and discussed the possibilities. Winslow believed that if the battle went badly for the Confederates, they would try to run the *Alabama* into the safety of French waters; therefore, the *Kearsarge* would have to draw the *Alabama* several miles beyond the breakwater before the fight began. It seemed incredible to the American officers that Semmes would risk his ship, and they concluded that he did so because he believed he could win. Should this be the case, they decided the *Kearsarge* would fight to the finish and, if necessary, would go down fighting; she would not surrender. The Americans settled down to wait, gunports open, guns pivoted to starboard, the entire battery loaded, and shell, grape, and canister ready. Thursday passed, then Friday; the *Alabama* remained in port.[37]

On Thursday, June 16, 1864, Semmes made the last entry in the *Alabama*'s journal: "The enemy's ship still standing off and on the harbor."[38]

He had already sent ashore the ship's operating funds, about 4,700 gold British sovereigns, along with payroll accounts, bonds on the ransomed prizes, and the collection of chronometers, all consigned to Bonfils's care. When a message was sent to the wardroom asking if the officers wanted their valuables sent ashore, Lieutenant Wilson commented that his only concern was his guitar, and it would not fit in Bonfils's safe.[39]

On Friday, Winslow again addressed his crew: "My lads. Captain Semmes says he will come out and fight us if we will wait one or two days for him. I have no intention of going away. He is a man of his word and will do as he says he will. I knew him in Mexico and he is a brave man." A drill showed that the men of the *Kearsarge* could come to general quarters in ninety seconds. Confident in themselves and their ship, the Americans relaxed through Saturday.[40]

The Cherbourg hotels and rooming houses were full of tourists who had come to see the fight. Captain Evan P. Jones of the British yacht *Deerhound,* in Cherbourg to pick up the yacht's owner, John Lancaster, and his family, called with some of his crew and asked permission to tour the ship. For the first time in the *Alabama*'s career, the officers refused; they were too busy preparing for battle. "Little did we imagine at the time that these brave fellows we were treating with scant courtesy were to be the means of saving the lives of so many of our officers and crew," Sinclair remarked.[41]

Outside the breakwater, the *Kearsarge* waited. By Saturday night, preparations on the *Alabama* were completed. Semmes notified the port admiral that he intended to leave Cherbourg the following morning.[42]

13

The Death of the Alabama

SUNDAY, JUNE 19, 1864, WAS A BEAUTIFUL DAY, MUCH LIKE the one almost two years before when the *Alabama* was commissioned.[1] On this particular Sunday, Napoleon III had returned from Biarritz and was staying at Fontainbleau, where he planned to attend the races that afternoon. Many government and court officials would be there, and Slidell, aware that Semmes planned to fight, went out to Fontainebleau to discuss the dry-dock issue one last time and, if necessary, assess blame for the outcome of any battle.[2]

In Cherbourg, the sun was bright, the sea smooth, and there was a gentle breeze. Semmes was still in his bunk when he received word from the port admiral that the ironclad frigate *Couronne* would escort the *Alabama* to the limit of French waters to ascertain that there would be no violations of neutrality in the coming fight. Contrary to its usual behavior in port, the crew had reported back to the ship early Saturday night and had gotten a good night's sleep. Aside from those necessary to get up steam, Semmes allowed them to have a leisurely breakfast and did not turn them out until 9:00 A.M.[3]

Crowds had gathered on the heights above the city and on the upper floors of any building that had a view of the sea. Several French pilot boats were putting to sea, along with the British yacht *Deerhound*. It seemed that everyone wanted to see the battle. The marine prefect of Cherbourg had a better vantage point than most: the seawall at the entrance to the harbor. Another spectator was George T. Sinclair, Confederate naval constructor and uncle of Arthur Sinclair of the *Alabama,* whose operations in Scotland had been shut down by increasingly vigilant enforcement of the Foreign Enlistment Act. He had arrived in Cherbourg the night before and had managed to slip aboard the *Alabama* for a brief visit. French officials were blocking shipboard visits by most Confederates to avoid any chance that Semmes might augment his crew. They had refused to allow several officers recently returned from the *Tuscaloosa* to rejoin the ship or even go aboard, despite Semmes's plea that they had been among the *Alabama's* original officers.[4]

Shortly after 9:00 A.M., the *Couronne* weighed anchor and started toward the entrance to the harbor. The *Alabama* followed, passing the ship-of-the-line *Napoléon,* whose crew manned the rigging and whose band played a Confederate air. Officers and men of the *Alabama* were in uniform, the crew looking particularly neat. Guns were pivoted to the starboard, the side on which Semmes planned to engage. As they cleared the breakwater, they could see the *Kearsarge,* standing out to sea about nine miles away.[5]

Once under way, Semmes summoned the ship's company aft and mounted a gun carriage. It was the first time he had formally addressed the entire company since the day *Alabama* was commissioned.

Officers and Seamen of the *Alabama!*
You have, at length, another opportunity of meeting the enemy—the first that has been presented to you, since you sank the *Hatteras!* In the meantime, you have been all over the world, and it is not too much to say, that you have destroyed, and driven for protection under neutral flags, one half of the enemy's commerce, which, at the beginning of the war, covered every sea. This is an achievement of which you may well be proud; and a grateful country will not be unmindful of it. The name of your ship has become a household word wherever civilization stands. Shall that name be tarnished by defeat?

The crew interrupted with shouts of "Never! Never!" Semmes continued:

The thing is impossible! Remember that you are in the English Channel, the theatre of so much of the naval glory of our race, and that the eyes of all Europe are at this moment, upon you. The flag that floats over you is that of a young Republic, who bids defiance to her enemies, whenever, and wherever found. Show the world that you know how to uphold it! Go to your quarters.[6]

At their stations, the crewmen were told to lie down and rest. The men were now stripped to the waist. The decks had been sanded to prevent slipping on blood during the fight, and tubs of water had been set out. The *Alabama* was ready.[7]

On the *Kearsarge,* the crew turned out for inspection and was dismissed for church services. Despite Winslow's assurances, they had waited for so long without seeing the *Alabama* that many speculated she would not come out, particularly after Minister Dayton's son arrived with a message from his father in Paris, doubting Semmes would fight. Even so, special lookouts had been posted on the masts to watch for the Confederate ship, and every gun was loaded. In the boiler room, all furnaces were burning. At 10:00 A.M., Winslow made Sunday inspection of the ship and crew. Twenty minutes later, the officer of the deck reported a steamer coming out from Cherbourg, but that was a frequent occurrence and no one paid attention. The bell was sounding for services when someone shouted, "She's coming, and heading straight for us!"

The officer of the deck checked the steamer through his glasses and shouted, "The *Alabama!*" The drum beat general quarters. Captain Winslow closed his prayer book, picked up his speaking trumpet, and ordered the ship about and the starboard guns run out. Ready for battle in just under three minutes, the *Kearsarge* headed for sea, drawing the *Alabama* away from the coast and allowing the Union ship time to build steam in all her boilers. A spare U.S. flag was run up on the masthead in stops, to be unfurled if the flag at the peak was shot away. Closer to shore, the *Couronne* came about and began cruising up and down the three-mile limit of French territorial waters as the *Alabama* steamed on into the channel.[8]

It had taken the *Alabama* about forty-five minutes to draw near to the *Kearsarge.* When she was within about a mile and a quarter,

Union gunners fire on the *Alabama* from one of the *Kearsarge*'s pivot guns.
(from *Battles and Leaders of the Civil War*)

the Union ship suddenly came about with her head to shore and presented her starboard battery to the Confederates. At 10:57 A.M., with the range closed to one mile, the *Alabama* opened fire. The solid shot passed through the rigging and splashed down on the other side of the *Kearsarge*. Winslow needed closer range because his guns were loaded with shells timed to explode in five seconds. He ordered more speed, but within two minutes the *Alabama* had let loose a second broadside, followed shortly by a third. So far, all the shots had passed overhead, but Winslow saw that the Confederate ship was maneuvering to rake. He ordered the *Kearsarge* to sheer, and at 11:00 A.M., opened fire on the *Alabama*.[9]

The two ships began steaming in a circle to maintain their range. Semmes was now within what he considered "good shell range" and ordered his guns loaded with shell. Soon the *Alabama*'s gunners scored a hit that might have ended the battle. A shell lodged in the *Kearsarge*'s sternpost and, had it exploded, would have blown out the stern, sinking her; it was a dud.[10]

There was no question now that the *Alabama*'s powder was practically useless. Witnesses watching from the heights along the shore noted a dull flame and "mass of sluggish grey smoke" coming from the *Alabama*'s guns, compared to the "fine blue vapor" from the *Kearsarge*. The *Alabama*'s gunners were not trained to judge distance, and, as naval agent Bulloch later noted, "were wholly without the skill, precision and coolness which come only with practice and habit of firing at a visible object and noting the effect."[11] Although Semmes ordered them to fire low and ricochet the shots off the water,[12] gunnery was generally wild. Some hits were scored, but many bounced off the chain armor, and projectile after projectile passed overhead. Despite orders, the gunners were firing high. When a shell flew over, the Union sailors flattened themselves on deck until it passed, then jumped up and back to their guns. Crewman Charles Fisher believed that was the reason the *Kearsarge*'s casualties were so low. "To those who have never heard the whistle of a shell there is something unearthly and terrible in the sound," Fisher wrote. "One is led to imagine that all the devils in hell are let loose to play around one[']s ears."[13] Meanwhile, the *Kearsarge*'s shots slammed into the *Alabama*'s hull.

Seeing that his shells had no effect, Semmes switched back to solid shot, then alternated between shot and shell. Two projectiles passed through the *Kearsarge*'s gun ports, one coming to rest in the hammock netting and the other going clear across the ship and exiting through the opposite port. Remarkably, no one was injured. Another Confederate shot knocked loose the stops from the flag on the *Kearsarge*'s main truck, and the banner unfurled in the breeze. The Union crew let out a wild cheer.[14]

It was different on the *Alabama*. A shot from the *Kearsarge* had carried off the spanker gaff with the ensign, and the flag now flew from the mizzen peak. The deck was a shambles, and the ship was taking water. A Union shell tore through the crew of the after pivot gun, and the men from the quarterdeck thirty-two-pounder secured their gun to work the pivot, throwing mangled bodies overboard to give themselves room. The ship was becoming sluggish with a bad starboard list, but the engines still worked. Semmes ordered the headsails set to assist in keeping her straight, then told Kell to set the trysails in an effort to reach the French coast. At the same time, he ordered the ship put about to bring her on an even keel. The

Alabama responded, and port guns were run out to continue the fight from that side as the dash for France began.[15]

Kell went to the hatchway and called down to First Assistant Engineer William P. Brooks to give more steam. Brooks shouted that there was "every inch of steam that was safe to carry without being blown up!" "Let her have the steam," Second Assistant Engineer Matthew O'Brien shouted. "We'd better blow her to hell than to have the Yankees whip us!"[16]

Suddenly a shell slammed into the hull below the waterline, spraying water over one of the gun crews. The ship shuddered from stem to stern as the shell exploded in the engine room, and tons of water poured in, putting out the fires. Chief Engineer Freeman came on deck and reported that the pumps could no longer handle the water.[17] Semmes turned to Kell. "Go below, sir, and see how long the ship can float." Kell hurried through the ship. In the wardroom, which had been converted to a surgery, he found Dr. Llewellyn standing over an empty space that had, a moment before, been filled with an operating table and a patient. An eleven-inch shell from the *Kearsarge* had swept through the room, carrying off the table and patient and opening a large hole in the side. Water rushed in.[18]

Kell reported back to Semmes that the ship had maybe ten minutes left. Semmes responded: "Then, sir, cease firing, shorten sail, and haul down the colors. It will never do in this nineteenth century for us to go down and the decks covered with our gallant wounded."[19]

The colors were struck and the two quarterboats lowered, the midship boats having been smashed. Incredibly, the *Kearsarge* let loose with another broadside. The reasons for this have never been fully explained. Winslow always maintained that the *Alabama* fired after the colors were struck, and Surgeon Browne of the *Kearsarge* said he understood later that some young officers of the *Alabama* had continued firing in defiance of orders, bringing on the broadside from the American ship. The Confederate officers were unanimous that they had ceased firing when Semmes gave the order. What really happened will never be known. Sinclair called the *Kearsarge*'s broadside "an accident." Semmes gave the *Kearsarge* the benefit of the doubt with the comment, "It is charitable to suppose that a ship of war of a Christian nation could not have done this, intentionally."[20]

Semmes now ordered a white flag run up and told Kell, "Dispatch an officer to the *Kearsarge* and ask that they send boats to save our wounded—ours are disabled."[21]

Fullam was sent with some of the wounded and, as he drew alongside the *Kearsarge,* Winslow called down, "Does Captain Semmes surrender his ship?"

"Yes."

Fullam then received permission to return to assist those who were in the water, giving his word, according to the Union officers, that he would return to the *Kearsarge* and report himself as a prisoner of war.[22]

On the *Alabama* the wounded were being loaded on boats, as were those who reported that they could not swim. Among the wounded was James King II,[23] called "Connemara" by his mates, for his place of birth in Ireland. Hot-tempered and a chronic discipline case, he had been one of Kell's more frequent problems throughout his service on the *Alabama*. Now, mortally wounded and being loaded into a boat, King asked for Kell.

"I have sent for you, Mr. Kell, to ask your forgiveness for all the trouble I've caused you since my enlistment on the ship. Please forgive poor Connemara now he is going to his long home."

Kneeling and holding the man's head, Kell replied, "My poor, dear boy, I have nothing to forgive; nothing against you, my brave lad; and I trust you will be in better trim soon."

"No," King said. "Connemara is going fast. Good-by, Mr. Kell. God bless you, Mr. Kell." He took Kell's hand and kissed it. Kell never saw him again; King died on the *Kearsarge*.[24]

The *Alabama* was going fast. Sinclair went below to get a bottle of rum for a wounded man in his division and found Dr. Llewellyn knee deep in water, attending to the wounded.

"Why, Pills!" Sinclair called, "You had better get yourself and wounded out of this, or you'll soon be drowned!"

"I must wait for orders," the surgeon replied. At that moment a gang of men arrived to transfer the wounded to the boats.[25]

The order now went out, "Every man save himself who can!"

Kell moved up and down the deck, shouting for every man to grab an oar, a spar, or a grating for support, jump overboard, and

Lieutenant Fullam approaches the *Kearsarge* to offer the
Alabama's surrender to Captain Winslow. Note the exposed
chain armor visible through the shell hole at left.
(from *Battles and Leaders of the Civil War*)

The *Alabama*'s wounded are removed as water rushes into the sinking ship.
(from *Battles and Leaders of the Civil War*)

get as far away from the ship as possible to avoid being sucked down by the vortex. The dead were lying about the decks, and the roar of the water could be heard as it rushed through the holes into the hull. There was no panic or confusion. Men calmly rigged something to help them float, looked for their mates, or saw to the safety of favorite officers. Several gathered around Semmes and urged him to look after himself.[26]

Semmes sent Michael Mars and George Freemantle down to his cabin to retrieve the ship's journal and papers. They waded into the cabin, got the journal and papers, and returned with Bartelli. Kell and Semmes, having thrown their swords into the channel, were now stripping down to swim away from the ship. Semmes was having trouble because a shell fragment had hit him in the right hand. Though not serious, the wound was painful, and together with his generally poor physical condition, it exhausted him. The men helped strip him down to his trousers and vest, while Kell stripped to his drawers. As he assisted Semmes, the tearful Bartelli told him a shell had gone through the cabin, destroying a painting of the *Alabama*. Bartelli failed to mention that he could not swim. Nor could Dr. Llewellyn and David White, the former slave from Delaware. All had remained at their posts when nonswimmers were ordered to the boats. Semmes took a life preserver, Kell a grating, and both went into the water.[27]

The stern of the ship was now underwater. Up forward, Sinclair and a member of his gun division were preparing to abandon. Sinclair was sitting on deck, water lapping his legs, trying to secure some gold sovereigns in a handkerchief around his neck, when Matthew O'Brien emerged from the engine room. "What are you loafing round here for?" O'Brien demanded. "Don't you see the ship is settling for a plunge? Over you go!" He shoved Sinclair into the water, making him drop his gold into the channel. The sailor and O'Brien followed. As they swam away, the bow of the *Alabama* shot high out of the water. The main topmast crashed over the side, followed by the foretop. She began a rapid slide to the bottom and was gone.[28]

From his vantage point on the breakwater, the marine prefect apparently mistook the white surrender flag for the new white Confederate ensign and remarked to George Sinclair, "The Confederates have lost their ship, but not their honor. The flag of the *Alabama* was the last thing to disappear."[29]

With or without a flag, Southern honor was preserved. But such sentiments would have been lost on the remaining officers and crew, who, at that moment, were concerned only with survival. Sinclair and his two companions were caught in the vortex and carried down with the ship "so deep, indeed, that with my eyes open in perfectly clear water, I found myself in the darkness of midnight." They struggled to reach the surface and swam until they were hauled into a boat. They were lying in the bottom catching their breath when the sailor noticed blue uniforms on the boat crew—she was from the *Kearsarge*. They took advantage of the general confusion to slip back over the side and swim away.[30]

A mass of struggling sailors and wreckage covered the water. Some of the men, worn out from the fight, began to sink. Kell noticed a makeshift float of empty shell boxes and sent a sailor who was a strong swimmer to investigate.

"It is the doctor, sir, dead," the sailor called. Dr. Llewellyn had apparently tried to rig a makeshift float but was unable to keep his head out of the water. Bartelli and David White also drowned.

Kell felt himself growing weaker. Midshipman E. A. Maffitt saw him and said, "Mr. Kell, you are so exhausted, take this life preserver," and began unfastening it.

Looking at Maffitt's face, Kell saw that the boy was too worn out to stay afloat without the life preserver and refused.

Then a voice called out, "Here's our first lieutenant."

Kell felt himself being picked up and hauled into a boat. It was from the yacht *Deerhound,* and in the stern sheets he found Semmes, unconscious but alive.[31]

It seemed to everyone that the *Kearsarge* was holding off long after she should have been launching rescue boats. Semmes later speculated that Winslow still feared a ruse; the log of the *Kearsarge* states that only two boats were available, the others having been disabled. Actually, Winslow did not seem to know what to do. For two years, the Northern propaganda machine had been grinding out lurid tales of Semmes's deceit and cruelty, and Winslow appears to have been genuinely afraid of the sinking ship and the helpless men in the

Her mainmast gone, the *Alabama* starts sinking by the stern.
(from *Battles and Leaders of the Civil War*)

water. Although he wrote Welles that he lowered his undamaged
boats "at once," the evidence is overwhelmingly against him.[32]

The English yachtsman John Lancaster had no such qualms and
ordered Captain Jones to bring the *Deerhound* to the scene. As the
yacht passed the *Kearsarge,* Winslow shouted, "For God's sake do
what you can to save them." Soon the *Deerhound*'s boats were moving
among the swimming Confederates.[33]

Richard F. Armstrong, second lieutenant of the *Alabama,* had been
wounded in the side. Exhausted and in pain, he managed to keep
his head above water with the help of some crewmen. A boat from
the *Kearsarge* was nearby but made no attempt to rescue, even though
Armstrong was sure that his officer's cap could be seen by the boat's
officer. Finally, he was pulled aboard a French boat. Michael Mars,
who still had the *Alabama*'s journal and papers, was taken aboard
the *Kearsarge* boat but jumped over the side and swam to the French
boat. On learning that Semmes was aboard the *Deerhound,* Mars

The *Alabama* takes her final plunge into the English Channel as the
Kearsarge steams in the background.
(from *Battles and Leaders of the Civil War*)

transferred to one of her boats and, once aboard the yacht, refused
to surrender the papers to anyone but Semmes. He was taken down to
the cabin where Semmes was resting and delivered them personally.[34]

On the *Kearsarge,* Dr. Browne was involved in an amputation when
Dr. Galt of the *Alabama* was brought on board. Galt introduced
himself with an offer to assist, and Browne asked him to tend to the
Alabama's wounded. It soon became obvious that Galt himself was
hurt and was so tired that Browne sent him to his own cabin to
rest.[35]

The only casualties on the *Kearsarge* were three men wounded, one
of whom, Ordinary Seaman William Gowin, later died of severe
blood loss from severed arteries. The *Alabama*'s losses were nine killed
in action, twenty-one wounded, and twelve drowned after the ship
sank.[36] The *Kearsarge* put into Cherbourg, where the *Alabama*'s
wounded were taken to hospitals, and Dr. Galt and the Confederate
enlisted personnel were paroled immediately. Lieutenant Wilson,
Chief Engineer Freeman, Third Assistant Engineer John M. Pundt,

and Boatswain Benjamin Mecaskey were detained on board and paroled later. Flag Officer Barron sent two Confederate surgeons to Cherbourg to see to the wounded, who were ordered kept on the books and paid until they recovered. The paroled crewmen were paid off and honorably discharged the night of June 19.[37]

On the *Deerhound,* Captain Jones raised the question of whether he was bound by international law to turn the *Alabama*'s survivors over to the *Kearsarge.* Kell offered the opinion that they were under the British flag and that Jones was under no obligation to the United States. Lancaster then asked Semmes where he wished to go and was told, "I am under English colors; the sooner you land me on English soil the better." The *Deerhound* steamed toward Southampton and landed that afternoon. In the channel, the *Kearsarge* hauled in her boats around 1:00 P.M. The crew was called to muster, and Winslow finished the church services interrupted that morning. He concluded with a prayer of thanksgiving for the victory. Two hours later, the *Kearsarge* steamed into Cherbourg.[38]

The battle over, Semmes and Winslow descended into pettiness. For all his attempts at charity, Semmes never forgave Winslow for firing after the *Alabama* had struck her colors or for the delay in rescuing the survivors. But in his view, the deepest cut of all was the chain armor, which he mentioned frequently afterward. In his report, he stated, "The enemy was heavier than myself, both in ship, battery and crew; but I did not know until the action was over, that she was also iron-clad." The fact of the chain armor was repeated over and over again until Semmes apparently convinced himself that was the only reason he lost the *Alabama*[39] and that defective powder and indifferent gunnery played no major part. Yet the chains had been installed on the *Kearsarge* more than a year earlier, after Farragut had proven their value when he ran his ships past the forts protecting New Orleans. The modification was general knowledge in Europe, and Sinclair maintained that Semmes had been informed of it in advance by the port admiral of Cherbourg. Add to this that the *Alabama* threw 370 projectiles, only about 8.5 percent of these even hit the *Kearsarge,* and few, if any, exploded, and the reasons for the Union victory are obvious.[40]

For his part, Winslow was furious over what he considered dishonorable conduct by Semmes and the officers of the *Alabama*. He believed
that they had become prisoners of war the moment the *Alabama*'s
colors were struck and were obligated to turn themselves over to
federal jurisdiction, specifically the *Kearsarge*. Fullam was castigated
for boarding the *Deerhound* after giving his word that he would return
to the Union ship. That Wilson could have easily gone to the yacht
but instead presented himself on the *Kearsarge* as a prisoner of war
made Fullam's conduct seem all the more reprehensible in Winslow's
eyes. In a lengthy exchange of correspondence, Winslow and Welles
berated the officers of the *Alabama* in general and Semmes in particular. Welles said he "resorted to any dishonorable means to escape
after his surrender," having "thrown overboard a sword that was no
longer his."[41]

In his outrage, Winslow began to see a conspiracy between the
Alabama and the *Deerhound,* which he accused of being a tender to
the Confederate ship. He repeated wild statements that the night
before the battle boats were seen going back and forth between the
Alabama and *Deerhound* and that the yacht had brought naval reservists
to serve as gunners. In his preliminary report, written two days after
the fight, Winslow admitted that he had "hailed and begged" the
Deerhound to pick up survivors. By June 30, however, the yacht had
been "edging to leeward, leading us to suppose she was seeking men
who were drifting in the current," then escaping to England with
Semmes and his leading officers.[42]

Winslow's allegations found their way into the *London Daily News,*
prompting Lancaster to write a scathing rebuttal. He pointed out that
as owner of the *Deerhound,* he presumed the yacht was in Cherbourg for
his own "pleasure and convenience" and not to serve the *Alabama*.
Although he was interested in watching the fight from a safe distance,
he said his wife and children were on board, and under no circumstances would he have risked them by actual participation.

As for the conduct of the rescue, Lancaster leveled a personal attack
at Winslow: "The fact is that when we passed the *Kearsarge* the
captain cried out, 'For God's sake do what you can to save them,'
and that was my warrant for interfering in any way for the aid and
succor of his enemies . . . if the captain and crew of the *Alabama*

had depended for safety altogether on Captain Winslow, not one-half of them would have been saved."[43]

In Richmond, a grateful government was unconcerned with over-seas disputes. On February 14, 1865, Congress passed a joint resolution of thanks to Lancaster, to which Jefferson Davis added his own appreciation for the "gallant and humane conduct displayed by yourself and the crew of your yacht."[44]

14

From History to Legend

THE DESTRUCTION OF THE *ALABAMA* BROUGHT JUBILATION in the United States, which needed good news after General Ulysses S. Grant's disastrous losses at Cold Harbor.[1]

"I would sooner have fought that fight than any ever fought on the ocean," Admiral Farragut wrote to his son, adding, "I go for Winslow's promotion."[2]

Winslow himself was more modest. "God be thanked that all is well, and to him be all the praise and glory," he wrote in a note dashed off the day after the battle.[3]

The *New York Times* of July 6, 1864, devoted the entire front page and a good portion of page 4 to the story, commenting:

The pirate *Alabama* has at last gone to the bottom of the sea. After a bloody and lurid career of two years on the high seas—in which career she has passed from one Continent to another, from the North and South Atlantic to the Indian Ocean, from the Gulf of Mexico to the China Seas, following the wake of our commercial ships wherever they would be found, and burning and destroying them wherever they were overtaken—she has been annihilated on the very first action that one of our ships-of-war was enabled to get an opportunity to measure metal with her.

The fight with the *Hatteras* and the *Alabama*'s remarkable lack of bloodshed were apparently forgotten in the midst of editorial deadlines and patriotic hyperbole.

Elsewhere, people made excuses. Commissioner Slidell, at Fontainebleau during the battle, had taken up the matter of dry-docking with Prince Murat and several other officials, telling them "what was probably then going on near Cherbourg, and my apprehension of the result of such a contest which had been in a great degree forced upon Captain Semmes by the manner in which he had been received there." The officials expressed concern, and Murat promised to discuss it with Napoleon III. The emperor arrived soon after and was handed a telegram informing him of the loss of the *Alabama*. Murat, who took the news to Slidell, said Napoleon was "deeply grieved." He also mentioned that the emperor told him Slidell must have been mistaken about dock facilities; he had granted permission for their use.[4]

Barron knew better. "It is pretended that permission had been given for the entry of the *Alabama* into the military port for repairs," he wrote to Semmes. "This I know not to have been the case."[5]

On hearing that the *Alabama*'s shell was still lodged in the sternpost of the *Kearsarge,* Lincoln ordered the entire piece sent to Washington as a trophy. When the *Kearsarge* arrived at the Boston Navy Yard for repairs, the damaged section was sawed out, crated, and sent to Norfolk for delivery to the capital.[6]

Welles was elated at the destruction of the "piratical craft" and told Winslow that Lincoln intended to recommend him for promotion to commodore. Yet the secretary was bitter that Semmes had escaped and took Winslow to task for his "grave error" in paroling the prisoners from the *Alabama.* Winslow, in no mood to deal with meddling bureaucrats, pointed out that the *Kearsarge* did not have room for prisoners, and because there were no other U.S. ships in port at the time, he had paroled them as a matter of expediency. Indeed, Lieutenant Wilson's parole had been specifically recommended by no less than Charles Francis Adams, and Winslow had acted accordingly.[7]

The South, reeling under the steady hammering of the Union army, was profoundly shocked at the *Alabama*'s loss. In Richmond, diarist Mary Chesnut blamed the captain: "Semmes, of whom we have been so proud—he is a fool after all—risked the *Alabama* in a sort of duel of ships! He has lowered the flag of the famous *Alabama* to the *Kearsarge.* Forgive who may! I cannot."[8] It was a poor commentary on a man who had given so much of himself for so long.

After recuperating in England, Semmes and Kell returned to the Confederacy. Kell finally reached his home in Macon, Georgia, in August 1864, after three years and four months. He had left three children behind; he found only one. His oldest son had died at the age of six, and his daughter, who was three months old the last time he had seen her, was also dead. A few days later, Kell went to Richmond, where Mallory formally appointed him commander, then returned home to take his family out of Macon until General William T. Sherman's forces had passed. In October he reported back to Richmond, where he was ordered to take command of the ironclad named for the Confederate capital. Early the next year, he caught a cold that developed into pneumonia and was invalided back to Macon, where he was recuperating when word reached him that Lee had surrendered. In July 1865, he and his wife, Blanche, had another son, whom they named after Semmes, "his dear name being associated with my last dream of glory." Later they had a second daughter.[9]

Several years after the war, Semmes stopped by to visit the Kells, and Blanche showed him the scrapbook she had kept during the war detailing the *Alabama*'s exploits. When Semmes noticed Kell's picture was first, she said, "Admiral, you will easily see who is the hero of the ship to me." "And so he is to me my right hand, and I knew he would be ready when I called him," Semmes replied. He remained with the Kells for a few days. Although he wrote frequently after that, they never saw him again.[10]

After the loss of the *Alabama,* Semmes had taken a blockade runner to the port of Bagdad, at the Mexican mouth of the Rio Grande, then proceeded upriver, where he reentered the Confederacy through Brownsville, Texas.[11] In February 1865 he was promoted to rear admiral and given command of the James River Squadron. During the fall of Richmond, he scuttled the squadron to prevent capture and transferred his command to the army, where he was given the rank of brigadier general. He surrendered in North Carolina on May 1, 1865.[12]

In December 1865, Welles ordered Semmes arrested. Colonel J. A. Bolles, solicitor and judge advocate, was preparing an extensive list of charges, but by now, tempers had cooled over Semmes's depredations at sea, and Welles could write: "That he and a million of others have been guilty of treason there is no doubt; that he ran the blockade, burnt ships after a semi-piratical fashion there is no doubt; so have others been guilty of these things, and I do not care to select and try Semmes on these points, though perhaps [he is] the most guilty." In Welles's mind, the only remaining issue was violation of parole. The secretary still insisted that Semmes had become a prisoner of war subject to exchange at the moment the *Alabama* surrendered and had returned to the South and continued fighting without being properly exchanged. In view of the general terms for demobilization of Confederate armed forces and the reincorporation of the South into the United States, this infraction was not enough to hold him.[13]

Considering all the furor in both government and press, why were the Confederate naval officers not tried for piracy, according to Lincoln's proclamation of April 19, 1861? After all, the Southern attempt to establish a separate nation had failed, those who had supported the Confederate war effort were once again under U.S. jurisdiction, and they had committed treason against the United States as defined in the federal Constitution. The reason is that it was not practical to charge them. When the proclamation was issued, the North did not realize the extent of Southern determination, but, as Soley noted: "The insurrection assumed such large proportions in the beginning, and was directed by such complete governmental machinery, that every consideration of policy and necessity, as well as of humanity and morality, prescribed a course of action under which the insurgents should be treated as belligerents, and, when captured, as prisoners of war."[14] There were already precedents for commerce raiding in the United States Navy; thus the Confederate depredations were legitimate acts of a naval power. And because captured Confederate soldiers were regarded as prisoners of war, rather than traitors in rebellion, there was no way Welles could justify treating Confederate naval personnel differently.

After a short term in prison, Semmes was released without trial and returned to Mobile to resume his legal practice. He died on August 30, 1877. Despite his remoteness from his officers, or perhaps because of it, he inspired an almost fanatical loyalty that lasted long after his death. Even Lieutenant Armstrong, who seemed to dislike Semmes personally, was adamant that nothing should defame his memory. Nowhere is this loyalty more apparent than in the controversy over the *Kearsarge*'s chain armor. Although it is indeed possible that Semmes was ignorant of the chains, the bulk of the evidence shows that it was common knowledge in Cherbourg and that surely he must have known about it. Yet for as long as they lived, Kell, Armstrong, and others insisted that Semmes had been duped into a fight with an armored ship. Sinclair's memoirs, first published in 1896, insisted that the admiral in Cherbourg had told Semmes about the chains. Kell flatly denied the allegation in his own memoirs, published four years later, and Armstrong never forgave Sinclair for the revelation. In 1900, shortly after her husband's death, Blanche Kell received a letter from Dr. Galt, stating that the existence of the chain armor was common knowledge among the officers of the *Alabama*. The statement infuriated her, and she destroyed the letter.[15] Regardless of whether he knew about the chains, Semmes was, in fact, a great captain and well deserved the efforts by his officers to defend his memory.

When the channel waters closed over the *Alabama*, she sailed from history into legend. Ironically, that legend is more appreciated in Europe and South Africa than in her own country. Except for dedicated Civil War buffs, the average person in the United States does not even realize the South had a navy. Her memory is preserved elsewhere—in England, where she was built; in France, where she rests; and in South Africa, which saw more of her than any other spot on the globe.

Perhaps the legend wears best in South Africa. The main dining room of the Holiday Inn in Cape Town is named for the *Alabama*.[16] There is also a song, originally written in Afrikaans:

Here Comes the *Alabama*

Here comes the *Alabama*, the *Alabama* comes o'er the sea,
Here comes the *Alabama*, the *Alabama* comes o'er the sea,
Girl, girl, the reed-bed girl, the reed-bed is made up,
The reed-bed is made for me
On which to sleep.
Girl, girl, the reed-bed girl, the reed-bed is made up,
The reed-bed is made for me
On which to sleep.[17]

Making more sense, if not historically accurate, is a sea chanty "Roll, *Alabama*, Roll," popular among seamen during the age of sail. As the term *chanty* implies, it is chanted, more than sung, with a cantor giving the verses and the chorus singing, "Roll, *Alabama*, roll."

When the *Alabama*'s keel was laid,
Roll, *Alabama*, roll,
She was laid in the yard of Jonathan Laird.
Oh, roll, *Alabama*, roll.

She was laid in the yard of Jonathan Laird.
Roll, *Alabama*, roll,
It was in the town of Birkenhead.
Oh, roll, *Alabama*, roll.

On the Mersey way she sailed then,
Roll, *Alabama*, roll,
She was Liverpool fitted with guns and men.
Oh, roll, *Alabama*, roll.

To the Western Islands she sailed forth,
Roll, *Alabama*, roll,
To destroy the commerce of the North.
Oh, roll, *Alabama*, roll.

To Cherbourg port she went one day,
Roll, *Alabama*, roll,
To take a share of prize money.
Oh, roll, *Alabama*, roll.

Oh many a sailor met his doom,
Roll, *Alabama,* roll,
When the *Kearsarge* she hove in view.
Oh, roll, *Alabama,* roll.

A shot from the forward pivot that day,
Roll, *Alabama,* roll,
Shot the *Alabama*'s keel away.
Oh, roll, *Alabama,* roll.

Off the three-mile limit in sixty-four,
Roll, *Alabama,* roll,
The *Alabama* sank to the ocean floor.
Oh, roll, *Alabama,* roll.[18]

What is the legend and what is the truth? This is hard to determine because, even before the war ended, the *Alabama*'s role was exaggerated. Mary Chesnut almost seemed to feel that her loss was a death blow to the Confederacy: "Oh, for one single port! If the *Alabama* in the whole world had had a port to take her prizes—refit—&c&c, I believe she would have borne us through—one single point by which to get at the outside world and *refit* the whole Confederacy. If we could have hired regiments from Europe or even imported army ammunition and food for our soldiers."[19]

This view was hardly realistic. In all, the South had perhaps a dozen cruisers either contracted for or delivered. Some, like the *Alabama, Shenandoah, Florida,* and *Georgia,* were ordered from foreign countries; others, such as the *Sumter, Chickamauga,* and *Tallahassee,* were wartime conversions undertaken in home yards. Regardless of their origins or capabilities, they had no real, long-term impact on the war, and even their impact on U.S. maritime history is disputed. In *The Flight from the Flag,* his now-classic study of the Confederate naval effort, George W. Dalzell contended that the effect on U.S. shipping was long term, dealing the American merchant marine a blow from which it never recovered. He maintained that the destruction inflicted by the Confederate cruisers forced up insurance rates, elevating shipping costs to an exorbitant level. When an insured ship and cargo were lost, the settlement generally was paid by Northern

The Grenadines of St. Vincent, in the Windward Islands of the West
Indies, honored the *Alabama* in a series of stamps issued in 1982,
portraying famous ships that have passed through Grenadine waters.
(author's collection)

underwriters, which simply transferred the financial loss from one
U.S. source to another without relieving the strain on American
resources. Additionally, the indemnities only compensated the immediate value of ship and cargo, thereby replacing the real purpose of
a merchant marine, which is, of course, trade.[20] The effect of Confederate depredations was to drive U.S. ships to foreign registry. In 1858
33 ships were transferred to other flags. In 1860 41 changes in
registration were recorded. The number jumped to 126 in 1861, the
year the war broke out, and by 1863 had reached 348.

Having demonstrated that the number of transfers jumped during
the war years, Dalzell then examined the reason these ships were not
returned to the U.S. flag when the war ended. Long before, in 1797,
Congress had passed an act denying repatriation to a ship transferred
to another country. Although application was made to Congress to
remove this ban, representatives of the western states ultimately
defeated it, claiming that an American merchant marine was of no

particular value so long as foreign hulls were available to transport western wheat. Thus the American ships then under other flags remained so.[21]

Yet some of Dalzell's arguments can be used to show that the Confederate cruisers did not deal the U.S. merchant marine its death blow; it was already dying. U.S. shipowners had begun registering their vessels under foreign flags even before the war because, as is still true, it was cheaper than using American registry.[22] After the war, control of seaborne commerce was no longer a high national priority. As Dalzell himself notes, the country's direction of development had changed because, for the first time, the United States functioned as a single nation rather than a federation of autonomous states. Given this new vision of itself, the nation concentrated on opening its interior. The settlement of the Great Plains and expansion of rail service ended the need for a vast fleet of merchant ships to connect East and West. If the Confederate cruisers drove the U.S. merchant fleet from the seas, they were only accelerating a process that was inevitable.[23] As World War II proved, maritime countries such as Great Britain and Norway will rebuild their postwar merchant marines, regardless of the extent of devastation. The U.S. merchant marine was not rebuilt after the Civil War because, very simply, it was not needed.

Most of all, the Confederate cruisers failed to draw vast numbers of ships away from the blockade. In that policy Welles remained inflexible. The ships he released to chase cruisers were those that were too large for efficient blockade work along the shallow Southern coast.[24]

Would a large Southern navy have made a difference? Had Mallory been able to acquire a dozen—two dozen—*Alabama*s, could the South have won? The idea is tempting and indeed possible, but the question will never be answered. Had the *Alabama* and her sisters broken the blockade, there still remains the question of how effective that would have been. The blockade itself has grown in public imagination over the last 130 years until it has been given much greater material importance than it actually had. Throughout the war, the vast majority of the blockade runners got through and landed their cargoes. Their failure to alleviate the South's military situation was logistical. Southern transportation was primitive; once a cargo had been landed, it could not reach all the places where it was needed. As the Northern scythe carved up more and more of the South, distribution of blockade goods became increasingly local.[25]

More than anything else, Northern victory was the result of superb leadership and unequivocal sense of purpose. The South's avowed goal—to be left alone—extended to purely local concerns, for which the national interest was sacrificed. Despite a towering intellect, Jefferson Davis was not an authoritarian figure. He lacked the ability to dominate men and twist and distort the forces of history to the common need. As the war dragged on, his hold on the government grew weaker when necessity should have made it stronger. Although Davis became the physical embodiment of the Confederate cause, he was unable to make the nation an extension of his own will, as Abraham Lincoln did in the United States. Had Davis been able to do so, it would have undermined the very reason for which the Confederacy was founded. In the end, the cause defeated itself.

Lincoln, by contrast, seemed to exist for only one purpose—to preserve the Union. He impressed this ideal onto the people of the United States and filled them with a single-minded resolve. Emancipation elevated this resolve to a holy crusade, and to that end the nation directed its resources. Lincoln's force of character was matched by his almost eerie ability to pick the best men for the most important positions. Thus Gideon Welles became secretary of the navy at a time when no one else could have handled the job. In the War Department, new generals were raised—innovative generals, who were not bound to the old military traditions. U.S. diplomacy grew to a height rarely seen in American history. The diplomatic truimph become complete in 1872, when an international board of arbitration determined that Great Britain had failed in its responsibilities as a neutral power and awarded the United States $15,500,000 in gold. Although the British indemnity was for damages by the *Alabama, Shenandoah,* and *Florida,* it is collectively known as the *Alabama Claims.*[26]

For Lincoln and Welles, the Confederate cruisers were nuisances, a naval and political embarrassment—nothing more. For the beleaguered South, their exploits provided a moral boost as the people starved and the Confederate armies fell back. They were ships without a home, wandering the world like Flying Dutchmen. Yet wherever they went, they brought admiration—not so much for the Southern cause as for the ships themselves and the men who sailed them.

After the battle with the *Kearsarge,* the *London Times* wrote the most fitting end to the *Alabama*'s story: "She was an outlaw; men called her a 'corsair,' and spoke of 'Semmes, the pirate captain' as though he had been some ruffianly Blackbeard sailing under the black flag with skull and cross-bones for his grisly ensign . . . we do not concern ourselves with legal quibbles; we decline to take a lawyer's view of her. She was a good ship, well handled and well fought, and to a nation of sailors that means a great deal."[27]

Epilogue

"THE WRECK OF THE *ALABAMA* LIES AT THE BOTTOM OF THE 'silver streak' which separates England and France. The remains of the *Hatteras* are rusting many fathoms down in the briny waters of the Gulf of Mexico. These are the facts which impartial history has already recorded, and no suggestions of what might, could or should have been can bring those two vessels again to the surface."[1] When Bulloch wrote these words, almost twenty years after the *Alabama* sank, he had every reason to believe that the two ships had disappeared from human eyes forever because sustained underwater activity existed only in the imagination of his French contemporary Jules Verne. The legend of the *Alabama* remained, however, and as a new century brought new technology, men began to believe they might once again stand on her decks.

Ironically, the first ship to be discovered was the *Hatteras*, whose wreck was officially confirmed when the builder's plate was recovered on February 27, 1976. The hunt for her started several years earlier, when Paul Cloutier, associate professor of space physics and astronomy at Rice University in Houston, met Jeff Burke, an agricultural aviator, diver, and part-time treasure hunter from Rio Hondo, Texas. Cloutier, involved in magnetometer design and development, wanted to work with someone who had diving experience, and Burke needed expertise in magnetometers. For several years, they worked together on the remains of the 1553 Spanish treasure fleet off Padre Island, Texas, until the state exercised sole jurisdiction and forbade further private activities.[2]

To avoid more legal problems, Burke and Cloutier began considering wrecks on the high seas, and the possibility arose of locating the *Hatteras*. They considered the historical significance of the ship, as well as its location on the continental shelf, beyond what they believed was U.S. or Texas salvage jurisdiction. "Paul and I decided to undertake looking for this [the *Hatteras*] and we did," Burke said.[3]

The search took more than two years, the workday beginning when their boat left Freeport shortly after midnight and ending when they returned shortly before the following midnight. Visibility at the bottom of the Gulf was often only inches, the diver working by feel alone. Because of the currents, divers were rigged to safety lines and carried flares to avoid being swept out to sea.[4]

"We went everywhere the history books said, and it wasn't there," Burke said. "We put in some pretty bad days." They were joined by Chuck Rose, another agricultural aviator from Rio Hondo, without whom, Burke said, "probably the *Hatteras* would have never been found. He was the guy with the Moxie and the will to make us go out on it. We were burnt out. We had looked for years." Cloutier compared the cost in time, discomfort, and money to "sitting, after twenty hours without sleep in a tub of ice water while tearing up $20 bills. If you're subject to seasickness, the simulation could be improved by first drinking a quart of cheap gin."[5]

By January 1976 the search area had narrowed down to a thirty-two-square-mile rectangle. Then, on the afternoon of January 17, the magnetometer registered "a terrific . . . magnetic field disturbance." It was already late and the sea was rising so they dropped marker buoys and returned to port. All night they listened to the wind and the water until Rose finally suggested that they go back out. At the wreck site, LORAN readings showed that the buoys had been blown off as much as a mile so another two hours were spent dragging the magnetometer before it registered again. Burke donned scuba gear and went down. Visibility was poor, and he returned without finding anything. After a brief rest he went down again; this time he found it. "The minute I saw that damned paddlewheel, I knew what we had," he said. "The paddlewheel, walking beam, a twenty-nine-foot paddlewheel. . . . The hull itself and the ribs are almost unbelievably preserved," Burke said. Marine life had covered the wreck almost immediately, encasing the iron hull and frames against the water. The upper deck was completely gone, and the second deck was almost gone. The third deck, however, was in good condition. The funnel could not be located, but Rose said most of the machinery, fittings, and miscellaneous equipment were still on board. "As the deck gave, it all fell into the hull," he explained. "Everything is there except the portside armament, which was jettisoned as the ship sank."[6]

On February 27 Rose recovered the builder's plate, which confirmed the ship's identity. Although the group had initially planned to salvage the ship, the state once again intervened. Having entered the Union as a sovereign republic, Texas never surrendered its jurisdiction over public lands to the federal government; the state defines public lands to include offshore areas, and the Texas Antiquities Commission maintained that the Hatteras was within that jurisdiction. The group, which by now had formed itself into a corporation, then sued the United States for title. In 1984, however, the U.S. District Court for the Southern District of Texas ruled that title and ownership remained with the federal government, although the Hatteras Corporation had a letter from the Navy Department abandoning interest. The corporation lacked funds to dispute the matter further in court. "It was illegal," Burke remarked in January 1992, "but we don't have the money to fight it, and the government can put up all those lawyers."[7] Since the late 1970s the Hatteras has remained, again undisturbed, where the Alabama sent her.

The discovery of the Hatteras, however, was a prelude to a much greater find. About 10:00 A.M. on November 7, 1984, Commander Max Guérout, chief of staff for the French navy's Mediterranean Flotilla in Toulon, received a telephone call from Cherbourg informing him that the Alabama had been discovered. The caller, Lieutenant Paul Henri Nargeolet, officer in charge of underwater exploration vehicles for the navy's underwater research and development section, told him the minesweeper Circé had located the ship and that divers had brought up two plates from a table service with the label "Davenport." Guérout immediately called the chief of staff for the marine prefect

of Cherbourg, who confirmed Nargeolet's information. They discussed the importance of the wreck to the United States, and Guérout
said that only "those objects absolutely required for identification of
the wreck" should be removed.[8]

The *Alabama* is in 195 feet of water about six miles off Cherbourg,
in what are now French territorial waters. The French navy apparently
used it as a deep diving practice site for years without bothering to
identify her among the many channel wrecks in the vicinity. The
navy began specifically looking for the *Alabama* in 1978 as a training
exercise for sonar operators, and in 1984 divers from the *Circé*
found it.[9]

Within a few days, Guérout was in Cherbourg on temporary
assignment to examine all information collected by the navy divers
and advise them on future investigations. In the *Circé*'s wardroom,
he studied a map of the wreck site, photographs, videos, and the
artifacts: the two Davenport plates and a third from Pankhurst, what
appeared to be a small chimney or ventilation pipe, and two copper
rails. Discussing the finds, he wrote:

> From the assembled evidence, it was possible to conclude
> that the wrecked vessel had had a mechanical propulsion
> system, as attested by the presence of a funnel and of coal,
> a wooden hull, and artillery composed of outdated cannons
> with tulip-shaped muzzles and a cascabel.
>
> These characteristics indicated a ship built and fitted out
> at a period when steam engines were already in use and old
> model artillery had not yet disappeared, that is, roughly
> between 1840 and 1890. In addition, the presence of several
> cannons . . . almost certainly designated a warship of a
> period when the differentiation with merchant ships was
> apparent.

Research of the plates showed that they had been manufactured
between 1850 and 1860, making the *Alabama* a candidate for the
wreck but not positively identified as such. As more equipment was
brought up and compared to the builder's plans, however, Guérout
said, "At last I felt justified in reporting to the navy my conclusion
that the wreck was very probably that of the *Alabama*.[10]

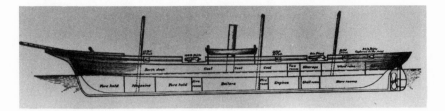

Cutaway profile plan of the *Alabama*
(from Ellicott, *John Ancrum Winslow*)

Although this conclusion was reached in 1985, it was not made public for two years. Guérout offered several reasons, among them previous naval and archaeological commitments, need for a preservation plan, and the need to protect the site from looters. Another factor may easily have been the close proximity of a French nuclear submarine base to the wreck site.[11] Guérout's promotion to captain, however, allowed him to retire and devote his full attention to the wreck and its international implications. During an underwater archaeological conference in Savannah in January 1987, initial contacts were made with U.S. experts. An administrative structure was established to oversee two nonprofit corporations, one French and one American.[12]

Even before the discovery of the *Alabama* became general knowledge, Confederate naval enthusiasts in Great Britain were taking steps to preserve sites and artifacts associated with her in their country. An organization called the Merseyside Confederate Navy History Society successfully lobbied for a government preservation order for the building at 10 Rumford Place, which had been Prioleau's offices and Bulloch's headquarters during the war. Then it won a "stunning victory" when the government issued an order protecting Number 4 Drydock at Laird's shipyards, the dock in which the *Alabama* had been fitted and prepared for trials. In 1987 the group formed the Birkenhead Ironworks and C.S.S. *Alabama* Trust to coordinate activities. Among its plans is full-scale replica of the *Alabama* to be built and displayed in Number 4 Drydock.[13]

Back at Cherbourg, a long and thorough investigation of the wreck site began. Because of the great depth and the currents, scuba divers could remain on the wreck for only fifteen minutes during restricted times of the month. Visibility is extremely limited. Consequently, it was necessary to obtain a small submarine with tender vessels. The survey showed about 30 percent of the ship intact, lying on her starboard side, partially buried in the sand. A portion of her funnel was visible, along with her hatchways and guns, machinery, propeller, and hoisting gear. The ship so closely resembled her builders' plans that it was possible to explore the wreck and identify features using the plans. The greatest reward came when the copper rims of the wheel were recovered (the wooden spokes had long since deteriorated). Still visible was the ship's motto, *"Aide-toi et Dieu t'aidera."*[14]

A major concern has been ownership. Since the battle with the *Kearsarge,* French territorial waters have been extended and now include the wreck site. British preservation groups contend that if she is raised, she should be displayed at Birkenhead. The United States, as legal heir to Confederate public property, maintains that it has never surrendered title to the *Alabama* and is therefore the rightful owner. The federal government entered that claim as early as 1962, and since the discovery of the wreck, the State Department has notified the French Foreign Ministry that the claim is still in effect. To reinforce the claim, Congress passed the C.S.S. *Alabama* Preservation Act (see Appendix 3).[15]

This brings up the case of the so-called *Alabama* bell, purportedly recovered from the wreck by a Guernsey salvage diver in 1936. The bell was ultimately found to be a not-so-elaborate hoax concocted in the early 1970s as a prank by a group of Englishmen. The joke got out of hand, however, when the bell was reportedly sold to Richard Steinmetz of Fort Lee, New Jersey, for an alleged price of $12,000.[16] The hoax is important only in that, during the year or two that the bell was thought to be genuine, it became involved in a court case which emphasizes the U.S. government's position on the ship and any artifacts recovered from her.

After supposedly purchasing the bell in London, Steinmetz offered to sell it to the U.S. Naval Academy, which refused. He then turned it over to a New York auction house for sale. Upon learning of the sale, William Dudley of the U.S. Naval Historical Center asked the Department of Justice to intervene, and the bell was seized. On

May 13, 1991, U.S. District Judge Dickinson Debevoise of Newark, New Jersey, ruled that the bell was the property of the United States. He based his decision on the contention that the United States had right of capture of the *Alabama* and her equipment and had not abandoned the claim, has right of succession to Confederate public property, and constitutional steps to abandon title to the property have never been taken. He also ruled that warships sunk in armed conflict and with clearly identifiable state of origin are subject to sovereign immunity and are indemnified against abandonment of title. Steinmetz disputes that and, hoax or not, the case is far from settled.[17]

As Steinmetz and the government continue to fight over what one editor calls "a very expensive doorstop," it appears that the United States and France are coming to terms about the ship. A joint commission has been appointed, consisting of two U.S. and two French members to coordinate future diving and salvage efforts. As a recent *Confederate Naval Historical Society Newsletter* noted, "This is just the beginning."[18]

Description of the Alabama

A. Internal Description Reported to Consul Dudley
by Matthew Maguire

State room right aft. The entrance to the cabin from the deck is abaft of the mizen mast, raised about 2 feet 6 inches. The state room is seated all round; there are two small glass cases in it. At the bottom of the stairs, the communication to the right leads to a small saloon in the centre of which, is a small dining table and on each side are state cabins. Passing from this to a little more forward, is a large saloon, where the chief officers' and chief engineers cabins are situated on each side, fitted up with a chart and book cases. From this you pass through a doorway into the engine room. There is a platform over the engines (which are two in number) and which are most complete and handsome pieces of machinery, only occupying a small space and lying entirely at the bottom; they are on the oscillating principle.

From here also you can pass in-to [*sic*] the stoke holes. Forward of this, but no communication, are the mens berths, which are quite open and spacious and run entirely forward, in the centre is the cooking apparatus. The hooks are slung to the deck for the mens hammocks. This is also seated all round. Under these seats are places for the mens bags with iron gratings which form the front of the seats. The entrance to this department is directly forward of the foremast. At the bottom of the stairs, a little to the fore

From the W. S. Hoole Special Collections Library, University of Alabama, Tuscaloosa.

part of the ship is a small hatch which leads to the magazines, two in number. The partition on each side of these magazines is of three thicknesses of oak, between each thickness is lined with lead. These magazines are under the main deck, of what I should call the mens berths in the fore part of the ship, about six or eight feet forward of the fore mast. The cannisters are fixtures on their sides, the screws lying one over the other. The magazines and entrances to them, are filled with water during action, by a pipe on each side, and by a pipe in the middle of the floor, the water descends to the bottom of the ship and is pumped out by steam power. The entrance to the cabin is abaft the mizen mast; each side is a brass ventilator about twelve inches high. Forward of the mizen mast is a skylight to the small saloon and forward of this skylight is a larger one, which gives light to the larger saloon. These skylights do not stand more than a foot high on deck and which have iron bars across. Forward of this skylight and abaft the funnel, is a skylight five or six feet long, which gives light to the engine room. The base of the funnel forms a square, about two feet high; each corner is latticed with iron rails, to throw light and air into the stoke room. Each side abaft the funnel, are two ventilators with round bell mouths and which stand about five or six feet high; more forward of the mainmast are two more ventilators of the same description. The entrance to the stoke hole is abaft the foremast. The entrance to the mens sleeping apartment, is raised, about 2 feet high. A small chimney, or brass or copper funnel rises here from the cooking apparatus. Each side of the gangway is carved oak, with an anchor and rope carved on.

B. External Description Reported by William Passmore, July 14, 1862

"Donkey" rigged barque. "No. 290" s.s. (gunboat) 1050 tons. Captain Butcher. Hull painted black. Round stern with twenty-two blank gallery windows in same. Carvings on stern, gilt. Billet head, gilt; red shield for figurehead, with gilt anchor, about 9 inches, on it. Bowsprit painted black. Jibboom, scrape spar, heel painted, black. Fore main Mizen, lower and topmasts bright. Spanker boom and gaff, yards crosstrees and booms, painted black. Black funnel or smoke stack with bright copper steam pipe forepart of same; funnel between fore and main masts. Mizen mast well aft and about 14 feet from stern-rail, with great rake aft. Rigging chains painted black, outside of bulwarks. A bridge forward of the funnel on iron stanchions; railing round bridge painted red. Four iron swivel davits, for two boats, each side between main and mizen masts; boats painted black outside and drab inside. Two iron swing davits at the stern for the captains gig. Flush deck. Has a lifting fan [propeller], which can be hoisted by steam power. The fan is solid brass. Entrances to cabin and engine room abaft main mast. Wheel abaft mizen mast, which has the following inscription round the rim "Aid Toi diever Dieu T-Aidira" [*sic*]. Ball racks forward of each of the masts. Skylights to cabin, engine room etc. covered with wooden gratings. Inside of bulwark painted drab. According to the chalk marks on the deck she will carry three swivel guns.[1] She has three double ports each side:— viz, forward amidships and aft, she will carry sixteen guns in all, swivels included.[2]

She is in a confused state and from her appearance will not be ready before the middle of next week.

She is built of oak and coppered. About 200 feet long and 18 feet deep. When loaded will draw from 10 to 14 feet and is about 1050 tons.

APPENDIX 2

U.S. Ships Overhauled
by the Alabama

During her career, the *Alabama* overhauled sixty-five United States ships on the high seas. Nine of these were bonded, one released without bond, one sunk in battle, one (*Tuscaloosa,* formerly *Conrad*) converted into an auxiliary cruiser, and one sold. The remaining fifty-two were burned.

Two ships were destroyed under questionable circumstances: the *Amanda,* a U.S. ship with a legal British cargo, and the *Martaban* (formerly *Texan Star*), which had transferred to Great Britain a few weeks before but ultimately adjudicated as American by an international claims commission. In each of these cases, Semmes declined to recognize British authority, which alienated British insurers and shippers, both from the *Alabama* and from the Confederate cause.

The total of the ransom bonds, which became worthless at the end of the war, was $562,250. The total value of the property she destroyed came to $4,613,914, or approximately eighteen times the cost of the *Alabama*'s construction. The damage inflicted by the *Alabama* more than justified the amount spent on her construction and operation and was a substantial amount for the British government when the United States entered claims against Great Britain for these losses.

Most of the captures occurred during the first year of operation. Beginning in the summer of 1863, months often passed before the *Alabama* encountered an American ship. As Semmes noted, the U.S. flag had been driven from the seas.

SOURCE: *ORN,* Ser. 1, 3:677–81.

The following list does not include U.S. ships encountered in neutral waters, which were allowed to proceed without penalty. The list includes date of capture and value as appraised by the officers of the *Alabama*, who sometimes valued ship and cargo separately and sometimes as a unit. Unless otherwise noted, all ships were burned.

1862

September 5, *Ocmulgee*, $50,000.

September 7, *Starlight*, $4,000.

September 8, *Ocean Rover*, $70,000.

September 9, *Alert*, $20,000.

September 9, *Weather Gauge*, $10,000.

September 13, *Altamaha*, $3,000.

September 14, *Benjamin Tucker*, $18,000.

September 16, *Courser*, $7,000.

September 17, *Virginia*, $25,000.

September 18, *Elisha Dunbar*, $25,000.

October 3, *Brilliant*, $164,000.

October 3, *Emily Farnham*, released without bond.

October 7, *Wave Crest*, $44,000.

October 7, *Dunkirk*, $25,000.

October 9, *Tonawanda*, bonded for $80,000.

October 11, *Manchester*, $164,000.

October 15, *Lamplighter*, $117,000.

October 23, *Lafayette*,[1] $100,337.

October 26, *Crenshaw*, ship, $11,680; cargo, $22,189.

October 26, *Laureatta*, ship, $15,000; cargo, $17,880.

October 29, *Baron de Castine*, bonded for $6,000.

November 2, *Levi Starbuck*, $25,000.

November 8, *Thomas B. Wales*, $245,625.

November 30, *Parker Cook*, $10,000.

December 5, *Union*, bonded for $1,500.

December 9, *Ariel*, bonded for $261,000.

1863

January 11, USS *Hatteras*, federal gunboat sunk in battle, value estimated at $160,000.

January 26, *Golden Rule*, $112,000.

January 27, *Chastelaine*, $10,000.

February 3, *Palmetto*, $18,430.

February 21, *Olive Jane*, $43,208.

February 21, *Golden Eagle*, $61,000.

February 27, *Washington*, bonded for $50,000.

March 1, *Bethia Thayer*, bonded for $40,000.

March 2, *John A. Parke*, $66,157.

March 15, *Punjaub*, bonded for $55,000.

March 23, *Morning Star*, bonded
   for $61,750.
March 23, *Kingfisher*, $2,400.
March 25, *Nora*, $76,636.
March 25, *Charles Hill*, $28,450.
April 4, *Louise Hatch*, $38,315.
April 15, *Lafayette*, $20,908.
April 15, *Kate Cory*, $10,568.
April 24, *Nye*, $1,127.
April 26, *Dorcas Prince*,
   $44,108.
May 3, *Sea Lark*, $550,000.
May 3, *Union Jack*, $77,000.
May 25, *Gildersleeve*, ship,
   $60,000; cargo, $2,783.
May 25, *Justina*, bonded for
   $7,000.
May 29, *Jabez Snow*, ship,
   $68,672; cargo, $4,109.
June 2, *Amazonia*, $97,665.

June 5, *Talisman*, $139,195.
June 20, *Conrad*, $100,936, fitted
   out as auxiliary cruiser and
   commissioned CSS *Tuscaloosa;*
   sold in South Africa.
July 2, *Anna F. Schmidt*,
   $350,000.
July 6, *Express*, ship, $57,000;
   cargo, $64,300.
August 5, *Sea Bride*, sold for
   $16,940.
November 6, *Amanda*, $104,442.
November 10, *Winged Racer*,
   $150,000.
November 11, *Contest*, $122,815.
December 24, *Texan Star*
   (Martaban), $97,628.
December 26, *Sonora*, $46,545.
December 26, *Highlander*,
   $75,965.

1864

January 14, *Emma Jane*, $40,000.
April 23, *Rockingham*, $97,878.

April 27, *Tycoon*, $390,000.

CSS Alabama *Preservation Act*

101st Congress
1st Session

H.R. 1563

In the House of Representatives
March 22, 1989

A BILL

To preserve the United States' title and interest in the CSS ALABAMA and to encourage its preservation.

Be it enacted by the Senate and House of Representatives of the United States of America in Congress assembled,

SECTION 1. SHORT TITLE.
This Act may be cited as the "CSS ALABAMA Preservation Act."

SEC. 2. FINDINGS.
Congress finds that—
(1) the CSS ALABAMA is an American Civil War vessel that was commissioned on August 24, 1862, by Captain Raphael Semmes, at the direction of Jefferson Davis, President of the Confederate States of America;
(2) on June 19, 1864, after seventy minutes of intense combat with the USS KEARSARGE off the coast of France, the CSS ALABAMA sank in

waters which were then the high seas but are now part of the French territorial sea;

(3) title to the CSS ALABAMA and her artifacts is vested in and has not been abandoned by the United States Government;

(4) the CSS ALABAMA is an important part of American history and culture which transcends regional interests;

(5) the Government of France and other foreign parties have evinced strong interest in the wreck of the CSS ALABAMA;

(6) the United States State Department has requested the Government of France to ensure that no further salvage operations are undertaken without the prior approval of the United States Government; and

(7) the National Park Service of the Department of the Interior and the National Oceanic and Atmospheric Administration of the Department of Commerce are recognized as possessing underwater archaelogical expertise and experience.

SEC. 3. DEFINITIONS.

In this Act—

(1) "CSS ALABAMA" means the sunken vessel CSS ALABAMA, and its cargo, ground tackle, deck auxiliaries, masts, rigging, armament, boilers, condensers, propulsion machinery, shafting, propeller, furniture, napery, cooking utensils, crockery, plate and cutlery, mails and specie, provisions and stores, items captured from prizes, crew's personal effects, and all other associated artifacts and detritus lying or once lying on the ocean floor in its vicinity.

(2) "Secretary" means the Secretary of the Interior, acting through the National Park Service;

(3) "Under Secretary" means the Under Secretary for Oceans and Atmosphere of the Department of Commerce.

SEC. 4. POLICY.

It is the sense of Congress that—

(1) the CSS ALABAMA should be preserved for the benefit of the citizens of the United States and for other interested international parties;

(2) the Secretary of State should enter into negotiations with the Government of France to ensure that the United States Government continues to maintain its title and interest in the CSS ALABAMA and to ensure that the CSS ALABAMA is preserved for the benefit of the citizens of the United States.

(3) The Secretary of State should enter into negotiations with the Government of France to allow the United States Government, in cooperation with the Government of France, to preserve the CSS ALABAMA from harm, begin

the recovery and conservation of its artifacts, and conduct other necessary activities, to explore and preserve the title and interest of the United States in this vessel.

SEC. 5. ADMINISTRATION.

(a) Subject to subsection (b), the Secretary of State shall conduct all bilateral negotiations regarding the CSS ALABAMA.

(b) The Secretary and Under Secretary are responsible for all scientific, cultural, and conservation activities of the United States directed at the CSS ALABAMA, unless, in the opinion of the Secretary of State, these activities would be detrimental to relations between the United States Government and the Government of France.

SEC. 6. REPORTS.

(a) Sixty days after the enactment of this Act, and annually thereafter, the Secretary of State shall prepare and transmit to Congress, the Secretary, and the Under Secretary, a report discussing the status of negotiations conducted under section 4 until the negotiations are completed.

(b) One year after the date of the enactment of this Act, and annually thereafter, the Secretary and the Under Secretary shall prepare and transmit to Congress a report on the plans for and status of the activities for which they are responsible under section 5 of this Act.

Notes

CHAPTER 1   The South Goes to Sea

1. Scharf, *Confederate States Navy*, 782.
2. Time-Life, *Blockade*, 143.
3. Semmes, *Service Afloat*, 402.
4. Hendrick, *Statesmen*, 367–68.
5. Ibid., 365.
6. Bulloch, *Secret Service*, 1:20.
7. Scharf, *Confederate States Navy*, 41–42.
8. Ibid., 42; Hendrick, *Statesmen*, 364; Soley, *Blockade and Cruisers*, 168.
9. Wise, *Lifeline*, 28.
10. Rhett, "Confederate Government," 107.
11. Scharf, *Confederate States Navy*, 41.
12. Nash, *Naval History*, 18–19; Hendrick, *Statesmen*, 373–74.
13. Soley, *Blockade and Cruisers*, 168.
14. Melton, "Pirate," 17; Semmes, *Service Afloat*, 93–94.
15. Semmes, *Service Afloat*, 94, 102, 107.
16. Hendrick, *Statesmen*, 365; Time-Life, *Blockade*, 143; Delaney, "'Old Beeswax,'" 11; Scharf, *Confederate States Navy*, 785n; Boykin, *Ghost Ship*, 30–31.
17. Delaney, "'Old Beeswax,'" 11–12; Scharf, *Confederate States Navy*, 785n; Boykin, *Ghost Ship*, 31.
18. Delaney, "'Old Beeswax,'" 11–12; quotation in Scharf, *Confederate States Navy*, 785n; Boykin, *Ghost Ship*, 31–34.
19. Scharf, *Confederate States Navy*, 785n; Delaney, "'Old Beeswax,'" 11–13.
20. Semmes, *Service Afloat*, 97.
21. Ibid., 98–99.
22. Ibid.

23. Bulloch, *Secret Service,* 2:294; Soley, *Blockade and Cruisers,* 170.
24. Semmes, *Service Afloat,* 103.
25. Ibid., 104–5.
26. Ibid., 105, 115–17, 127–28.
27. Ibid., 294–95, 297.
28. Ibid., 298–302.
29. Ibid., 303; Spencer, *Confederate Navy in Europe,* 33–34.
30. Semmes, *Service Afloat,* 306–9.
31. Ibid., 311–13, 329–32.
32. Ibid., 333–35.
33. Ibid., 342–45; Wise, *Lifeline,* 119; Nash, *Naval History,* 274.
34. Semmes, *Service Afloat,* 345.
35. Delaney, "Fight or Flee," 20.

CHAPTER 2   The Secret War of No. 290

1. Semmes, *Service Afloat,* 413; Summersell, *Alabama,* 4.
2. Bulloch, *Secret Service,* 1:57–58.
3. Ibid., 58–60.
4. Ibid., 226.
5. Semmes, *Service Afloat,* 347–48; Kell, *Recollections,* 178.
6. Semmes, *Service Afloat,* 348; Boykin, *Sea Devil,* 89.
7. Bulloch, *Secret Service,* 1:226–27.
8. Report of Matthew Maguire, May 16, 1862, in *Alabama* File; Hoole, *Four Years in the Confederate Navy,* 42–43.
9. Bulloch, *Secret Service,* 1:227, 251.
10. Ibid., 62; Semmes, *Service Afloat,* 400.
11. Maguire, March 28, 1862, *Alabama* File; Summersell, *Alabama,* 111. Before the days of electric lighting, a light room was placed next to the magazine, with a glass window opening into the powder storage area. Light from that room illuminated the magazine through the window, avoiding the need for an open flame around the powder.
12. Summersell, *Alabama,* 112; Bulloch, *Secret Service,* 2:287.
13. Maguire, July 15, 1862, *Alabama* File; Bulloch, *Secret Service,* 1:227–30; Boykin, *Ghost Ship,* 167. The sponsor's name was Henrietta. Her full identity has been lost to history.
14. Semmes, *Service Afloat,* 348–50; Semmes to Mallory, June 15, 1862, ibid., 352; Kell, *Recollections,* 181.
15. Semmes, *Service Afloat,* 349–51; Kell, *Recollections,* 180.
16. Semmes, *Service Afloat,* 351; Semmes to Commander J. H. North, June 8, 1862, *ORN,* Ser. 1, 1:771.
17. Semmes to Mallory, June 15, 1862, in Semmes, *Service Afloat,* 351–53. Lieutenant Howell was the brother-in-law of President Davis.
18. Semmes to North, June 8, 1862, *ORN,* Ser. 1, 1:771.
19. Semmes to Mallory, June 15, 1862, in Semmes, *Service Afloat,* 351–53.
20. Kell, *Recollections,* 182.

21. Duberman, *Adams,* 301, 293; Soley, *Blockade and Cruisers,* 190; Adams, *Charles Francis Adams,* 311, 313–14; Hoole, *Four Years in the Confederate Navy,* 43–44; Time-Life, *Blockade,* 121–22.

22. Adams, *Charles Francis Adams,* 307, 281–82, 310–11; Duberman, *Adams,* 294.

23. Maguire, June 13, 1862, *Alabama* File; Bulloch, *Secret Service,* 1:230–31, 236, 241; Sinclair, *Alabama,* 8, 262. Sinclair was the uncle of novelist Upton Sinclair.

24. Guernsey and Alden, comps., *Harper's Pictorial History,* 423; Adams, *Charles Francis Adams,* 314; Duberman, *Adams,* 293.

25. Bulloch, *Secret Service,* 1:238.

26. Adams, *Charles Francis Adams,* 314.

27. Guernsey and Alden, comps., *Harper's Pictorial History,* 423; Time-Life, *Blockade,* 122; Bulloch, *Secret Service,* 1:238–39; Hoole, *Four Years in the Confederate Navy,* 47–48.

28. Bulloch, *Secret Service,* 1:241–42.

29. Bulloch to J. M. Butcher, July 30, 1862, *ORN,* Ser. 1, 1:773–74; owners of the *Agrippina* to Alexander McQueen, July 28, 1862, ibid., 771–72; Bulloch, *Secret Service,* 1:245–48; Hoole, *Four Years in the Confederate Navy,* 50; Semmes had been promoted to captain that summer *(Service Afloat,* 368).

30. Semmes, *Service Afloat,* 353, 360, 402; Time-Life, *Blockade,* 142.

31. Semmes, *Service Afloat,* 402; Sinclair, *Alabama,* 109–10.

32. Kell, *Recollections,* 183.

33. Semmes, Journal of the *Alabama,* August 20, 1862, *ORN,* Ser. 1, 1:783. This source, parts of which appear in three volumes of the *ORN,* is hereafter cited as "Journal."

CHAPTER 3   The *Alabama*

1. Low, *Logs,* July 28–August 13, 1862, 1–3; Fullam, *Journal,* undated, 6. Fullam's name is sometimes spelled Fulham.

2. Fullam, *Journal,* undated, 6–10.

3. Ibid., August 18–20, 1862, 3–4; quotation in Semmes, *Service Afloat,* 404. The Confederate suspicion that the United States might violate neutrality was later confirmed when the USS *Wachusett* rammed, boarded, and captured the CSS *Florida* (formerly the *Oreto*) in a Brazilian port. Brazil protested and the United States apologized, but the South never regained the *Florida.*

4. Semmes, *Service Afloat,* 404; Sinclair, *Alabama,* 9.

5. Semmes, *Service Afloat,* 405; Journal, August 20, 1862, *ORN,* Ser. 1, 1:784.

6. Low, *Logs,* August 20, 1862, 4; Semmes, *Service Afloat,* 405.

7. Journal, August 20, 1862, *ORN,* Ser. 1, 1:784; Semmes, *Service Afloat,* 406.

8. Sinclair, *Alabama,* 9.

9. Low, *Logs,* August 21, 1862, 5; Semmes, *Service Afloat,* 406–7; Journal, August 21, 1862, *ORN,* Ser. 1, 1:784; Fullam, *Journal,* August 21, 1862, 12.

10. Low, *Logs,* August 22, 1862, 5–6.

11. Semmes, *Service Afloat,* 407–8; Journal, August 20–23, 1862, *ORN,* Ser. 1, 1:784–85; Sinclair, *Alabama,* 12.

12. Semmes, *Service Afloat,* 408–9; Sinclair, *Alabama,* 12.

13. Semmes (*Service Afloat*, 409–10), Kell (*Recollections*, 187), and Fullam (*Journal*, August 24, 1862, 14) state that the captain himself read the commission and orders. Low, however (*Logs*, August 25, 1862, 7), says that these were read by Smith, after which Semmes addressed the crew. In the Journal (August 24, 1862, *ORN*, Ser. 1, 1:785), Semmes makes no mention of a reading of orders or commission, only that he addressed the crew about the nature of the voyage. Low and Fullam both recorded the event shortly after it happened, but in view of the greater attention to detail in Low's account, it is the version used here.

14. Fullam, *Journal*, August 24, 1862, 14; Semmes, *Service Afloat*, 409–12; Journal, August 24, 1862, *ORN*, Ser. 1, 1:785.

15. Sinclair, *Alabama*, 14.

16. Semmes, *Service Afloat*, 412–13; Bulloch to Mallory, September 10, 1862, *ORN*, Ser. 1, 1:776–77; Journal, August 24, 1862, ibid., 785–86.

CHAPTER 4   Flames in the Azores

1. Semmes, *Service Afloat*, 413; Journal, August 25, 1862, *ORN*, Ser. 1, 1:785–86.

2. Figures from design specifications quoted in Summersell, *Alabama*, 108.

3. Ibid., 113; Semmes, *Service Afloat*, 402–3; Sinclair, *Alabama*, 3, 7.

4. Sinclair, *Alabama*, 20; Semmes, *Service Afloat*, 419–20.

5. Semmes, *Service Afloat*, 403; Summersell, *Alabama*, 108.

6. Semmes, *Service Afloat*, 403; Sinclair, *Alabama*, 7.

7. *ORN*, Ser. 1, 1:782; Sinclair, *Alabama*, 14; Maguire, Report, July 14, 1862, *Alabama* File.

8. Semmes, *Service Afloat*, 415–17. Semmes refused to mention Yonge by name, and his opinion of the paymaster seems to have been shared even by some Union officers. Until his defection to the Union side, however, Yonge appears to have done a credible job. When he joined the ship at Liverpool, Bulloch told him, "When Captain Semmes joins, you will at once report to him and act thereafter under his instructions. He will be a stranger to the ship and crew, and will be in a position of great responsibility and embarrassment. You have it in your power to smooth away some of his difficulties in advance . . . and I confidently rely upon your exertions to bring about such a state of things" (Bulloch to C. R. Yonge, July 28, 1862, *ORN*, Ser. 1, 1:773). In view of the "indiscretion" Fullam noted in the Azores, however, one wonders whether Yonge may have been a Union spy during his entire service aboard the *Alabama*.

9. Semmes, *Service Afloat*, 418–19. Some muster rolls list Bartelli as Portuguese, but Civil War muster rolls are not always accurate. Semmes always referred to him as Italian, and the name "Bartelli" does not occur in the Portuguese language.

10. Ibid., 419; Journal, August 25, 1862, *ORN*, Ser. 1, 1:786.

11. "A jack tar. . . . adventure and prize money," Wilkinson, *Narrative*, 161–62; "sustained their reputation nobly," Kell, "Cruise and Combats," 603n; Sinclair, *Alabama*, 19; Semmes, *Service Afloat*, 419.

12. Kell, *Recollections*, 301–2.

13. Sinclair, *Alabama*, 22–23.

14. Semmes, *Service Afloat,* 423–42; Low, *Logs,* September 6, 1862, 9; Journal, September 5–6, 1862, *ORN, Ser.* 1, 1:787–88; Fullam, *Journal,* September 5, 1862, 16.

15. Semmes, *Service Afloat,* 426–27.

16. Ibid., 428–29; Journal, September 7, 1862, *ORN,* Ser. 1, 1:788.

17. Journal, *ORN,* Ser. 1, 1:788; Semmes, *Service Afloat,* 429–30; Kell, *Recollections,* 191.

18. Semmes, *Service Afloat,* 430; Low, *Logs,* September 9, 1864, 11.

19. Journal, September 8, 1862, *ORN,* Ser. 1, 1:788.

20. Semmes, *Service Afloat,* 431–33.

21. Ibid., 433–35.

22. Kell, *Recollections,* 190–91; Journal, September 9, 1862, *ORN,* Ser. 1, 1:789.

23. Semmes, *Service Afloat,* 437–38.

24. Fullam, *Journal,* undated, 21.

25. Ibid., September 14, 1862, 22.

26. Journal, September 11, 1862, *ORN,* Ser. 1, 1:789; Kell, *Recollections,* 191–92.

27. Semmes, *Service Afloat,* 444.

28. Journal, September 19, 1862, *ORN,* Ser. 1, 1:791.

29. Journal, September 21–28, 1862, ibid., 791–92.

30. Journal, September 28, 1862, ibid., 792.

CHAPTER 5   Storm

1. Semmes, *Service Afloat,* 449.

2. Ibid., 450–51.

3. Ibid., 452.

4. Ibid., 453–55; Low, *Logs,* October 1, 1862, 21.

5. Journal, September 30–October 1, 1863, *ORN,* Ser. 1, 1:792; Semmes, *Service Afloat,* 457; Low, *Logs,* October 1, 1862, 21; Fullam, *Journal,* October 1, 1862, 28.

6. Semmes, *Service Afloat,* 458, 449; Fullam, *Journal,* October 3, 1862, 29. *ORN,* Ser. 1, 3:677, says the *Emily Farnum* was released without bond.

7. Fullam, *Journal,* October 3, 1862, 29.

8. Semmes, *Service Afloat,* 458; Low, *Logs,* October 5, 1862, 22–23.

9. Semmes, *Service Afloat,* 460–61; Journal, October 7, 1862, *ORN,* Ser. 1, 1:793.

10. Semmes, *Service Afloat,* 462.

11. Low, *Logs,* October 9, 1862, 24.

12. Journal, October 9, 1862, *ORN,* Ser. 1, 1:794; Semmes, *Service Afloat,* 464.

13. Journal, October 10, 1862, *ORN,* Ser. 1, 1:794; Semmes, *Service Afloat,* 462; Low, *Logs,* October 10, 1862, 25.

14. Semmes, *Service Afloat,* 467; Journal, October 12, 1862, *ORN,* Ser. 1, 1:795.

15. Journal, October 13, 1862, *ORN,* Ser. 1, 1:795.

16. Sinclair, *Alabama,* 32; Semmes, *Service Afloat,* 465–66.

17. Kell, *Recollections,* 193.

18. Journal, October 16, 1862, *ORN,* Ser. 1, 1:796; Kell, *Recollections,* 194; Sinclair, *Alabama,* 37–38; Semmes, *Service Afloat,* 473–74. Fullam (*Journal,* October 16,

1862, 36) says a storm trysail was bent, but no doubt he meant the staysail. A trysail was simply too much canvas to use in a storm of such magnitude.

19. Journal, October 16, 1862, *ORN,* Ser. 1, 1:796; Semmes, *Service Afloat,* 474–75; Low, *Logs,* October 16, 1862, 28.

20. Journal, October 16, 1862, *ORN,* Ser. 1, 1:796; Semmes, *Service Afloat,* 474; Kell, *Recollections,* 194. In a picture caption on page 39 of his memoirs, Sinclair credited Low's "superb seamanship and coolness in 'wearing' ship from the port tack, without awaiting the commander's orders," which he said, "*doubtless* saved the Alabama from foundering. Had he hesitated *five* minutes, the manoeuvre would have been impossible of execution, owing to the fury of the wind." Hoole quotes this caption on page 64 of his biography of Low. Sinclair, however, did not mention Low's action in his text, nor does Semmes say anything about it in his journal. In *Service Afloat* Semmes attributes their survival largely to the seakeeping abilities of the ship: "She behaved nobly, and I breathed easier after the first half hour of the storm." Low's account of the storm is primarily a report of the damage.

21. Journal, October 19–22, *ORN,* Ser. 1, 1:797; Fullam, *Journal,* October 23, 1862, 41.

22. Sinclair, *Alabama,* 37.

23. Journal, October 30, November 2, 8, 1863, *ORN,* Ser. 1, 1:802–3; Semmes, *Service Afloat,* 492–94. Semmes's message to the New York Chamber of Commerce is in Fullam, *Journal,* October 29, 1862, 45.

24. Journal, November 8, 1862, *ORN,* Ser. 1, 1:803–4; Semmes, *Service Afloat,* 494–96.

25. Semmes, *Service Afloat,* 495–96; Sinclair, *Alabama,* 42. Confederate accounts consistently refer to Fairchild as a U.S. consul, but there is no record of a consul by that name with the Department of State so he may have been a minor official (see ibid., 42n).

26. Semmes, *Service Afloat,* 497.

27. Ibid., 496.

CHAPTER 6   Lincoln's Dilemma

1. Scharf, *Confederate States Navy,* 41–42; Welles, *Diary,* November 4, 1862, 1:179; October 18, 1862, 1:175; and December 26, 1863, 1:497.

2. Sandburg, *Lincoln,* 3:344–45. Sandburg quotes a letter dated April 23, 1863, and ostensibly written by one Melton of the *Boston Gazette,* which was supposedly "printed in scores of newspapers, reaching a large section of the literate population of the country." There is some question as to the reliability of the account, particularly because the normally gossipy Welles makes no mention of any séance in his diary during the month of April 1863.

3. Sandburg, *Lincoln,* 2:107–8.

4. Ibid., 2:524; Welles, *Diary,* September 25, 1863, 1:443.

5. Duberman, *Adams,* 300–302; Welles, *Diary,* December 26, 1863, 1:497.

6. Journal, November 11–12, 1862, *ORN,* Ser. 1, 1:804.

7. Journal, November 11, 16, 1862, ibid., 804–5; Semmes, *Service Afloat,* 509.

8. Semmes, *Service Afloat,* 509–14; Journal, November 18, 1862, *ORN,* Ser. 1, 1:805.

9. Semmes, *Service Afloat,* 510–11.

10. Ibid., 511–13; Kell, *Recollections,* 197–98; Journal, November, 18, 1862, *ORN,* Ser. 1, 1:805; Fullam, *Journal,* undated, 53–54. Semmes and Kell, writing after the war, recalled that the men shouted defiance while being doused. Fullam, however, writing within days of the event, says the men were gagged "with a few exceptions." Fullam's account, being more timely, is used here.

11. Semmes, *Service Afloat,* 514; Journal, November 19, 1862, *ORN,* Ser. 1, 1:805; Sinclair, *Alabama,* 43.

12. Semmes, *Service Afloat,* 514–16; Journal, November 19, 1862, *ORN,* Ser. 1, 1:805–6; Fullam, *Journal,* undated, 53.

13. Quotation in Semmes, *Service Afloat,* 517; Kell, *Recollections,* 199.

14. Journal, November 21, 1862, *ORN,* Ser. 1, 1:806.

15. Kell, *Recollections,* 199.

16. Semmes, *Service Afloat,* 517–18; Journal, November 25, 1862, *ORN,* Ser. 1, 1:807; Sinclair, *Alabama,* 46.

17. Journal, November 26, 28, 1862, *ORN,* Ser. 1, 1:807; Semmes, *Service Afloat,* 519.

18. Semmes, *Service Afloat,* 519–20.

19. Ibid., 519.

20. Journal, November 28, 1862, *ORN,* Ser. 1, 1:807; Fullam, *Journal,* December 1, 1862, 59.

21. Semmes, *Service Afloat,* 520.

22. Journal, November 29, 1862, *ORN,* Ser. 1, 1:807.

23. Semmes, *Service Afloat,* 522. The *Iroquois* was a favorite ruse of Semmes's, probably because she had blockaded the *Sumter.*

24. Ibid., 523.

25. Sinclair, *Alabama,* 30.

26. Semmes, *Service Afloat,* 527–28; Kell, *Recollections,* 203.

27. Journal, December 5, 1862, *ORN,* Ser. 1, 1:810.

28. Journal, December 7, 1862, ibid., 811; Semmes, *Service Afloat,* 529–30.

29. Kell, *Recollections,* 203.

30. Journal, December 7, 1862, *ORN,* Ser. 1, 1:811; Read, *Pioneer,* 132.

31. Journal, December 7, 1862, *ORN,* Ser. 1, 1:811; Semmes, *Service Afloat,* 532–33; Read, *Pioneer,* 132–33 and 133n.

32. Kell, *Recollections,* 205–6. Low's log does not comment, other than to note that the capture occurred.

33. Read, *Pioneer,* 134–35; Kell, *Recollections,* 205.

34. Journal, December 8–9, 1862, *ORN,* Ser. 1, 1:811.

35. Journal, December 9, 1862, ibid., 811–12. According to Kell (*Recollections,* 204–5), the *Ariel*'s women passengers waved and cheered when the *Alabama* departed. Sinclair (*Alabama,* 54) added that the boarding officers were entertained with a champagne dinner in the *Ariel*'s saloon with toasts to Presidents Lincoln and Davis. This may have been true, but from the passenger side, Read (*Pioneer,* 137–38) said: "I never felt so indignant as I did when cut throats were over me with sword and pistol, and I a prisoner. . . . All in all [*Alabama*] is an ugly, a very ugly, customer. I hope

to hear soon that one of our men of war has met and captured her." If the passengers and crew seemed cheerful at the *Alabama*'s departure, it could well have meant they were glad to see the last of her.

36. Journal, December 10–15, 1862, *ORN*, Ser. 1, 1:812; December 21, 1862, ibid., 813; December 23, 1862, ibid., 814.

37. Sinclair, *Alabama*, 56.

38. Kell, *Recollections*, 207; Fullam, *Journal*, December 25, 1862, 68.

39. Journal, December 25, 1862, *ORN*, Ser. 1, 1:814–15.

CHAPTER 7   Battle

1. Welles, *Diary*, December 29, 1862, 1:207.

2. Fullam, *Journal*, January 5, 1863, 69–70.

3. Welles, *Diary*, January 1, 1863, 1:212.

4. Journal, January 1, 1863, *ORN*, Ser. 1, 1:816.

5. Welles, *Diary*, September 4, 1862, 1:109.

6. Charles Wilkes to Welles, January 2, 1863, *ORN*, Ser. 1, 2:5–7.

7. Wilkes to Welles, January 2, 1863, second letter, ibid., 7–8.

8. Wilkes to Commander D. B. Ridgely, January 3, 1863, ibid., 9; Welles, *Diary*, January 6, 1863, 1:217. Condemned blockade runners and their cargoes were sold and the prize money prorated among the officers and men of the ship that made the capture. The largest share, of course, went to the commander of the blockading squadron, in this case, Admiral Wilkes.

9. C. H. Baldwin to Welles, January 17, 1863, *ORN*, Ser. 1, 2:37–38.

10. Sinclair, *Alabama*, 57–58n.

11. Fehrenbach, *Lone Star*, 369.

12. Journal, January 11, 1863, *ORN*, Ser. 1, 2:721.

13. Ibid.

14. Semmes, *Service Afloat*, 541; Sinclair, *Alabama*, 60. After the 1900 hurricane, in which about six thousand people drowned in the storm surge, the elevation of the island under the entire city of Galveston was raised six feet and seawalls constructed, giving the island a higher profile.

15. Journal, January 11, 1863, *ORN*, Ser. 1, 2:721; H. C. Blake to Welles, January 21, 1863, ibid., 18.

16. Semmes, *Service Afloat*, 542; Journal, January 11, 1863, *ORN*, Ser. 1, 1:721.

17. Blake to Welles, January 21, 1863, *ORN*, Ser. 1, 2:18; Statistical Data of U.S. Ships, *ORN*, Ser. 2, 1:100. The Statistical Data do not mention the Parrott gun, which was listed in Blake's report to Welles.

18. Journal, January 11, 1863, *ORN*, Ser. 1, 2:721; Blake to Welles, January 21, 1863, ibid., 19; Low, *Logs*, undated, 33; Kell, *Recollections*, 208; Sinclair, *Alabama*, 61. Blake reported that the *Alabama* identified herself as the British warship *Vixen*, and L. H. Partridge, who commanded the boarding party, said he heard the name *Spitfire*. The Confederates are unanimous that the name *Petrel* was used. The Confederate sources, viz., the ship's journal and accounts by Low, Semmes, Sinclair, and Kell are accepted here.

19. Quotation from Journal, January 11, 1863, *ORN*, Ser. 1, 2:721; Blake to Welles, ibid.; Sinclair, *Alabama*, 61; Low, *Logs*, undated, 33; Kell, *Recollections*, 208; Semmes, *Service Afloat*, 543. In their memoirs, Semmes, Kell, and Sinclair indicated that they heard Blake say that he was sending a boat. The ship's journal and Low's account, written soon after the fight, however, both stated that the Union reply could not be understood. Semmes wrote *Service Afloat* after the war, and Kell and Sinclair compiled their memoirs decades later. Semmes and Kell had both read Blake's report, Semmes quoted it in full, and it is probable that they and Sinclair worked it into their own narratives.

20. Kell, *Recollections*, 208–9; Sinclair, *Alabama*, 61.

21. L. H. Partridge to Rear Admiral D. G. Farragut, January 12, 1863, *ORN*, Ser. 1, 2:21.

22. Fullam, *Journal*, January 11, 1863, 76.

23. Blake to Welles, January 21, 1863, *ORN*, Ser. 1, 2:19; Journal, January 11, 1863, ibid., 722; Sinclair, *Alabama*, 62; Fullam, *Journal*, January 11, 1863, 71–72.

24. Blake to Welles, January 21, 1863, *ORN*, Ser. 1, 2:19; Journal, January 11, 1863, ibid., 722; Partridge to Farragut, ibid., 21–22; Low, *Logs*, undated, 33.

25. Journal, January 11, 1863, *ORN*, Ser. 1, 2:722; Blake to Welles, January 21, 1863, ibid., 19; Edward S. Matthews, assistant surgeon, U.S. Navy, to Blake, January 21, 1863, ibid., 20–21.

26. Bell to Farragut, January 12, 1863, *ORN*, Ser. 1, 19:506–7.

27. Bell to Farragut, January 12, 1863, ibid., 507; Farragut to Welles, January 15, 1863, ibid., 506. The *Florida* escaped from Mobile and put to sea.

28. Parole of officers of USS *Hatteras*, January 11, 1863, *ORN*, Ser. 1, 2:21; Sinclair, *Alabama*, 61, 64; Low, *Logs*, undated, 34.

29. Blake to Welles, January 27, 1863, *ORN*, Ser. 1, 2:22.

30. Kell, *Recollections*, 209.

31. Sinclair, *Alabama*, 64–66; Journal, *ORN*, Ser. 1, 2:722–23.

32. Journal, January 20–24, 1863, *ORN*, Ser. 1, 2:724–25; Kell, *Recollections*, 210; Sinclair, *Alabama*, 67–68.

33. Semmes, *Service Afloat*, 559; Sinclair, *Alabama*, 68. Although Paymaster Yonge reportedly found work as one of Charles Francis Adams's agents, not all U.S. officials were impressed with him. Captain Baldwin of the *Vanderbilt* was told, probably by Vice-Consul John Camp, that Yonge was a "worthless fellow," a statement Baldwin repeated to Secretary Welles (Baldwin to Welles, February 16, 1863, *ORN*, Ser. 1, 2:86).

34. Semmes, *Service Afloat*, 559–61; Sinclair, *Alabama*, 69; Journal, January 25, 1863, *ORN*, Ser. 1, 2:724.

35. Journal, January 25, 1863, *ORN*, Ser. 1, 2:724; Blake to Welles, January 27, 1863, ibid., 22; Semmes, *Service Afloat*, 547, 561–62.

36. Blake to Welles, January 27, 1863, *ORN*, Ser. 1, 2:22.

37. Welles to Blake, March 23, 1863, ibid., 22–23.

CHAPTER 8   The Glory Days

1. Semmes, *Service Afloat*, 564.

2. Ibid., 561, 564–65; Sinclair, *Alabama*, 69.

3. Journal, January 26–29, 1863, *ORN*, Ser. 1, 2:724–25.
4. Sinclair, *Alabama*, 99.
5. Baldwin to Welles, February 16, 1863, *ORN*, Ser. 1, 2:85–88.
6. Journal, January 29–February 1, 1863, ibid., 725–26.
7. Journal, February 2, 1863, ibid., 726; Semmes, *Service Afloat*, 575–76.
8. Journal, February 3, 1863, *ORN*, Ser. 1, 2:726; Sinclair, *Alabama*, 71.
9. Sinclair, *Alabama*, 72.
10. Semmes, *Service Afloat*, 582–83.
11. Journal, February 11, 1863, *ORN*, Ser. 1, 2:727; March 25, 1863, ibid., 735.
12. Journal, February 15, 1863, ibid., 728.
13. Journal, February 21, March 1–2, 15–23, 1863, ibid., 730–31, 733–34.
14. Journal, March 2, 25–27, 1863, ibid., 731–32, 735–36.
15. Journal, April 4–10, 1863, ibid., 736–38.
16. Kell, *Recollections*, 216; quotation from Semmes, *Service Afloat*, 595; Boykin, *Ghost Ship*, 290.
17. Bulloch, *Secret Service*, 2:267.
18. Sinclair, *Alabama*, 89; Semmes, *Service Afloat*, 597–98.
19. Semmes, *Service Afloat*, 598; Sinclair, *Alabama*, 90–91; Journal, April 11, 1863, *ORN*, Ser. 1, 2:738.
20. Semmes, *Service Afloat*, 598–99; Journal, April 12, 1863, *ORN*, Ser. 1, 2:739; Sinclair, *Alabama*, 90, 92, 95.
21. Kell, *Recollections*, 218; Sinclair, *Alabama*, 92; Journal, April 18, 1863, *ORN*, Ser. 1, 2:740.
22. Journal, April 11, 1863, *ORN*, Ser. 1, 2:738.
23. Journal, April 15, 1863, ibid., 740; Sinclair, *Alabama*, 93.
24. Journal, April 16–17, 21, 1863, *ORN*, Ser. 1, 2:740–41.
25. Journal, April 19, 1863, ibid., 741.
26. Journal, April 22, 1862, ibid., 741; Semmes, *Service Afloat*, 611; Bulloch, *Secret Service*, 2:267.
27. Journal, April 22–May 5, 1863, *ORN*, Ser. 1, 2:741–43.
28. Journal, May 7, 1863, ibid., 743; Semmes, *Service Afloat*, 613.
29. Sinclair, *Alabama*, 101–2.
30. Ibid., 101.
31. Ibid., 107; Semmes, *Service Afloat*, 615–18; Journal, May 11–12, 1863, *ORN*, Ser. 1, 2:743.
32. Journal, May 13, 1863, *ORN*, Ser. 1, 2:743; Sinclair, *Alabama*, 101. Pernambuco is now Recife.
33. Sinclair, *Alabama*, 108.

CHAPTER 9   The *Tuscaloosa* and Cape Town

1. Kell, *Recollections*, 219–20; Sinclair, *Alabama*, 109; Journal, May 15, 1863, *ORN*, Ser. 1, 2:744. Kell has little to say about this entire portion of the cruise, passing it off in a few pages, which are largely an inventory of ships encountered. Instead

of his usual day-to-day entries, Low's account for this period is a brief synopsis of events since late December.

2. Journal, May 12, 1863, *ORN*, Ser. 1, 2:743; Semmes, *Service Afloat*, 617.

3. Journal, May 15, 1863, *ORN*, Ser. 1, 2:744.

4. Journal, May 16–20, 1863, ibid., 744–45; Semmes, *Service Afloat*, 618–19.

5. Bulloch, *Secret Service*, 2:268–69.

6. Semmes, *Service Afloat*, 621; Sinclair, *Alabama*, 111.

7. Semmes, *Service Afloat*, 622; Journal, May 29, 1863, *ORN*, Ser. 1, 2:746. Semmes (*Service Afloat*, 622) and Sinclair (*Alabama*, 112) both list the *Jabez Snow* as being from Buckport, but the ship's journal says Rockport.

8. Sinclair, *Alabama*, 112.

9. Semmes, *Service Afloat*, 623–24; Sinclair, *Alabama*, 112–14.

10. Journal, June 2–5, 1863, *ORN*, Ser. 1, 2:748.

11. Semmes, *Service Afloat*, 625. Just as New Englanders viewed Southern slavery as odious, many Southerners considered New England's opium trade with China equally reprehensible. The regional misunderstandings were aggravated even more by New England's laissez-faire brand of Calvinism, which made business and religion extensions of each other and supported an aggressive missionary effort in China. As Southerners saw it, New England's evangelical work went hand-in-glove with the narcotics trade and thus cloaked it in hypocrisy.

12. Sinclair, *Alabama*, 115; Journal, June 5, 1863, *ORN*, Ser. 1, 2:748.

13. Journal, June 6, 1863, *ORN*, Ser. 1, 2:749.

14. Journal, June 7–16, 1863, ibid., 749–50.

15. Wilkes to Welles, June 9, 1863, ibid., 262–63; Welles, *Diary*, May 29, 1863, 1:316.

16. Welles, *Diary*, May 29, 1863, 1:316; May 16, 1863, 304–5.

17. Ibid., May 16, 1863, 304–5. Elsewhere in this diary entry, Welles indicated that he had two options: permanently dry-dock Wilkes without any command position or reassign him from the West Indies to the Pacific command. He also stated that he considered Wilkes too unstable to hold a position of command and power.

18. Ibid., May 29, 1863, 1:316.

19. Baldwin to Welles, July 23, 1863, ibid., 407–9.

20. Journal, June 20, 1862, *ORN*, Ser. 1, 2:750–51; Semmes, *Service Afloat*, 627; Low, *Logs*, June 21, 1862, 35.

21. Semmes, *Service Afloat*, 627.

22. Journal, June 21, 27, 1863, *ORN*, Ser. 1, 2:751–52; Kell, *Recollections*, 221.

23. Journal, June 28, 29, 1863, *ORN*, Ser. 1, 2:752–53.

24. Journal, July 2–29, 1863, ibid., 753–57.

25. Kell, *Recollections*, 222–23; Journal, July 30–August 1, 1863, *ORN*, Ser. 1, 2:757–58.

26. Journal, July 30–August 3, 1863, *ORN*, Ser. 1, 2:757–58; Sinclair, *Alabama*, 126–27.

27. Sinclair, *Alabama*, 130–31; Semmes, *Service Afloat*, 640.

28. Semmes, *Service Afloat,* 641; Sinclair, *Alabama,* 131.
29. Journal, August 5, 1863, *ORN,* Ser. 1, 2:759; Sinclair, *Alabama,* 133.

CHAPTER 10   Hound and Hare with the *Vanderbilt*

1. Quoted in Soley, *Blockade and Cruisers,* 199–200.
2. Journal, August 5–6, 1863, *ORN,* Ser. 1, 2:759.
3. Journal, August 6–8, 1863, ibid., 759–60; Kell, *Recollections,* 229.
4. Kell, *Recollections,* 228–29.
5. Journal, August 6–7, 1863, *ORN,* Ser. 1, 2:759; Kell, *Recollections,* 229.
6. Sinclair, *Alabama,* 134–35.
7. Edward Cooper to Messrs. C. J. and F. W. Coggill, August 19, 1863, *ORN,* Ser. 1, 2:428–29.
8. Journal, August 9–30, 1863, ibid., 760–62; Low, *Logs,* August 19–20, 1863, 53.
9. Journal, September 13, 1863, *ORN,* Ser. 1, 2:765.
10. Baldwin to Welles, August 17, 1863, ibid., 426–27. Union and Confederate accounts both state that coal sold for $11 to $12 per ton in the Brazilian ports.
11. Baldwin to Welles, August 20, 1863, ibid., 429–30.
12. Baldwin to Welles, September 11, 1863, ibid., 445–47.
13. Kell, *Recollections,* 229.
14. Sinclair, *Alabama,* 140–42; Journal, September 4, 1863, *ORN,* Ser. 1, 2:763.
15. Journal, September 16, 1863, *ORN,* Ser. 1, 2:765; August 14, 1863, ibid., 760.
16. Semmes, *Service Afloat,* 668. The *Alabama* got around the neutrality proclamation by dividing her time between Saldanha Bay, Cape Town, and Simon's Bay, leaving British waters when she moved from one anchorage to the other.
17. Ibid., 668–69.
18. Kell, *Recollections,* 230.
19. Semmes, *Service Afloat,* 669–70, 672; Journal, September 18–20, 1863, *ORN,* Ser. 1, 2:765–66.
20. Fullam, *Journal,* September 23, 1863, 140, October 25, 1863, 146.
21. Journal, September 23–24, 1863, *ORN,* Ser. 1, 2:766; Sinclair, *Alabama,* 272–73.
22. Journal, September 24–27, 1863, *ORN,* Ser. 1, 2:766–68.
23. Baldwin to Welles, October 5, 1863, ibid., 466–68.
24. Baldwin to Welles, October 30, 1863, ibid., 480–81.

CHAPTER 11   "My Ship Is Weary"

1. Semmes, *Service Afloat,* 674, 678; Sinclair, *Alabama,* 152.
2. Journal, October 3, 6, 14, 16, 1863, *ORN,* Ser. 1, 2:769, 771, 773–74; Semmes, *Service Afloat,* 685.
3. Journal, October 22–26, 1863, *ORN,* Ser. 1, 2:776–77; Sinclair, *Alabama,* 153.
4. Journal, October 26–28, 1863, *ORN,* Ser. 1, 2:777–78; Semmes, *Service Afloat,* 687.
5. Wilson, "*Alabama* in Southeast Asian Waters," 34–35.
6. Ibid., 39; Semmes, *Service Afloat,* 687–88; Journal, October 30–November 6, 1863, *ORN,* Ser. 1, 2:779; Sinclair, *Alabama,* 155; Summersell, commentary on Fullam, *Journal,* 152.

7. Semmes, *Service Afloat,* 689–92; Sinclair, *Alabama,* 159; Journal, November 8–11, 1863, *ORN, Ser.* 1, 2:779–80.

8. Journal, November 12, 1863, *ORN,* Ser. 1, 2:781; Semmes, *Service Afloat,* 693–95; Sinclair, *Alabama,* 161–63.

9. Sinclair, *Alabama,* 160; Journal, November 13, 17, 1863, *ORN,* Ser. 1, 2:781–82; Wilson, "*Alabama* in Southeast Asian Waters," 39; Fullam, *Journal,* November 17, 1863, 160.

10. Journal, November 19–20, 1863, *ORN,* Ser. 1, 2:782.

11. Journal, November 22, 1863, ibid.

12. Journal, November 22–December 2, 1863, ibid., 782–84.

13. Sinclair, *Alabama,* 164.

14. Journal, December 3–7, 1863, *ORN,* Ser. 1, 2:785–86.

15. Sinclair, *Alabama,* 167–68, 172.

16. Journal, December 5, 7, 1863, *ORN,* Ser. 1, 2:785–86.

17. Journal, December 7, 1863, ibid., 786; Sinclair, *Alabama,* 170.

18. Journal, December 9–10, 1863, *ORN,* Ser. 1, 2:787–88.

19. Wilson, "*Alabama* in Southeast Asian Waters," 37, 41–42.

20. Journal, December 15, 1863, *ORN,* Ser. 1, 2:789.

21. Ibid.

22. Journal, December 22–23, 1863, ibid., 791–92; Sinclair, *Alabama,* 178–79; Semmes, *Service Afloat,* 711.

23. Journal, December 22–23, 1863, *ORN,* Ser. 1, 2:791–92; Semmes, *Service Afloat,* 709.

24. Wilson, "*Alabama* in Southeast Asian Waters," 45.

25. Sinclair, *Alabama,* 180–81.

26. Kell, *Recollections,* 237; Semmes, *Service Afloat,* 717; Journal, December 24, 1863, *ORN,* Ser. 1, 2:792; Wilson, "*Alabama* in Southeast Asian Waters," 47–48.

27. Semmes, *Service Afloat,* 718; Kell, *Recollections,* 238; Summersell, commentary on Fullam, *Journal,* 168.

28. Wilson, "*Alabama* in Southeast Asian Waters," 47–50.

29. Journal, December 25–26, 1863, *ORN,* Ser. 1, 2:793, January 16, 1864, ibid., 795; Kell, *Recollections,* 398–99.

30. Journal, January 16, 1864, *ORN,* Ser. 1, 2:796; Kell, *Recollections,* 239.

31. Journal, February 28, 1864, *ORN,* Ser. 1, 2:803; Sinclair, *Alabama,* 205–6; Fullam, *Journal,* February 27, 1864, 177, March 6, 1864, 178.

32. Journal, March 4, 1864, *ORN,* Ser. 1, 2:804; March 11, 1864, ibid., 804, March 20, 1864, ibid., 806.

CHAPTER 12   Cherbourg

1. Journal, March 21, 1864, *ORN,* Ser. 1, 2:806; Wodehouse to the Duke of Newcastle, Secretary of State for Colonies, January 11, 1864, ibid., 714; Low, *Logs,* December 26–28, 1863, 86–87.

2. Low to Flag Officer Samuel Barron, February 29, 1864; Newcastle to Wodehouse, March 4, 1864, both in *ORN,* Ser. 1, 2:715. Because it was no longer feasible to

operate the *Tuscaloosa,* she was sold at auction to Simon's Town Ship Co. for £350; see Hoole, *Four Years in the Confederate Navy,* 105–7.

3. Journal, March 29, 1864, *ORN,* Ser. 1, 2:807; Semmes to Walker, quoted in Semmes, *Service Afloat,* 739–42.

4. Semmes, *Service Afloat,* 745; Sinclair, *Alabama,* 213–16; Kell, *Recollections,* 241–42.

5. Semmes, *Service Afloat,* 745.

6. Ibid., 745; Journal, March 25, 1864, *ORN,* Ser. 1, 2:806.

7. Semmes, *Service Afloat,* 745–48; Kell, *Recollections,* 242.

8. Journal, April 3, 1864, *ORN,* Ser. 1, 3:669.

9. Journal, April 17, 1864, ibid., 670; Sinclair, *Alabama,* 216. This *Express* is not on the official list of prizes (see Appendix 2).

10. Journal, April 23, 1864, *ORN,* Ser. 1, 3:671; Sinclair, *Alabama,* 217.

11. Journal, April 27–28, 1864, *ORN,* Ser. 1, 3:672; Sinclair, *Alabama,* 218, also "General Muster Roll" at the end of the book, no pagination.

12. Kell, *Recollections,* 242.

13. Journal, May 21, 1864, *ORN,* Ser. 1, 3:674.

14. Journal, May 21, 25–26, 1864, ibid., 674.

15. Journal, May 12, 1864, ibid., 673, May 24, 1864, ibid., 674; Semmes to Barron, July 5, 1864, ibid., 664.

16. Journal, June 10, 1864, ibid., 676.

17. Ellicott, *Winslow,* 194.

18. Journal, June 11, 1864, *ORN,* Ser. 1, 3:676.

19. Semmes to Barron, June 13, 1864, ibid., 651; Semmes, *Service Afloat,* 749–50; Spencer, *Confederate Navy in Europe,* 190.

20. Spencer, *Confederate Navy in Europe,* 178–80, 184–85; John Slidell to Secretary of State (Judah P. Benjamin), June 30, 1864, *ORN,* Ser. 1, 3:658.

21. Semmes, *Service Afloat,* 751; Browne, "Duel," 615; Fisher, *Diary,* undated, 82. A North Carolinian, Winslow opted to remain in U.S. service when his state seceded. Although he doubtless suffered the anxieties that many felt over disruption of the Union, there never appears to have been any question that he would remain loyal to the federal government (see Ellicott, *Winslow,* 67–70).

22. Semmes, *Service Afloat,* 751; Semmes to Barron, June 14, 1864, *ORN,* Ser. 1, 3:651.

23. Journal, June 13–14, 1864, *ORN,* Ser. 1, 3:677.

24. Browne, "Duel," 615.

25. Semmes, *Service Afloat,* 753.

26. Quoted in Delaney, "End of the *Alabama,*" 58.

27. Ibid., 59–60; Kell, *Recollections,* 245.

28. Semmes to Ad. Bonfils, June 14, 1864, *ORN,* Ser. 1, 3:648.

29. Delaney, "End of the *Alabama,*" 60; Fisher, *Diary,* June 16, 1864, 83.

30. Journal, June 14, 1864, *ORN,* Ser. 1, 3:677; Fullam, *Journal,* June 14, 1864, 190. The reference to mizzen yards, which appears in several Confederate sources, is confusing. As a three-masted bark, the *Alabama* was square-rigged with crossyards only on the fore- and mainmasts; the mizzen had gaff and spanker booms in place of crossyards. All plans and drawings of the *Alabama,* as well as the builder's model,

show this sail plan. Therefore, one wonders exactly what yards might have been on the mizzenmast.

31. Sinclair, *Alabama*, 222.

32. Bonfils to Slidell, June 18, 1864, *ORN*, Ser. 1, 3:661–62; Slidell to Bonfils, June 19, 1864, ibid., 662–63.

33. Journal, June 15, 1864, ibid., 677.

34. Kell, *Recollections*, 245, 252; Winslow to Welles, June 20, 1864, *ORN*, Ser. 1, 3:59–60; Semmes, *Service Afloat*, 752–53; Spencer, *Confederate Navy in Europe*, 187–88.

35. The Minister of the Marine and the Colonies to Monsieur the Vice-Admiral, Maritime Prefect at Cherbourg, June 15, 1864, *ORN*, Ser. 1, 3:58–59.

36. Spencer, *Confederate Navy in Europe*, 185–86.

37. Ellicott, *Winslow*, 194–95; Browne, "Duel," 615.

38. Journal, June 16, 1864, *ORN*, Ser. 1, 3:677.

39. Semmes to Barron, July 14, 1864, ibid., 651; Sinclair, *Alabama*, 224; Semmes, *Service Afloat*, 755.

40. Fisher, *Diary*, June 17, 18, 1864, 83.

41. Sinclair, *Alabama*, 224.

42. Semmes, *Service Afloat*, 755.

CHAPTER 13   The Death of the *Alabama*

1. Semmes, *Service Afloat*, 755.

2. Slidell to Secretary of State, June 30, 1864, *ORN*, Ser. 1, 3:658.

3. Semmes, *Service Afloat*, 755–56.

4. Kell, *Recollections*, 246; George Sinclair to Barron, June 20, 1864, in Merli, ed., "Letters," 216–17. Sinclair's letter is erroneously dated; it was written on June 19.

5. Semmes, *Service Afloat*, 755; Semmes to Barron, Official Report, June 21, 1864, reprinted ibid., 757, hereafter cited as Official Report; Sinclair, *Alabama*, 226–27.

6. Semmes, *Service Afloat*, 756; Kell, *Recollections*, 246–47.

7. Sinclair, *Alabama*, 227.

8. Browne, "Duel," 615–16; Sinclair, *Alabama*, 226; Ellicott, *Winslow*, 193, 196; Fisher, *Diary*, June 19, 1864, 84.

9. Official Report, 757; Log of USS *Kearsarge*, June 19, 1864, *ORN*, Ser. 1, 3:64–65; Browne, "Duel," 616; Winslow, Supplementary report of the engagement between USS *Kearsarge* and the CSS *Alabama*, *ORN*, Ser. 1, 3:79, hereafter cited as "Winslow."

10. Official Report, 757; Winslow, 79; Sinclair, *Alabama*, 228; Bulloch, *Secret Service*, 2:284.

11. Bulloch, *Secret Service*, 2:279, 286.

12. Semmes, *Service Afloat*, 761.

13. Fisher, *Diary*, 85.

14. Official Report, 757; Winslow, 80; Kell, *Recollections*, 251; Ellicott, *Winslow*, 204–5.

15. Official Report, 757; Sinclair, *Alabama*, 230; Kell, "Cruise and Combats," 609.

16. Kell, *Recollections*, 248.
17. Ibid.; Sinclair, *Alabama*, 231.
18. Kell, "Cruise and Combats," 610.
19. Kell, *Recollections*, 248.
20. Official Report, 757–58; Winslow, 80; Browne, "Duel," 619; Kell, *Recollections*, 248; Sinclair, *Alabama*, 231.
21. Kell, *Recollections*, 248.
22. Browne, "Duel," 619–20.
23. Two crewmen with the same name were designated "I" and "II" on the ship's muster roll.
24. Sinclair, *Alabama*, 241–42; Kell, *Recollections*, 249.
25. Sinclair, *Alabama*, 237–38.
26. Semmes, *Service Afloat*, 763; Kell, *Recollections*, 249.
27. Kell, *Recollections*, 249–50; Semmes, *Service Afloat*, 764; Sinclair, *Alabama*, 244, 224; Kell, "Cruise and Combats," 611.
28. Semmes, *Service Afloat*, 765; Sinclair, *Alabama*, 239–40. The log of the *Kearsarge*, (*ORN*, Ser. 1, 3:65) states that the *Alabama* sank at 12:24 P.M.
29. George Sinclair to Barron, June 20 (*sic*), 1864, in Merli, ed., "Letters," 217.
30. Sinclair, *Alabama*, 239–40.
31. Kell, *Recollections*, 250.
32. Semmes, *Service Afloat*, 759; Log of the *Kearsarge*, June 19, 1874, *ORN*, Ser. 1, 3:65; Winslow to Welles, June 21, 1865, ibid., 60.
33. Statement of Captain Evan P. Jones, in Sinclair, *Alabama*, 246–47; John Lancaster to *London Daily News*, June 27, 1864, in *ORN*, Ser. 1, 3:665–67.
34. R. F. Armstrong to Barron, June 21, 1864, *ORN*, Ser. 1, 3:653; Sinclair, *Alabama*, 244.
35. Browne to W. Whelan, Chief, Bureau of Medicine and Surgery, U.S. Navy, July 23, 1864, *ORN*, Ser. 1, 3:69–70.
36. Ibid.; Official Report, 758; Sinclair, *Alabama*, 248.
37. Browne, "Duel," 622; Barron to Mallory, June 22, 1864, *ORN*, Ser. 1, 3:655.
38. Jones, in Sinclair, *Alabama*, 248; Kell, *Recollections*, 251; Ellicott, *Winslow*, 207–8.
39. Semmes, *Service Afloat*, 759–62; Official Report, 758.
40. Browne, "Duel," 624; Sinclair, *Alabama*, 223; Spencer, *Confederate Navy in Europe*, 185.
41. Browne, "Duel," 621; Winslow, letter of reference for Lieutenant J. D. Wilson, C.S. Navy, July 14, 1864, *ORN*, Ser. 1, 3:76.
42. Winslow to Welles, July 30, June 21, 1864, *ORN*, Ser. 1, 3:77; 60.
43. John Lancaster to *London Daily News*, June 27, 1864, *ORN*, Ser. 1, 3:665–67. Almost twenty years later, when the passions of war had died down, James R. Soley wrote his assessment of the Winslow-Lancaster dispute in a letter to the editors of *Century* magazine. According to Soley, Winslow waived the right of capture when he asked the *Deerhound* to assist the survivors of the *Alabama*. Once they were in the *Deerhound*, Lancaster was not only under no obligation to Winslow but, to the contrary, was legally prohibited from turning them over to him as prisoners because, in doing so, he would have violated the *Deerhound's* neutrality. Likewise, the *Kearsarge* could

not legally detain the *Deerhound* and remove the *Alabama*'s survivors. The editors of *Century* reprinted Soley's observations in a footnote to Browne's account, "Duel," 621n–622n. They noted, however, that this did not resolve the question of whether Fullam was legally obligated to return to the *Kearsarge* and surrender himself. In our own time, of course, it is generally agreed that the first duty of a prisoner of war—surrendered or otherwise—is to escape.

44. Joint Resolution of the Confederate Congress, February 14, 1865; Jefferson Davis to Lancaster, March 1, 1865, both in *ORN,* Ser. 1, 3:668.

CHAPTER 14   From History to Legend

1. Welles, *Diary,* July 6, 1864, 2:67.
2. From *Life and Letters of Admiral D. G. Farragut,* by Loyall Farragut, 403, quoted in Bulloch, *Secret Service,* 2:107.
3. Quoted in Ellicott, *Winslow,* 219–20.
4. Slidell to Secretary of State, June 30, 1864, *ORN,* Ser. 1, 3:658. Winslow was promoted to commodore retroactive to the date of the battle.
5. Barron to Semmes, June 21, 1864, ibid., 654.
6. S. H. Stringham, commandant, Boston Navy Yard, to Welles, January 28, 1865, ibid., 81–82.
7. Welles to Winslow, July 6, 12, 1864, ibid., 72–75; Winslow to Welles, July 15, 30, 1864, ibid., 75, 78; Charles Francis Adams to Winslow, July 13, 1864, ibid., 75–76.
8. Woodward, *Mary Chesnut's Civil War,* 623.
9. Kell, *Recollections,* 263, 265–76.
10. Ibid., 276–77.
11. Semmes, *Service Afloat,* 791–93.
12. Delaney, " 'Old Beeswax,' " 21–22. Biographical sketches of all the *Alabama*'s officers and their postwar activities may be found in Sinclair, *Alabama,* 253–84.
13. Delaney, " 'Old Beeswax,' " 21–22; Welles, *Diary,* December 27, 1865, 2:404, January 3, 1866, 2:410, and April 6, 1866, 2:476.
14. Soley, *Blockade and Cruisers,* 170–71.
15. Delaney, " 'Old Beeswax,' " 22, and "Fight or Flee," 26–27; Kell, *Recollections,* 245.
16. Information on the Holiday Inn was sent to Malcolm MacDonald, University of Alabama Press, by U.S. Representative William L. Dickson in April 1986. Mr. MacDonald passed it on to the author in a letter of November 6, 1990.
17. English translation of Afrikaans original, both quoted in Hoole, *Four Years in the Confederate Navy,* 87.
18. *The X-Seamen Sing.*
19. Woodward, *Mary Chesnut's Civil War,* 659.
20. Dalzell, *Flight from the Flag,* 239–41.
21. Ibid., 245, 249.
22. Miller, *U.S. Navy,* 180.
23. Dalzell, *Flight from the Flag,* 249–52; McPherson, *Battle Cry,* 859–60.

24. Semmes, *Service Afloat,* 746.
25. Wise, *Lifeline,* 221, 165–66.
26. Boatner, *Dictionary,* 4–5.
27. *London Times,* June 21, 1864, quoted in Kell, *Recollections,* 255.

Epilogue

1. Bulloch, *Secret Service,* 2:110.
2. Cloutier, *"Hatteras,"* 6, 4; Robinson, "Civil War Shootout," 82.
3. Robinson, "Civil War Shootout," 82.
4. Ibid.; Cloutier, *"Hatteras,"* 5.
5. Robinson, "Civil War Shootout," 82; Cloutier, *"Hatteras,"* 6.
6. Robinson, "Civil War Shootout," 82.
7. Jeff Burke and Chuck Rose, various conversations with Charles M. Robinson III; *Confederate Naval Historical Society Newsletter* 7 (June 1991):3.
8. Guérout, "Last Remains of a Legend," 1–2.
9. Ibid., 3.
10. Ibid., 4–5.
11. Lambert, "Lost and Found," 34–35.
12. Guérout, "Last Remains of a Legend," 5.
13. Sirett and Williams, "Liverpool," 119–21.
14. Lambert, "Lost and Found," 35–36; Guérout, "Last Remains of a Legend," 5, 9, 13.
15. Lambert, "Lost and Found," 36–37n.
16. *Confederate Naval Historical Society Newsletter* 6 (February 1991):1; 10 (June 1992):1–3. Peter James Trickett of Hastings, England, one of the perpetrators of the hoax, does not believe the bell was sold "for anything like" $12,000.
17. Ibid. 6 (February 1991):1; 7 (June 1991): 1, 3.
18. Ibid. 10 (June 1992): 3; 6 (February 1991):6.

Appendix 1

1. The *Alabama* actually carried two pivot guns.
2. The actual number was eight: three in each broadside and two pivoting on the centerline.

Appendix 2

1. The *Alabama* destroyed two ships named *Lafayette.*

Bibliography

* Denotes works that were particularly useful in preparing this book.

Manuscripts

* *Alabama* File. W. S. Hoole Special Collections Library, University of Alabama, Tuscaloosa.

Books—Primary

Adams, Charles Francis. *A Cycle of Adams Letters, 1861–1865*. Edited by Worthington C. Ford. 2 vols. Boston: Houghton Mifflin, 1920.

* Bulloch, James D. *The Secret Service of the Confederate States in Europe*. 2 vols. 1883. Reprint. New York: Burt Franklin, 1972.

Delaney, Caldwell, ed. *Raphael Semmes, Rear Admiral, Confederate States Navy, Brigadier General, Confederate States Army: Documents, Pertaining to Charges Preferred against Him by the United States Government, with a Pictorial History of the Voyage of the* Sumter *and* Alabama *and the* Alabama *Claims Commission.* Mobile: Museum of the City of Mobile, 1978.

Edge, Frederick Milnes. *The* Alabama *and the* Kearsarge: *An Account of the Naval Engagement in the British Channel, on Sunday June 19th, 1864, from Information Furnished to the Writer by the Wounded and Paroled Prisoners of the Confederate Raider* Alabama *and the Officers of the United States Sloop-of-War* Kearsarge, *and the Citizens of Cherbourg.* London: W. Ridgeway, 1864.

*Fisher, Charles B. *Diary of Charles B. Fisher.* Transcribed and edited by Paul E. Sluby, Sr., and Stanton L. Wormley. Washington, D.C.: Columbian Harmony Society, 1983.

Fullam, George Townley. *The Cruise of the* Alabama, *Raphael Semmes, Commander, from her Departure from Liverpool July 29, 1862. By an Officer on Board, with Gleanings from Other Sources.* N.p.: N.p., 1864.

* ———. *The Journal of George Townley Fullam, Boarding Officer of the Confederate Sea Raider* Alabama. Edited and annotated by Charles G. Summersell. University, Ala.: University of Alabama Press, 1973.

———. *Our Cruise in the Confederate States War Steamer* Alabama: *The Private Journal of an Officer.* London: A. Schulz, 1863.

* Kell, John McIntosh. *Recollections of a Naval Life.* Washington, D.C.: Neale, 1900.

* Low, John. *The Logs of the C.S.S.* Alabama *and C.S.S.* Tuscaloosa, *1862–1863.* Edited with an introduction by W. Stanley Hoole. University, Ala.: Confederate Publishing Co., 1972.

* Read, Georgia Willis, ed. *A Pioneer of 1850: George Willis Read, 1819–1880, The Records of a Journey Overland from Independence, Missouri, to Hangtown (Placerville), California, in the Spring of 1850, with a Letter from the Diggings in October of the Same Year to an Account of a Journey from New York to California, via Panama, in 1862, Capture by the Confederate Raider* Alabama, *etc., and a Visit to the Nevada Silver Mining District in 1863.* Boston: Little, Brown, 1927.

* Semmes, Raphael. *Memoirs of Service Afloat during the War Between the States.* Baltimore: Kelly, Piet and Co., 1869.

* Sinclair, Arthur. *Two Years on the* Alabama. 1896. Reprint. Annapolis: Naval Institute Press, 1989.

* U.S. Department of the Navy. *The War of the Rebellion: Official Records of the Union and Confederate Navies.* 30 vols. Washington, D.C.: U.S. Government Printing Office, 1894–1927.

* Welles, Gideon. *Diary of Gideon Welles.* 3 vols. Boston: Houghton Mifflin, 1911.

Wilkes, Charles. *Autobiography of Rear Admiral Charles Wilkes, U.S. Navy, 1788–1877.* Edited by William James Morgan et al. Washington, D.C.: U.S. Government Printing Office, 1978.

Wilkinson, John. *The Narrative of a Blockade-Runner.* 1877. Reprint. Alexandria, Va.: Time-Life Books, 1981.

* Woodward, C. Vann, ed. *Mary Chesnut's Civil War.* New Haven: Yale University Press, 1983.

Books—Secondary

* Adams, Charles Francis, Jr. *Charles Francis Adams.* Boston: Houghton Mifflin, 1900.

Adams, Ephraim Douglass. *Great Britain and the American Civil War.* New York: Longmans, Green, 1925.

Badlam, William H. *The* Kearsarge *and the* Alabama: *Personal Narratives of Events in the War of the Rebellion, Being Papers Read before the Rhode Island Soldiers and Sailors Historical Society.* Ser. 5, No. 2. Providence, R.I.: N. B. Williams, 1884.

* Boatner, Mark Mayo III. *The Civil War Dictionary.* New York: David McKay, 1959.

Boykin, Edward. *Ghost Ship of the Confederacy: The Story of the* Alabama *and Her Captain, Raphael Semmes.* New York: Funk & Wagnalls, 1957.

———. *Sea Devil of the Confederacy: The Story of the* Florida *and Her Captain, John Newland Maffitt.* New York: Funk & Wagnalls, 1959.

Bradlee, Francis Boardman Crowninshield. *The* Kearsarge-Alabama: *The Story as Told to the Writer by James Magee of Marblehead, Seaman on the* Kearsarge. Salem, Mass.: Essex Institute, 1921.

Bradlow, Edna, and Frank Bradlow. *Here Comes the* Alabama: *The Career of a Confederate Raider.* Cape Town: A. A. Balkema, 1958.

Cook, Adrian. *The* Alabama *Claims: American Politics and Anglo-American Relations, 1865–1872.* Ithaca: Cornell University Press, 1975.

Dalzell, George Walton. *The Flight from the Flag: The Continuing Effects of the Civil War upon the American Carrying Trade.* Chapel Hill: University of North Carolina Press, 1940.

Davis, Evangeline, and Burke Davis. *Rebel Raider: A Biography of Admiral Semmes.* New York: J. B. Lippincott, 1973.

* Delaney, Norman C. *Ghost Ship: The Confederate Raider* Alabama. Middletown, Conn.: Southfarm Press, 1989.

———. *John McIntosh Kell of the Raider* Alabama. University, Ala.: University of Alabama Press, 1973.

* Duberman, Martin B. *Charles Francis Adams, 1807–1886.* Boston: Houghton Mifflin, 1961.

* Ellicott, John M. *The Life of John Ancrum Winslow, Rear-Admiral, United States Navy.* New York: G. P. Putnam's Sons, 1905.

Fehrenbach, T. R. *Lone Star: A History of Texas and the Texans.* New York: American Legacy Press, 1983.

* Guernsey, Alfred H., and Henry M. Alden, comps. *Harper's Pictorial History of the Civil War.* New York: Fairfax Press, 1977.

* Hendrick, Burton J. *Statesmen of the Lost Cause: Jefferson Davis and His Cabinet.* New York: Literary Guild of America, 1939.

* Hoole, William Stanley. *Four Years in the Confederate Navy: The Career of Captain John Low on the C.S.S.* Fingal, Florida, Alabama, *and* Ajax. Athens: University of Georgia Press, 1964.

Jones, Virgil Carrington. *The Civil War at Sea, January 1861–March 1862.* 3 vols. New York: Holt, Rinehart and Winston, 1960–62.

* McPherson, James M. *Battle Cry of Freedom: The Civil War Era.* New York: Oxford University Press, 1988.

Merli, Frank J. *Great Britain and the Confederate Navy, 1861–65.* Bloomington: Indiana University Press, 1970.

* Miller, Nathan. *The U.S. Navy: An Illustrated History.* New York: Simon and Schuster for American Heritage Publishing Co. and the United States Naval Institute Press, 1977.

* Nash, Howard P., Jr. *A Naval History of the Civil War.* South Brunswick and New York: A. S. Barnes and Co., 1972.

* Sandburg, Carl. *Abraham Lincoln: The War Years.* 4 vols. New York: Harcourt, Brace, 1939.

* Scharf, J. Thomas. *History of the Confederate States Navy from Its Organization to the Surrender of Its Last Vessel.* New York: Fairfax Press, 1972.

* Soley, James Russell. *The Blockade and the Cruisers.* New York: Charles Scribner's Sons, 1883.

* Spencer, Warren F. *The Confederate Navy in Europe.* University, Ala.: University of Alabama Press, 1983.

* Summersell, Charles Grayson. *C.S.S.* Alabama, *Builder, Captain, and Plans.* University, Ala.: University of Alabama Press, 1985.

* Time-Life Books, Editors of. *The Blockade: Runners and Raiders.* Alexandria, Va.: Time-Life Books, 1983.

* Wise, Stephen R. *Lifeline of the Confederacy: Blockade Running during the Civil War.* Columbia: University of South Carolina Press, 1988.

Articles—Primary

* Browne, John M. "The Duel between the 'Alabama' and the 'Kearsarge.'" In Robert U. Johnson and Clarence C. Buel, eds., *Battles and Leaders of the Civil War.* 4 vols. 4:615–25. 1887–88. Reprint. New York: Thomas Yoseloff, 1956.

* Cloutier, Paul A. "The Search for the *Hatteras.*" *Rice University Review,* Spring–Summer 1976, 3–7.

* Guérout, Max. "The Last Remains of a Legend: The Modern Discovery of the C.S.S. *Alabama.*" *Journal of Confederate History* 4 (1989): 1–14.

* Kell, John McIntosh. "The Cruise and Combats of the 'Alabama.'" In Robert U. Johnson and Clarence C. Buel, eds., *Battles and Leaders of the Civil War.* 4 vols. 4:600–614. 1887–88. Reprint. New York: Thomas Yoseloff, 1956.

* Merli, Frank J., ed. "Letters on the *Alabama,* June 1864." *Mariner's Mirror* 58 (May 1972): 216–18.

* Rhett, R. Barnwell. "The Confederate Government at Montgomery." In Robert U. Johnson and Clarence C. Buel, eds., *Battles and Leaders of the Civil*

War. 4 vols. 1:99–110. 1887–88. Reprint. New York: Thomas Yoseloff, 1956

Articles—Secondary

* Delaney, Norman C. "The End of the *Alabama.*" *American Heritage* 23 (April 1972): 58–69, 102.
* ———. "Fight or Flee: Raphael Semmes' Decision to Engage the *Kearsarge,* June 1864." *Journal of Confederate History* 4 (1989): 15–28.
* ———. " 'Old Beeswax': Raphael Semmes of the 'Alabama.' " *Civil War Times Illustrated* 12 (December 1973): 10–22.
* Lambert, C. S. "CSS 'Alabama'—Lost and Found." *American History Illustrated* 23 (October 1988): 32–37.
* Melton, Maurice. "Pirate: Cruise of the Rebel Sea Wolf *Sumter,* Her Career of Triumph." *Civil War Times Illustrated* 20 (January 1982): 16–25.
* Robinson, Charles M. III. "Civil War Shootout: USS 'Hatteras' vs. CSS 'Alabama.' " *Sea Combat* 3 (February 1980): 12–13, 81–82.
* Sirett, K. F., and K. J. Williams. "Liverpool and the American Civil War: A Confederate Heritage in England." *Journal of Confederate History* 4 (1989): 113–31.
* Wilson, Harold S. "The Cruise of the C.S.S. *Alabama* in Southeast Asian Waters." *Journal of Confederate History* 4 (1989): 29–55.

Miscellaneous

* *Confederate Naval Historical Society Newsletter* 4 (July 1990): 6; 6 (February 1991): 1; 7 (June 1991): 1, 3; 10 (June 1992): 1–3.
New York Times, July 6, 1864.
The X-Seamen Sing at South Street Seaport, Songs of Sailing, Whaling, Fishing. Vol. 4 of the *Sea Heritage Library of Sailing Songs,* notes by Bernie Klay. New York: Sea Heritage Foundation, 1987.

Index

ABOUT THE AUTHOR

CHARLES M. ROBINSON III was born in Harlingen, Texas. As a boy he spent summers along the coasts of Mississippi and North Carolina, whose islands and inlets had sheltered both blockade runners and Union naval forces. He dropped out of high school at seventeen and shipped out of Houston on a Norwegian freighter, ultimately sailing many of the same waters as the *Alabama*. He has a bachelor's degree in history from St. Edward's University in Austin, Texas, and is working on his master's degree at the University of Texas–Pan American. He is a member of the Western Writers of America, the Texas State Historical Association, the Montana Historical Society, the Custer Battlefield Museum and Preservation Association, and the Descendants of Mexican War Veterans. Most of his work focuses on the Old West. His book *Bad Hand: A Biography of General Ranald S. Mackenzie* won the Texas Historical Commission's prestigious T. R. Fehrenbach Book Award.

The **Naval Institute Press** is the book-publishing arm of the U.S. Naval Institute, a private, nonprofit society for sea service professionals and others who share an interest in naval and maritime affairs. Established in 1873 at the U.S. Naval Academy in Annapolis, Maryland, where its offices remain, today the Naval Institute has more than 100,000 members worldwide.

Members of the Naval Institute receive the influential monthly magazine *Proceedings* and discounts on fine nautical prints and on ship and aircraft photos. They also have access to the transcripts of the Institute's Oral History Program and get discounted admission to any of the Institute-sponsored seminars offered around the country.

The Naval Institute also publishes *Naval History* magazine. This colorful bimonthly is filled with entertaining and thought-provoking articles, first-person reminiscences, and dramatic art and photography. Members receive a discount on *Naval History* subscriptions.

The Naval Institute's book-publishing program, begun in 1898 with basic guides to naval practices, has broadened its scope in recent years to include books of more general interest. Now the Naval Institute Press publishes more than seventy titles each year, ranging from how-to books on boating and navigation to battle histories, biographies, ship and aircraft guides, and novels. Institute members receive discounts on the Press's nearly 400 books in print.

For a free catalog describing Naval Institute Press books currently available, and for further information about subscribing to *Naval History* magazine or about joining the U.S. Naval Institute, please write to:

Membership & Communications Department
U.S. Naval Institute
118 Maryland Avenue
Annapolis, Maryland 21402-5035
Or call, toll-free, (800) 233-USNI.

*T*HE ENGLISH-BUILT CONFEDERATE COM-
merce raider *Alabama* is easily the best-
known ship from the American Civil War.
This book is essentially the biography of that
ship — how she came to be, her mission, her
cruises, and her destruction. Under the command of Captain Raphael Semmes, the *Alabama* wreaked havoc on the flow of food and
military supplies to the North with devastat-
ing raids on both sides of the Atlantic as well
as the Gulf of Mexico. The U.S. government
considered the ship a major obstacle to Union
victory and spared no effort in its attempts to
locate and dispose of her. This eventually led
to the dramatic confrontation between the
USS *Kearsarge* and the *Alabama* off Cherbourg,
France, while many French citizens looked on
from the shore. The *Alabama* was sunk, ending the career of a ship that became legendary.

By far the most inclusive, thorough book
yet written on this famous American warship,
it chronicles everything from construction
to destruction, as well as her recent salvage.
The author details shipboard life from the per-
spectives of both officers and seamen and re-
counts the *Alabama*'s triumphs, frustrations,
and deterioration from continued operation, as
well as world opinion of her, and more. He includes material on the discovery of the wreck
off Cherbourg in the 1980s and the subse-
quent controversy over rights to the ship and
the archaeological investigation. This story is
certain to satisfy general readers and critical
scholars alike.